"While Dr. Indick focuses on facilitating the process of screenwriting, anyone who likes movies will find his analysis of the psychology behind the plot and characters to be a treat. Screenwriters, filmmakers, psychologists, and film enthusiasts alike will find his book engaging and enlightening."

— **Dr. Kendell Thornton**
Assistant Professor of Psychology
Dowling College

"*Psychology for Screenwriters: Building Conflict in Your Script* is a must read for screenwriters, filmmakers, film analysts, and students of film and psychology. This book is destined to become an essential volume for all those who aspire to write a successful script or make a successful movie. Dr. Indick's treatment of complex psychological concepts, character traits, and plot lines is clear and direct. His book lends itself to immediate application in character development, portrayal, and script analysis."

— **Dr. Suzanne Johnson**
Professor of Psychology
Author of *For Lesbian Parents* (Guilford Press, 2001)
and *The Gay Baby Boom* (New York University Press, 2002)

"Dr. Indick's book is a comprehensive and insightful account of how psychological knowledge can elucidate and guide any filmmaking experience. Unquestionably, it is must-read material for screenwriters and anyone who might be interested in understanding the intricacies of storytelling in the motion picture industry."

— **Dr. Maura Pilotti**
Assistant Professor of Psychology
Dowling College

"You cannot find a clearer or more concise guide on the psychology of cinema than this book. A brilliant and insightful companion for the screenwriter and film aficionado alike, this lucid and lyric guide provides a 'Let's Go' tour of the most powerful psycho-literary theories of our age as they apply to hundreds of great films."

— **Marcus C. Tye, Ph.D.**
Clinical Psychologist
Associate Professor of Psychology
Dowling College

"Even the most experienced writer may have misplaced the knowledge needed to right the course of a script that has lost its creative rudder or stayed too close to the surface of human conflict. Indick's book can be the trade wind that helps bring the screenwriter's solitary voyage into harbor, on time and under budget."

— **Stuart Fischoff, Ph.D.**
Screenwriter
Senior Editor, *Journal of Media Psychology*
Professor of Media Psychology
California State University, Los Angeles

# Psychology *for* Screenwriters

## Building Conflict *in your* Script

William Indick, Ph.D.

Published by Michael Wiese Productions
11288 Ventura Blvd., Suite 621
Studio City, CA 91604
tel. (818) 379-8799
fax (818) 986-3408
*mw@mwp.com*
*www.mwp.com*

Cover Design: MWP
Book Layout: Gina Mansfield
Editor: Arthur G. Insana

Printed by McNaughton & Gunn, Inc., Saline, Michigan
Manufactured in the United States of America

© 2004 William Indick

Library of Congress Cataloging-in-Publication Data

Indick, William, 1971-
  Psychology for screenwriters : building conflict in your script / William Indick.
      p. cm.
  Filmography: p.
  Includes bibliographical references and index.
  ISBN 0-941188-87-6
  1. Motion picture authorship. 2. Motion picture authorship--Psychological aspects. I. Title.
  PN1996.I53 2004
  808.2'3--dc22
                                        2004002056

*For M²*

# TABLE OF CONTENTS

# ACKNOWLEDGEMENTS

The author must give much thanks to Mustafa Lokmaci, a graduate assistant in the Psychology Department at Dowling College, for compiling the filmography and subject index. Much of the information in the filmography was retrieved from the Internet Movie Database, *IMDB.com*. Thanks to Victoria Cook for her excellent legal advice. Much appreciation goes to Jim Garbarino at Cornell University, Suzanne Johnson at Dowling College and Frank Madden at SUNY Westchester Community College for their mentorship, guidance, and advice. A debt of gratitude is owed to the faculty and administration of Dowling College in Oakdale, New York, for their support of the author's research and writing projects. And many thanks to Michael Wiese and Ken Lee at Michael Wiese Productions for making this book possible.

# INTRODUCTION

*"Drama is life, with the dull bits cut out."*
— Alfred Hitchcock

In *Stardust Memories* (1980), Woody Allen's protagonist has a death fantasy in which his psychiatrist eulogizes him, saying: *"he had a faulty denial mechanism... he was unable to block out the harmful truths of life... or, as a famous movie producer put it: 'People don't want to see too much reality'... "* People go to the movies to experience fantasy. While they watch the film-fantasy projected in front of them, they project their own fantasies onto the characters on the screen. The theater experience itself — a dark, quiet, cavernous room — is evocative of the unconscious mind. As a projection of the human imagination, film is the greatest medium of fantasy ever created.

Very early on in its existence, the "Hollywood Dream Factory" realized that fantasy sells. At the movies, the depths of unconscious fantasy and desire — love and sex, death and destruction, fear and anger, revenge and hatred — can all be indulged in safely, without risk of embarrassment and with a virtual guarantee of a happy ending. A thorough understanding of the unconscious mind — the birthplace of fantasy, dreams, and imagination — is a fundamental point of departure for creating psychologically resonant scripts and films.

## A PSYCHOANALYTIC APPROACH

Film's visceral appeal as a larger than life medium on both visual and auditory levels makes it an extremely powerful psychological force. Viewers are literally absorbed in a movie, becoming so emotionally connected with the characters and plot that the illusion on the screen becomes intertwined with their own psychological lives. Through the unconscious process of **"identification,"** the people in the audience actually become the characters that they identify with in the film, and they experience, vicariously, the same psychological development and catharsis that the characters on the screen experience.

Movies reach deep down inside the audience's unconscious minds, affecting the way they think and feel about themselves and the world around them. A psychoanalytic approach to understanding and creating film images, characters, and stories is an invaluable resource for filmmakers and screenwriters. Audiences are not consciously aware of the subtle manipulation achieved through a film's activation of their primal fears, childhood anxieties, unconscious issues, and repressed desires. Yet, they experience heightened states of arousal when viewing the film, because they are emotionally and psychologically integrated with the characters and images on the screen. By learning about the inner workings of the human mind, filmmakers and screenwriters bring more skill and depth to their craft, and create more powerful and resonant films.

## KNOW YOUR AUDIENCE

The key to success in any field of endeavor – whether it be teaching, writing, filmmaking, acting, etc. – is to know your audience. The brilliant theories of **Sigmund Freud**, **Erik Erikson**, **Carl Jung**, **Joseph Campbell**, **Maureen Murdock**, **Alfred Adler**, and **Rollo May** are all designed to increase our knowledge of the human mind. Psychoanalytic theory is the study of the "primary subject," aimed at what Socrates believed was the ultimate intellectual goal: "To know thyself."

Any task that deals mainly in creative interpretation and extrapolation is inherently subjective, and therefore not an objective science. True psychoanalysis is not a science... it is an art. In this sense, psychoanalysis and screenwriting are two sides of the same coin. They are both creative arts aimed at the investigation and understanding of the human character, mind, and soul. They are both intrinsically engaged in the personality and personal development of their subjects. They are both immersed in the world of archetypal symbols and mythological figures. And they both are rooted firmly in the unconscious realm of human experience.

## MAJOR THEORIES OF PSYCHOANALYSIS

Christopher Vogler, author of *The Writers Journey: Mythic Structure for Writers* (1998), once said that "screenwriting isn't brain surgery... but then again, maybe it is?" Both brain surgery and screenwriting are intricate, painstaking processes that involve the dissection, examination, and reconfiguring of basic structural elements in the human mind. As such, it is no coincidence that the father of psychoanalysis – Sigmund Freud – was a research neurologist before he became a clinical psychiatrist. Freud's groundbreaking and seminal theories of psychoanalysis changed the way that people think of the human mind and behavior. His thoughts influenced and inspired generations of theorists, and his ideas still are a groundswell in every area of scholarship. Though Freudian psychology has lost favor among most of the new generation of psychologists – the "scientist-practitioners" – who believe that psychology as a field must adhere to the rigid constraints of objective, empirical science, Freudian thought has been embraced by the non-scientists... the artists, actors, creative writers, and filmmakers.

## FREUDIAN ANALYSIS

The first part of this book will explain the basic principles of Freudian theory, and show you how to apply it to the characters and plot in your script. The essence of Freudian theory is the notion that the majority of emotions, anxieties, behaviors, and issues that rule our lives are essentially enigmas to us, because we are unconscious of them. The point of Freudian analysis is to reveal these latent motivations to the conscious mind. The first chapter focuses on the Oedipal Complex, the intellectual nucleus of Freudian analysis and the forerunner of Freud's highly controversial theories of infantile sexuality, repressed taboo desires, and castration anxiety. The Oedipal Complex provides the very basis of drama and conflict, as it explores the issues of love and sex, hatred and aggression, creation and destruction, and life and death.

In Freudian theory, neurotic conflict is an internal psychological conflict between what we desire and the rigid constraints of civilized society. Chapters Two and Three focus on neurotic conflict, following the primary conflicts faced by children as they progress through the psycho-sexual stages of ego development. These chapters will show you ways of expressing internal conflict as psychologically resonant external conflicts between characters that can be visualized on the movie screen. Chapter Four explores the ego defense mechanisms, elements of Freudian theory that were codified by his daughter, Anna Freud. The defenses are common ways that people deal with their neurotic conflicts. As such, they are essential aspects of neurotic behavior that can add depth to the characters in your script. Chapter Five focuses on "Dreamwork," the Freudian method of dream analysis. This chapter draws out the parallels between the film and dream experiences, and shows you how to employ dream symbolism and imagery in your script.

## ERIKSONIAN ANALYSIS

Though the field of psychoanalysis started with Freud, by no means does it end with him. Erik Erikson's theory of identity development is the subject of Part Two of this book. While Freud focused on repressed sexuality and internal conflict, Erikson focused on "normative conflict" — the conflict between the individual's "will to be oneself," and the obstructive pressures of the environment that surround him. Chapters Six and Seven explore Erikson's eight stages of ego identity development (the "Identity Crises"), showing you how to apply his model of identity development to your own structure of character development in your script. To my knowledge, this book offers the first model of character development for screenwriting based on Eriksonian theory.

## JUNGIAN ANALYSIS

Carl Jung's theories of archetypes and the collective unconscious have arguably become even more influential among creative artists than Freud's theories. Jung believed that there is an essential element within the unconscious that integrates and expresses universal or collective psychological images and themes, which he called "archetypes." Throughout history, archetypal figures and stories have depicted universal human needs, such as the need for mother and father, the need for love and personal achievement, the need for spiritual healing and connection with others, and the need for existential rebirth.

Whereas the archetypes have been depicted for thousands of years through mythology, religion, legends, stories, and art — the primary instrument for the expression of contemporary archetypes is the modern mass medium of movies. In the third part of this book, the archetypes are presented as points of character and plot in films that are psychologically resonant for all people. Chapters Eight and Nine show you how to integrate Jungian archetypes into your script, so you can link your personal story with the collective figures and plots that communicate to everyone on a primary unconscious level.

## THE HERO'S JOURNEY

In his book, *The Hero With a Thousand Faces* (1948), Joseph Campbell provided a psychological analysis of the structure within the mythological hero's saga. Drawing freely from his study of psychoanalytic theory, and applying this insight to his vast knowledge of ancient, classical, and world mythology, Campbell configured a discrete set of "stages" to the mythological hero's journey. Due in no small part to the tremendous success of George Lucas' *Star Wars* films, which were inspired by Campbell's theories, the "journey model" of script and hero structure has become a template for screenwriters and filmmakers around the world. Books such as Christopher Vogler's *The Writer's Journey* and Stuart Voytilla's *Myth and the Movies* (1999) have applied Campbell's theories to film and screenwriting, increasing the popularity of the journey model and spreading the word to a new generation of writers and filmmakers. In Part Four of this book, the journey model is explored in the light of its psychoanalytic roots. Each stage is addressed in terms of its psychological function, as well as the archetypes that the hero must encounter and integrate in order to develop toward the resolution of his story.

Other books on Campbell and film/screenwriting tend to simplify Campbell's stages, because his theory requires a certain amount of psychological knowledge and background in order for it to be understood. Since this book provides the necessary background of Freudian, Eriksonian, and Jungian theory in the first three parts, the Campbell part of the book is not simplified or rearranged. Campbell's model of the Hero's Journey is presented using Campbell's original configuration from *The Hero With a Thousand Faces*. In Chapter 10, the stages of the journey are explored using two running examples, *Braveheart* (1995) and *Gladiator* (2000), modern film versions of the mythological hero's journey. Though Campbell's stages are interpreted for application to the screen, the interpretations stay true to Campbell's original model, and Campbell's original terminology is left intact.

## THE HEROINE'S JOURNEY

A basic truth of the hero's journey model is that it is based primarily on classical mythology and the traditional legends and stories of Western cultures. As such, the structure is descended from male-dominated societies, and the hero archetype itself represents an inherently male xvi Psychology *for* Screenwriters ~ *William Indick*

version of an inherently male character's story. In Chapter 11, Maureen Murdock's model – drawn from her book, *The Heroine's Journey* (1990) – is explored, using the film *Erin Brockovich* (2000) as a running example.

The heroine's journey model reconfigures Campbell's stages for the modern age of female heroes – women who are struggling with issues of independence, autonomy, equality, and self-determination. While the hero's journey deals mainly with victory and transformation in the realm of conquest, the heroine's journey deals with the modern woman's quest for balance. The heroine is seeking to balance the traditional feminine goals of child-bearing, nurturing, and love, with the modern goals of success in the traditionally male realm of personal ambition and competition. To my knowledge, this book offers the first application of the heroine's journey model to screenwriting or filmmaking.

## ADLERIAN ANALYSIS

Part Five of this book focuses on the theories of Alfred Adler. In Chapter 12, Adler's theory of the inferiority complex is explained as a potent means of character motivation, especially in movies with child heroes. The "child hero formula" is drawn out in detail, specifying the unique motivations, goals, conflicts, and obstacles faced by the child hero in films by Disney and other movie studios. The rivalry relationship is a universal theme in movies, as it is rife with psychological symbolism and conflict. In Chapter 13, Adler's theory of sibling rivalry is explained as a basic template for rivalry themes in all stories and films. And in Chapter 14, Adler's theory of "life styles" is presented as a model for both character development and psychological conflict between characters.

## EXISTENTIAL ANALYSIS

Rollo May was a pioneering scholar and psychoanalyst who successfully merged the concepts of existential philosophy with the principles and practice of psychoanalysis. May's theories explore the most basic neurotic conflict... the existential anxiety that arises from the fundamental questions: "Who am I?" "Why do I exist?" "What is my purpose?" and "What is the meaning of life?" Chapter 15 interprets Rollo May's theories of existential conflict and his stage model of self-consciousness into a cogent model of motivation and character development that you can use in your script.

Rollo May labeled the late 20th Century, "The Age of Narcissism," referring to the narcissistic quality of modern American heroes and the apparent loss of traditional values in American culture. Chapter 16 explores the modern narcissistic archetypes provided to us by our contemporary mythmaker – Hollywood – and the screenwriters and filmmakers of the 20th and 21st Centuries. This final chapter breaks down the elements of common screen character types, revealing them as archetypes for the age of narcissism and explaining their unique challenges, conflicts, and motivations.

## WHO CAN USE THIS BOOK

This book is intended primarily for screenwriters, though it provides insights and theories that will be of interest to all filmmakers, as well as psychoanalysts, film analysts, and more generally – all students of psychology and/or film, and anyone with more than just a passing interest in these areas. If you are a screenwriter, this book may be useful to you at any stage of script development. If you don't even have an idea for a script, this book may turn you on to the classical themes and characters from mythology, drama, and film, and inspire you with an idea or story. If you have an idea for a script, this book will be of great use in helping you with plot structure, creating essential elements of conflict in your characters, and setting up the path of character development for your protagonists. If you are "in full career" of your writing journey, this book may serve as both a guide and inspiration. The fruitful world of psychoanalytic and mythological theory provides a boundless supply of ideas for character and plot. And if you are finishing, revising, or rewriting your script, this book may help you to work out some of the bugs in your script by finding the weak points in the plot or character development. It also may help you figure out why certain parts of your script don't work, and even give you direction for revamping the script so that it does work.

## HOW TO USE THIS BOOK

The usefulness of this book is completely dependent upon your needs as a reader and as a writer. The chapters on Freud provide the basics of internal psychological conflict, a topic that is addressed and developed throughout this book. If you feel that your script lacks a strong or engaging sense of conflict, then the different interpretations of psychological conflict in this book may give you the inspiration you need. The second major leitmotif in this book is character development. The chapters on Erikson and Jung focus on the different psychological elements of character development, providing two very different yet complementary approaches to creating fully developed film characters.

The chapters on the Hero's Journey and Heroine's Journey focus more on form, providing plot points and development schemes for the traditional hero and heroine story structures. If you feel that you need help with structure, these chapters may help you immensely, though I suggest that you read the chapters on Freud and Jung first, as the book is designed to provide a progression of ideas that build upon each other. Finally, the chapters on Adler and May focus on alternative psychoanalytic models for story structure, character development, psychological motivation, and conflict. There are no other books that provide Adlerian or existential models for screenwriting.

Whether you are reading this book to gain specific help or insight, or whether you just wish to increase your palette of knowledge for screenwriting or filmmaking, there is an abundance of ideas in this book for you to consider. The brilliant theories of the scholars covered in this book are a consummate source of wisdom and guidance. While learning about these theories, you may find that a flood of new ideas for movies and screenplays will come upon you. You may find yourself brainstorming a plethora of different symbols and unconscious figures, either for the script you are writing, the film you are making, or the movie you happen to be watching in the theater or on television. Leave yourself open to this flow of unconscious images and ideas. The greatest thing this book can offer you is an entrance into your own unconscious mind, because this is the place where fantasies, dreams, and movies are born.

# PART ONE

*Sigmund Freud*

*Chapter One*

# THE OEDIPAL COMPLEX

The central theory in Freudian analysis is his conception of the Oedipal complex, which is drawn from the myth of Oedipus. Within this seminal paradigm lies the groundwork for many of Freud's greatest ideas, such as his structural model of the psyche, drive theory, castration anxiety, and a host of other theories. Oedipal themes are ubiquitous in movies because they portray the two most basic elements of character development: the integration of **moral wisdom** and the formation of a mature **romantic relationship**. As you write your script, many different elements of plot and character development will arise, but the core issues in the story rarely diverge significantly from these two elements. Whatever happens in the film, the main character is generally aiming at some kind of moral victory, or the character is trying to win over the heart of the person he loves. Many movie plots contain both of these elements. A thorough understanding of the Oedipal complex is an essential base for any writer who wishes to tell a story that addresses these fundamental psychological issues of character development.

The Oedipal complex could be interpreted on either a literal or figurative level. In Freud's "psychosexual" perspective, the infant boy desires sexual union with his mother. Freud was outspoken in his theory of "infantile sexuality" — the belief that babies and small children have raging sexual desires, just like adults. According to this view, suckling at the breast, hugging, bathing, kissing, and every other intimate act shared by the infant and his mother are inherently sexual experiences. A less literal interpretation sees the Oedipal complex as a metaphor for the son's desire for his mother's love and affection, rather than a desire for sexual union. A comprehensive understanding of Freud's theory requires an inclusive approach that understands the son's desire for mother as a need for love and affection that may be sexually charged, as well. Eventually, the son will grow into a young man and his desires for love and sex will be projected onto another woman. Hence, the resolution of the Oedipal complex is a key element in the formation of romantic relationships.

## THE ELECTRA COMPLEX

Freud's ideas have been broadly criticized for being **"androcentric,"** (focusing solely on male viewpoints and perspectives). Freud himself was unapologetic about his tendency to explain intrinsically male issues as universal psychological issues. Even though his clinical work was almost exclusively dedicated to analysis with female patients, Freud admitted: *"Despite my 30 years of research... I have not been able to answer the great question that has never been answered: What does a woman want?"* Certainly, the Oedipal complex is an example of Freud's androcentrism. Nevertheless, Freudian revisionists have adopted the "Electra complex" as a female counterpart to the Oedipal complex, in which the infant daughter develops a passionate desire for her father.

## EROS & THANATOS

The son's conflicted desire for his mother is only one side of the Oedipal coin. The son inevitably realizes that his father is a rival for his mother's love and attention, and that this rival is infinitely more powerful than he is. This **rivalry** results in feelings of aggression and hostility toward the father. Like Oedipus, who killed his father Laius and married his mother Jocasta, the son wishes he could destroy his rival for his mother's love, so he could have her all to himself. According to Freud, the boy's divergent feelings toward his parents (love for mother and aggression toward father), reflect the two basic primal drives – Eros and Thanatos. In keeping with the mythological theme of the Oedipal complex, Eros and Thanatos are mythological figures, as well. As the attendant of his mother, Aphrodite, Eros was a god of love and sex, pro-viding the Greek root to the word "erotic." As the son of Nyx, the Greek goddess of night, Thanatos was the personification of death. In Freudian theory, Eros represents the drives that create and foster life (**love** and **sex**), while Thanatos represents the drives toward death (**hate** and **aggression**). Within Eros and Thanatos are the great dramatic devices that will add spice to any film. If you mix love, hate, sex, and violence with the classical themes of internal conflict, jealousy, and rivalry, you have all the ingredients for an exciting plot.

## NEUROTIC CONFLICT AS AN OBSTACLE TO LOVE

In writing your script, it is important to remember that the core of the Oedipal complex is neurotic conflict. As the child grows, he realizes that sexual desire for his mother is socially inappropriate due to the universal "**incest taboo.**" The boy represses his desire for mother, creating an **internal conflict** within his character. In movies, this internal neurotic conflict is usually represented by an **external obstacle** that blocks a character from his object of love and desire.

Almost every script includes some kind of **love interest.** In romance movies, the love interest is the central plot; but even in other genres, a film may feel empty or lacking if there is no love interest. A movie without love lacks "heart." Since the parent/child relationship represents the **primary love relationship** in a person's life, the Oedipal complex is intrinsically symbolic of every romance, and the resolution of the Oedipal complex has an extremely significant impact on every subsequent love relationship in a person's life. A comprehensive understanding of Oedipal themes is every writer's touchstone for creating psychologically resonant love stories.

## OEDIPAL RIVALRY

Just as the son sees his father as a rival for his mother's love, film characters often face a rival for their love interest. In *The Graduate* (1967), Ben (Dustin Hoffman) gains Mr. Robinson (Murray Hamilton) as a rival, when he gets involved in an affair with Mrs. Robinson (Anne Bancroft). Later on, the rivalry reappears on a different level, when Ben falls in love with Mr. Robinson's daughter, Elaine (Katherine Ross), and he tries to run away with her against Mr. Robinson's wishes. First, Ben is a rival for the love of Mr. Robinson's wife, and then he becomes a rival for the love of his daughter. Typically, the rivalry theme is not as overtly Oedipal as the rivalry between Ben and Mr. Robinson. In *Gone With the Wind* (1939), Scarlet (Vivien Leigh) experiences a more straightforward rivalry with Melanie (Olivia de Havilland) over the love of Ashley (Leslie Howard).

The rivalry theme is not limited to romantic plot lines. Movie characters often face rivals in their various goals and objectives. In *Jerry Maguire* (2000), Jerry (Tom Cruise) is forced out of his agency by Bob

(Jay Mohr), his obnoxious rival. In sports movies such as *Rocky* (1976) and *The Karate Kid* (1984), the main character is driven throughout the film by a desire to best his formidable rival. Even the horse, *Seabiscuit* (2003), is driven to succeed by his infamous rivalry with "War Admiral," a bigger, younger, and stronger horse with far better breeding and training. In *Tin Cup*, Roy (Kevin Costner) is competing against his rival (Don Johnson) for both his primary goal (victory in the golf tournament), and the heart of his love interest (Rene Russo). This double whammy approach to rivalry themes is a typical device in scripts that want to build high levels of conflict between the hero and his rival. In the end, the hero can claim victory over his rival by winning both the championship, and the love of the beautiful maiden.

### Forbidden Fruit

Some movies depict a somewhat literal version of the Oedipal complex, in which a boy actually wants to have sex with his mother. In *Spanking the Monkey* (1994), a young son is seduced by his middle-aged mother into an illicit incestuous affair. And in *Tadpole* (2002), a high school boy desires a sexual relationship with his stepmother. But more often than not, the mother complex is displaced onto an unrelated mother figure. In *The Graduate*, Ben is seduced by an older woman who is his mother's close friend, Mrs. Robinson. And in *Harold and Maude* (1971), Harold (Bud Cort) enters a sexual relationship with Maude (Ruth Gordon), a woman 60 years his senior. In all of these cases, the heroes seem to impart a sense of **emotional neediness** and **immaturity**. They are little boys in men's bodies, who are looking for a mother figure to take care of their emotional needs, and an enticing woman to satisfy their sexual desires.

A key element in all of these love stories is the forbidden fruit factor. Just as the opposite sex parent is forbidden to the child as an object of sexual desire, sex with the older woman is a figurative violation of cultural taboos. The forbidden fruit factor is an extremely common element in love stories. Shakespeare's *Romeo and Juliet*, the most famous love story ever told, is about two teens falling in love, even though marriage between them is forbidden by their feuding families, the Montagues and Capulets. When writing a love story with a forbidden fruit element, keep in mind that these stories typically resolve in **tragedy**.

*Forbidden Fruit: The title characters (Bud Cort and Ruth Gordon) consummate their love in* Harold and Maude *(1971)*

Romeo and Juliet commit suicide. Oedipus, when realizing that he married his mother, gouges his own eyes out, and Jocasta commits suicide. Ben and Mrs. Robinson's relationship in *The Graduate* ends with the two hating each other, and Harold and Maude's relationship ends with Maude committing suicide. While the ever popular "love conquers all" denouement tends to work in plots with external obstacles to love, the forbidden fruit plot line almost always ends in tragedy, because the internal conflict is born out of the illicit nature of the relationship itself. In order for the conflict to be resolved, the romantic relationship must end or transform itself into something else.

## ADULTERY

The most common application of the forbidden fruit theme is seen in the adultery plot. This conflict is even stronger when the love object is married to a close friend. The adultery theme is figuratively Oedipal, because it replays the same basic emotions. The character desires some-one who is morally and socially taboo. The character is also thrust into rivalry with the love object's spouse, just as the son is pitted into rivalry against his father. The adultery plot line is somewhat tricky to resolve, because while audiences tend to sympathize with the forbidden fruit theme, they also respect the sanctity of marriage. But your character can have his cake and eat it, too (he can win the girl while avoiding massive punishment), if it is established that his rival is undeserving of the love object. In *Titanic* (1997), the audience is pleased when Jack (Leonardo DiCaprio) wins over Rose's (Kate Winslet) heart, because her fiancé (Billy Zane) is a mean and insensitive snob. Similarly, in *Ocean's Eleven* (2001), it's okay for Danny (George Clooney) to steal Tess (Julia Roberts) away from her fiancé (Andy Garcia), because he is clearly a controlling, manipulative, and rich jerk, who is not nearly as cool as Danny. When the rival is established as a **bad guy** or loser, the love story can end in triumph for the main character.

It is difficult to write a triumphant love story when the rival is not established as a bad guy. In *Unfaithful* (2002), Connie (Diane Lane) indulges in a passionate adulterous affair, even though her husband Edward (Richard Gere) is an attractive, loving, and all-around nice guy. Connie's conflict is doubly troubling, because on top of breaking a taboo, she is hurting the man she loves. The tables are turned in this film, as Edward discovers the relationship and finds himself in the precarious position of being a rival for his own wife's love. Now Edward is Oedipus, driven by love and desire to seize Jocasta, and driven by hatred and rage to kill Laius. The twin passions of Eros and Thanatos overpower Edward and he kills Connie's lover. While the adultery and subsequent murder function well in the story, the absence of punishment for Connie constitutes a hole in the plot. Screenwriters must be aware that the primal Oedipal themes (love, hate, sex, and violence), need little justification because they are self-explanatory. However, the more subtle themes of **punishment** and **retribution** need to be carefully structured and woven into the plot. *Unfaithful* was set up as a tragedy, but the filmmakers backed out in the end. They were probably afraid to punish the heroine of the film too harshly, since she was the character that viewers identified with. Nevertheless, sophisticated audiences are subconsciously aware of the dramatic structure of tragedies, and they know when a film cheats them out of an emotional wallop in the end.

## CASTRATION ANXIETY

While Oedipus himself was able to kill his father, the little boy in the throes of an Oedipal complex has no chance against his massive rival. Furthermore, since the son harbors feelings of aggression toward his father, he also assumes that his father harbors similar aggressive feelings toward him. This assumption is confirmed when the father punishes or spanks his son for naughty behavior. According to Freud, the young boy fears that his father wants to eliminate him as a sexual rival by castrating him. Even the staunchest Freudians typically apply a figurative interpretation to the concept of "castration anxiety," focusing on the feelings of **powerlessness** and **impotence** that a small boy feels in the presence of an angry and violent father. These early childhood fears were exploited to the maximum degree in *The Shining* (1980), in which a psychotic axe-wielding father (Jack Nicholson) chases his son through a haunted hotel. The little boy in this film is literally afraid that his father is going to chop him into pieces.

### POWERLESSNESS

Powerlessness in the presence of danger is an extremely terrifying experience that can be used to elicit gut reactions of fear in audiences. Horror films often employ the device of an evil man, monster, or psycho stalking a helpless child or a maiden in distress. Even though "Slasher" films like the *Halloween* and *Friday the 13th* movies overused this device for decades, the device still retains the power to terrify. Horror movies utilize a similar device when the menacing figure attacks his victims in states of **defenselessness**. In "Slasher" films, there is always a scene in which a victim is attacked in bed, in the bath, in the shower or while having sex. At these moments, the victims are powerless to defend themselves. Incidentally, they are also naked — their genital regions precariously exposed to the slasher — who is invariably wielding a knife. Castration anxiety in these scenes is related to a literal fear of the character having his genitals slashed off.

### ROLE REVERSAL

A role reversal in which a **caregiver** becomes a menacing figure is particularly terrifying. The young boy experiencing an Oedipal complex expects his father to love and take care of him. When he suspects his father of wanting to kill him, he has no defense and no one to run to. In *The Night of the Hunter* (1955), the menacing figure (Robert Mitchum) is even more terrifying because the helpless children that he is hunting are his stepchildren. In *Flowers in the Attic* (1987) and *Mommie Dearest* (1981), the menacing figures are the children's mothers. And in *Rosemary's Baby* (1968), *Suspicion* (1941), and *Gaslight* (1944), frail and frightened women suspect that their menacing husbands are plotting against them. *Misery* (1990) is an especially horrifying film, because a woman who starts out as a caring nurse (Kathy Bates), gradually turns into a sadistic and brutal psycho. Meanwhile, her powerless victim (James Caan) is confined in the **emasculated** positions of a sickbed and wheelchair. A role reversal in which a caring figure becomes menacing elicits fear because it defies the viewers' expectations, while also creating the sense that the victim is trapped with no one to help and nowhere to run. On an unconscious level, the role reversal recalls childhood fears of parental punishment.

BODY SWITCHING

Several films have used the "body switching" scenario to generate literal role reversals between parent and child — typically to a comical effect. In *Freaky Friday* (1976 & 2003), mother and daughter are magically trans-figured into each other's bodies. The same device was employed in a male version of this plot in *Like Father, Like Son* (1987). In each case, children experience a sense of **freedom** and **release** when they are sud-denly elevated from their state of second class citizenship as mere kids, and get to indulge in all the privileges of adulthood. Josh (Tom Hanks) in *Big* (1988) initially revels in his newfound independence when his wish is granted by a magical carnival game, and he grows big overnight. And Kevin (Macaulay Culkin) in *Home Alone* (1990) relishes his freedom from his restrictive elders when he suddenly finds himself unfettered in his big house, all alone.

Parents also experience a psychological release when their adult roles as responsible parents and workers are relinquished, and they can enjoy being careless kids again. These movies tend to be successful because they key in to fantasies that reach a crossover audience. Both parents and kids can experience vicarious pleasure by identifying with these role-switching characters. However, the simplicity of the plot device leaves little room for variation in the resolution of the story. In the end, parent and/or child must return to their original states, having learned valuable lessons from their time spent in the others' shoes. They both gain a sense of respect for each other's struggles, (i.e., "the grass is always greener... "). And they also learn to work together and cooperate in order to rectify their freaky predicament.

## THE POSSESSIVE PARENT

Role reversal and body switching themes in movies address a real psychological need in parent/child relationships. Parents and children often do not see eye-to-eye on many crucial issues. Though there are an infinite number of ways in which parents and children can disagree, these conflicts can typically be broken down to the fundamental issue of **independence**. Children want the freedom to determine their own lives. Parents, in their desire to protect their children from the perils of the adult world, may display their care through **possessiveness** — a desire to control every aspect of their children's lives. This basic conflict is Oedipal in nature, because it recalls the parent's desire to monopolize the emotions of their children, and the child's emerging need to escape from the claustrophobic state of love and fear within the Oedipal relationship. Nowhere is the conflict of parental possessiveness more apparent than in stories in which daughters wish to marry suitors against their parents' wishes. In these situations, the young suitor and possessive parent become true rivals, as the daughter is torn between an infantile love for the parent and a passionate love for her suitor.

In *Fiddler on the Roof* (1971), Tevye's inability to accept his daughter's choice of a goy for her suitor leads Tevye (Topol) to denounce his daughter, losing her love forever. The conflict can be a source of terror, as well. In *Psycho* (1960), Norman Bates' (Anthony Perkins) mother was so overpowering and possessive that she devoured Norman's identity and controlled his psyche, even after her death. When writing your script, remember that the Oedipal themes of rivalry and possessiveness are excellent sources for internal conflict, violence, and drama. Originality does not require finding new sources of conflict — it merely demands unique and creative ways of expressing these ancient mythical themes.

## CHAPTER ONE SUMMARY POINTS

- *The Oedipal complex*, in which the infant boy feels psychosexual love toward his mother and jealous aggression toward his father, provides the basic template of neurotic conflict. Neurotic conflict can be represented externally as conflict in the script, when the characters want what they should not have, fear awesome powers, desire love, hate tyranny, experience sexual desire, or express violent aggression.
- *The Electra complex* can be interpreted as the female version of the Oedipal complex, in which the infant girl experiences psychosexual love for the father, and feels jealous aggression toward her mother.
- *Eros and Thanatos*, respectively, are the primary drives toward life and death. Eros represents the need for love, sex, and affiliation; Thanatos represents the urge toward aggression, violence, and destruction.
- *Neurotic conflict* in the Oedipal complex arises from the "incest taboo" – the illicit desire for mother. This theme is commonly represented as an obstacle to love in films in the ubiquitous "forbidden fruit" plot line.
- *Adultery* is an example of a popular "forbidden fruit" plot line, in which the illicit desire for a married man or woman recapitulates the infant's illicit desire for sexual union with his mother.
- *Oedipal rivalry* between the infant son and his father over the love and attention of the mother is recapitulated in film in the rivalry plot line between the hero and another character over the heart of a mutual love interest.
- *Castration Anxiety* is the infant son's fear of his father.
- *Powerlessness* makes the infant son's castration anxiety even more intense, as the small child is powerless and defenseless in the presence of his adult father.
- *Role reversals* in films, such as when a nurturing caregiver becomes a menacing figure, recall the Oedipal fears of early childhood, in which the small child fears that the same sex parent will destroy him.
- *Body switching* is a popular theme in films because it indulges two fantasies. The child's fantasy of becoming a powerful and independent adult is indulged, and so is the adult's fantasy of returning to a state of childhood, in which there are fewer obligations and responsibilities.

• *The possessive parent* is a universal figure in movies. The parents try to control their children's lives because they love and care for them, while the children crave freedom and independence.

## CHAPTER ONE EXERCISES

1. Analyze the Oedipal themes in the following classic films: *Mildred Pierce* (1945), *White Heat* (1949), *Psycho* (1960), *The Graduate* (1967), and *Chinatown* (1974).
2. Identify at least five more films in which a major aspect of the Oedipal complex is symbolically represented.
3. Now identify five films in which the Electra complex is symbolically represented.
4. Identify five films in which the hero must overcome powerlessness in order to succeed.

## ADDRESSING OEDIPAL THEMES IN YOUR SCRIPT

1. Is there a love interest in your script? If not, do you think adding a love interest would add drama to your story?
2. If there is a love interest in your script, is there a conflict between the characters? Could this conflict be intensified by adding Oedipal themes such as the "forbidden fruit" factor, a rivalry, or an obstacle that must be overcome?
3. Does the hero in your script have a rival? If not, consider how a rival may add conflict or tension to your plot.
4. If the hero in your script does have a rival, could this rival be developed to a higher degree? Consider tying the hero's rival in with the primary love interest, and how this may increase tension in your plot.
5. Are you writing a script or scene that should be scary? If so, can you employ the "castration anxiety" themes of powerlessness or role reversal to make the menacing figure more terrifying?
6. Does your script contain a parent/child relationship or love relationship? If so, could conflict be added to this relationship by including the theme of possessiveness?

## THE OEDIPAL COMPLEX AT A GLANCE

| ELEMENTS OF THE OEDIPAL COMPLEX | CHARACTERISTICS | CHARACTER MOTIVATIONS | EXAMPLES IN FILM |
|---|---|---|---|
| Eros & Thanatos | The primal drives toward sex and aggression | Love & Hate Sex & Violence Revenge & Spite | *Duel in the Sun* *Natural Born Killers* *Death Wish* |
| Oedipal Rivalry | Aggression toward the father | Rivalry for Love Rivalry for a Goal | *Gone With the Wind* *Rocky* |
| Incest Taboo (Forbidden Fruit) | Guilt over sexual desire for mother | Incestuous Desire Adultery | *Tadpole* *Unfaithful* |
| Castration Anxiety | Fear of the father | Powerlessness Role Reversals | *The Shining* *Freaky Friday* |
| Parental Possessiveness | Parental desire to control the lives of their children | Possessiveness Drive toward Independence | *Fiddler on the Roof* *The Wild One* *Rebel Without a Cause* |

*Chapter Two*

# NEUROTIC CONFLICT

Freud's structural model of neurotic conflict was born out of his theory of the Oedipal complex. In order to illustrate this internal psychological conflict, Freud separated the unconscious into three separate structures. The **Id** represents the primal, animalistic drives that are present in the infant at birth. A literal translation from Freud's German term – "das es" – is "**the it**." The id is pure instinct, driven entirely by the "**pleasure principle**" and interested only in satisfying its own impulses. The power behind the Id is "**libido**," the primal life force that empowers every animal with the basic instincts of **sex** and **aggression**, (the biological drives at the heart of Eros and Thanatos). The Id is the bestial part of the unconscious that wants to make love with Mother and kill Father.

## THE ID AS VILLAIN

The villain character in films is often a representation of id energy. In *Cape Fear* (1991), Max Cady (Robert De Niro) is a villain whose fearsome presence arises from his primal motives and behavior. When he appears for the first time, he is in prison... a caged animal. He has "love" tattooed on one hand and "hate" tattooed on the other, symbolizing the two drives behind his character – **sex** and **aggression**. Max's primary goal is to get revenge against Sam (Nick Nolte), the lawyer who sent him to jail. Max indulges his sexual drives as a means of satisfying his aggressive impulse toward revenge. In a truly terrifying sequence, Max seduces/rapes a young woman and, while having sex with her, bites off a chunk of her flesh. In that moment, Max is pure id. He is all sex and aggression, combined into one evil villain. The psychological power behind the villain comes from the sense that his character is a wild animal in human clothing. You never know how far he might go in order to satisfy his primal urges.

While not all villains are as evil as Max, the basic quality of the villain's character is typically related to either sex, aggression, or both. **Vampires** are excellent examples of id monsters, because they derive sexual pleasure from the aggressive act of sucking blood from the soft throats of their maiden victims. Serial killers such as Hannibal (Anthony Hopkins) from *Silence of the Lambs* (1991) also tend to mix their aggressive business with sexual pleasure. Other villains direct their aggression into evil schemes of destruction, domination, or conquest. Villains such as Dr. No (Joseph Wiseman) and Goldfinger (Gert Fröbe) in the James Bond movies are always out to destroy or conquer the world in some way.

Whether a villain is out to destroy the world or just one person, the villain is usually the character who is the most fun to write. Immune from all inhibitions, morals, guilt, or regret, the villain is free to express his id desires completely. Audiences secretly love the villain because they can release their own inhibitions and satisfy their own id desires vicariously through him. The secret to writing a good villain is to get in touch with your inner id. Lose control, drop your inhibitions, let all of your primal impulses flow out onto the page, and express your darkest fears, dreams, drives, and desires through your villain character.

### The Id as Prisoner

The id is like a caged animal inside our unconscious minds. Id drives are always trying to get out, but we repress them constantly and keep our primal urges locked up. As a representation of the id, the villain is often cast as a prisoner behind bars. This villain's plot line begins with him escaping or being released from jail. Max Cady in *Cape Fear* starts out in prison, as does Lex Luthor (Gene Hackman) in *Superman II* (1980). The villain escaping or leaving prison represents the **release of id energy**. Audiences vicariously enjoy this release. Escape movies such as *The Great Escape* (1963), *Papillon* (1973), and *Escape from Alcatraz* (1979) are popular because audiences identify with the feeling of being caged by a repressive society, and they vicariously enjoy the freedom of released inhibitions.

While the villain is out of his cage (while the id is temporarily unrepressed), you should try to give the audience its money's worth. Have fun with the lawless immorality of the id. Lex Luthor was a great supervillain because he enjoyed being an evil scamp who did exactly what he wanted to do without a second's thought. The villains in Bond movies are so entertaining because they revel in their evilness, and take pleasure in concocting their diabolical plots. Every script and story has different demands, but if a plot calls for a villain, fill him up with as much gas as possible and then let him loose. Typically, the entertainment level in a film is not based on how good the hero is, but on how bad the villain is.

## THE RETURN OF THE VILLAIN

It's no secret that audiences enjoy the unrepressed villain more than the goody-goody hero. As the representative of the id, the villain is a sinner, and sinners have much more fun. Many scripts intentionally leave gateways at the end of the story so that the villain, if he is popular with audiences, can make a return in a sequel film. Instead of being killed by the hero, the villain may be imprisoned, exiled from the country, or he may even get away. Hannibal Lecter (voted the American Film Institute's #1 villain), escapes from prison at the end of *The Silence of the Lambs* (1991), only to return in *Hannibal* (2001), in which he escapes once again at the end. By leaving the door open at the end of the script, the writer retains the option of resurrecting the villain and giving him one more chance to wreak havoc on society with his perverse plans.

## THE VILLAIN'S COMEUPPANCE

The key to the villain's character is that he is **amoral**. As an expression of id energy, the villain could care less about the moral quality of his behavior. Guilt, remorse, and regret are anathema to his character. So, just as the naughty child must be punished for his immoral behavior by his parents, the evil villain must be punished by the hero. The villain must get his comeuppance. Furthermore, the villain's comeuppance should ideally be **tantamount to his crimes**. If the villain raped, ravaged, and murdered his way through a host of the hero's closest family members and friends, a punch in the face or a jail sentence does not provide a sense of dramatic justice to the viewer. The villain must suffer greatly, preferably at the hands of the hero.

At the end of the original *Dracula* (1931), the Count's (Bela Lugosi) demise is not even shown on screen, it is merely indicated by a short grunt as we see Von Helsing (Edward Van Sloan), from a distance, drive a stake into Dracula's coffin. This uneventful death lacks the emotion needed at the climax of the film, and it also cheats the audience out of a necessary sense of dramatic justice. In Hammer Films' 1958 remake with

Christopher Lee as Dracula, the Count's comeuppance is suitably dramatic and painful — complete with screams of agony and gory violence splattered with lots and lots of blood.  One popular way to punish the villain, as seen in *Die Hard* (1988), is to have him fall to his death off a tall building or cliff.  The **falling death** allows for a long, drawn out shot of the villain's screaming face as he drops 100 stories to his doom.  The agonizing fall also symbolizes his **descent to hell** — where his soul will be punished for eternity.  Being blown to pieces, hacked up, eaten by wild animals, or ironically destroyed by his own elaborate killing device are also popular ways of killing the villain, which are much more dramatic than a simple gunshot.

## THE EGO AS HERO

After the id, the next unconscious structure to develop is the "ego." While the id represents the "pleasure principle," the ego represents the **"reality principle"** — the need for the individual to reconcile his id drives with parental and societal demands for appropriate behavior. Translated from Freud's German, "das Ich," the ego is the "I" — the central representation of the self.  The ego is constantly developing, constantly learning new ways to adjust to the demands of society, and hopefully becoming stronger and healthier as each day passes.  In this way, the psychological function of the ego is directly parallel to the function of the hero.  The hero is also developing.  He is trying to master his environment, overcome obstacles, and defeat the depraved villains out to get him.  If the hero is not in some way better, healthier, or stronger by the end of the film, then his character has not developed.  While the plot of a film may deal with any number of issues, the heart and lifeblood of the movie is the development of the hero's character.  The hero is the "Ich" of the film, and his character *must* develop in order for the film to communicate on a psychological level.  And, just as the ego's job in the unconscious is to repress and control the id, the hero's job in a film is to capture and defeat the villain.

The triumph of the hero over the villain symbolizes the triumph of the ego over the id.  In the traditional plot structure of "the maiden in distress," a villain or monster kidnaps the maiden to satisfy his own immoral and libidinous desires.  For example, in *Dracula* (1931), the vampire (Bela Lugosi) takes Mina back to his castle to make her a demonic undead creature. In rescuing the maiden, the hero foils the villain's unholy schemes and redeems the maiden so they can be married in a wholesome and socially appropriate manner. In this sense, the hero's triumph recalls the Oedipal drama, in which primal libidinous desires are defeated by the symbol of social restraint. In destroying his rival and rescuing the maiden, the hero symbolically destroys the troublesome id drives, and transforms the taboo desire for mother into a socially appropriate desire for the nubile young maiden.

### THE SUPEREGO AS MENTOR

Often times, films have no external villain character. The problem of libido desires is an **internal conflict** within the hero, represented by inner demons and temptations. The internal force needed to control the dark power of the libido is supplied by the third unconscious structure, the "superego." Translated from Freud's German, "das uber-Ich," the superego is the "**over-I**," the unconscious representation of the morals and social conventions instilled into the individual by authority figures such as the father. As the son grows older, his feelings of aggression toward the father transform into a sense of respect and admiration. By **identifying with the father as a role model**, the son internalizes all of the father's moral values and beliefs. In essence, the superego is the psychological embodiment of the boy's identification with his father.

### VISUALIZING THE MENTOR

Neurotic conflict between the id and superego is resolved by the ego. Since film is a visual medium, it is difficult to represent internal conflict on the screen without a physical embodiment of the two forces in conflict. While the id and superego in the unconscious are internal figures, the conflicting forces of primal impulses and moral conscience in film are usually represented by external figures. The id usually plays the part of the villain, and the superego is typically cast as a **mentor** character. The mentor provides the hero with a **father figure** or **role model** who informs the hero of his moral obligations and gives him the psychological strength he needs to succeed. Obi Won Kenobe (Alec Guiness) in *Star Wars* (1977) inspires his hero, Luke, to accept the moral challenge of fighting against the evil Empire. Obi Won also tutors Luke in the use of the "force," giving him the spiritual and psychological power he will need to face the Dark Lord.

*The Mentor: Alec Guinness as Obi Won in* Star Wars *(1977).*

In writing your script, it might be useful to add a physical representation of the superego, to give the audience a visual cue to the internal conflict going on in the hero's psyche. In *Jerry Maguire*, Jerry recalls some wise words given to him by his mentor, an old sports agent he worked with long ago. Though this mentor figure only appears once in a brief flash-back, it adds a much needed physical and visual presence to the ethereal sense of moral integrity that Jerry is trying to achieve. Similarly, *The Natural* (1984) begins with a short sequence in which the hero plays catch with his father. The father is not seen again in the film, but the short scene creates an indelible link in the audience's mind between Roy's internal representation of his father (his superego), and Roy's ardent desire to succeed as a baseball player. When the film ends with another short scene of Roy playing catch with his own son, a sense of emotional resolution is expressed in a way that could not have been achieved through dialogue, voice over, or a written epilogue.

The emotional power of film is linked directly with its appeal as a visual art form. Even if the hero's conflict is internal, your primary job as a screenwriter is to express this internal struggle *visually*, so that the conflict is readily apparent on the screen, and not just through words. Creating external representations of internal psychological structures (i.e., id as villain and superego as mentor), is a traditional method of visualization.

## THE CRISIS OF CONSCIENCE

When a character does not have a strong or present mentor figure, his struggle may center around the issue of an **underdeveloped superego**. This character's weakness may be displayed through egoism, selfishness, or a general unwillingness to dedicate himself to the heroic cause at the core of the plot. Han Solo (Harrison Ford) in *Star Wars* exemplifies this sort of self-involved hero. (The character's name, "Solo," gives away his predisposition toward going his own way and avoiding selfless causes.) While Luke dedicates himself to the rebel's struggle early on, Han expresses his unwillingness to join in the rebellion against the Empire throughout the film. He constantly maintains that he is only involved in Luke's mission for the money, and he refuses to help Luke in the big battle to destroy the Death Star, because there's nothing in it for him. Characters like Han develop through a crisis of conscience, in which they must reevaluate their priorities. The **guilt** behind this crisis comes from the character's role model or mentor – the physical embodiment of that character's superego.

Luke's heroism develops quickly because he has a strong superego, represented by his mentor and role model, Obi Won. Han lacks a mentor figure, so his development as a hero is stunted. By the end of the film, Luke's character has developed so much that he becomes a mentor to Han, setting up the sudden change of colors at the climax of the film, when Han suddenly appears out of nowhere to save Luke from certain death – finally sacrificing himself for the sake of the cause. When writing the character that is struggling to develop his own superego, remember that the superego develops when the boy **identifies with his father** as his primary role model. When your character finally develops his or her superego and is ready to fight the good fight, ask yourself: "**Who is this character's role model**?" The answer to this question will typically provide the key to your character's primary motivation for fighting.

### COWARDLY CHARACTERS

Often times, the character struggling with his own conscience or integrity can be a comical figure, a **cowardly sidekick** whom the hero must drag unwillingly into dangerous situations. Scooby and Shaggy from the *Scooby Doo* cartoons epitomize this kind of cowardly character. These figures recall the humorously chicken-hearted antics of comic heroes such as Abbot and Costello, Laurel and Hardy, and the Marx Brothers. Whether the cowardly heroes are the stars of the movie or just comic relief, their reluctance to face danger throughout the film is a typical set up for a surprise development in the end, when the cowards suddenly overcome their fear and courageously face the dangerous foe and save the day. No matter how many times this formula is used, it still remains effective, because it addresses a universal psychological issue of character development that everyone can identify with. Nevertheless, the coward-who-finds-courage theme should be used with care and subtlety. Don't make it too obvious that this character will eventually change colors, because audiences (especially children), can still be joyfully surprised when the goosey scaredy-cat becomes a brave hero in the end.

### THE ANTIHERO

American movie heroes tend to be men who are dominated by their id drives rather than their moral consciences. Western outlaws, mobsters, thieves, and criminals are just as often cast as heroes as the typical do-gooders. The antihero is a character with a strong libido and a seriously underdeveloped superego. He gets his way by breaking laws rather than enforcing them. John Wayne, James Cagney, Humphrey Bogart, Henry Fonda, Robert Mitchum, and many other movie superstars became popular as antiheroes in Westerns, Film Noir, gangster, and heist films. While the initial goal for these figures is to break the law and satisfy their own primal urges, the antihero usually gets involved with another goal which is related to the development of his moral character. The resolution of this second goal is the psychological crux of the film, because it represents the progression of the hero's character from selfish egoist to selfless champion.

The antihero (Alan Ladd) in *Shane* (1953) starts out as a lone outlaw, a wandering gunslinger running away from his shady past. He is interested only in self-preservation and the possibility of making a fresh start. But as Shane's relationship with a family of homesteaders grows closer, he cares less about himself and dedicates himself more and more to the homesteaders' struggle against the evil cattle baron. In the end, Shane sacrifices his chance for a new beginning and puts his own life on the line to help the homesteaders defeat the bad guys. Shane's courageous act of selflessness epitomizes this type of character's primary goal – to develop from an id-centered antihero who only cares about himself, into a true hero who sacrifices himself for others.

When writing the antihero character, it is crucial to link his goal with more than just physical rewards such as money, prestige, or power. These antiheroes may be fun for a while, but they lack psychological depth because their motivations are one-dimensional. The antihero's original egoistic goals must be replaced by a need to redeem himself, creating a second dimension to his character. A third dimension arises from an internal conflict, when the antihero realizes that the only way he can redeem himself is by belying the nature of his original character, and committing himself to **self-sacrifice** rather than self-indulgence.

### The Fallen Hero

When writing your script, you need to be very clear about the motivations behind your characters, as motivation provides the key to character development, and consequently determines the dramatic structure of the entire story. If the hero breaks the law in order to help others, then he is a two-dimensional antihero… like Jesse James or Robin Hood. If the hero breaks the law merely to help himself, then he is a one-dimensional antihero, like the crooks in *The Score* (2001) and *The Heist* (2001). These heroes are quickly forgotten because their motivations are too simple. When these heroes triumph in the end, we feel a vicarious sense of pleasure in the fact that they got away with the loot, but there is no feeling that the character has developed at all. He started out as a crook, and he ended as a crook. But when the bad man's dark acts lead to his own downfall, the dramatic structure of the triumphant hero is transformed into a tragedy, and the character gains some crucial psychological depth. He is not just a crook or a criminal – he is a fallen hero.

The dramatic quality of the fallen hero's story lies in his motivation. The fallen hero wants to better himself in some way. Unfortunately, the fallen hero chooses a shady path toward self-redemption, which inevitably leads to his own destruction. The tragedy within the story emerges from the **irony** of the fallen hero's situation. It is his own desire for redemption that precipitates his demise. In *Scarface* (1983), Tony (Al Pacino) robs, kills, and intimidates his way to the top of the drug world. He has done far too many evil things for his character to be redeemed, yet his final downfall comes after he refuses to kill the innocent wife and children of a man whom he was supposed to assassinate. Ironically, despite all his evil deeds, it is Tony's one moral act that destroys him.

Similarly, in **The Godfather** trilogy, Michael Corleone's (Al Pacino) primary motivation is to extricate himself and his family from their insidious life of organized crime. However, his attempts to legitimize his family's name always lead him into more killings and more illicit conspiracies. The tragic irony in the fallen hero's story elicits compassion and sympathy in the viewer, and gives the character a tremendous amount of psychological depth. The fallen hero is **doomed**. Like a man stuck in quicksand, every effort to pull himself out just plunges him further in. The key to writing the fallen hero character lies within this sense of doom and dread – the character's desperate struggle against himself – and his true desire to be better than the man that he's become.

## THE GUILT COMPLEX

The classical heroes – the white knights on white horses – typically start out with well-developed superegos. Rather than having too much libido, these heroes often suffer from too much guilt. Despite their superpowers, the superheroes in *Superman* (1978) and *Spider-man* (2002) are defenseless against their own superegos, and the crippling guilt that rules their lives. When Clark Kent's adoptive father (Glenn Ford) dies of a heart attack, young Clark (Jeff East) inexplicably blames himself. He doesn't understand why he has so many awesome powers, if he couldn't even save his own dad. This guilt complex leads Clark into his new identity as a selfless superhero, which Superman (Christopher Reeve) sees as a way of redeeming himself and justifying his special abilities.

Spider-man's genesis is an even more direct portrayal of a guilt complex. In the 1st act, Peter Parker (Tobey Maguire) is using his superpowers to benefit himself, as an undefeatable professional wrestler. Peter doesn't even stop a criminal after the lowlife robs Peter's boss. But when the criminal goes on to kill Peter's uncle (Cliff Robertson), Peter believes that he must justify his own existence in order to atone for his sin. As Spider-man, Peter will use his powers only for good, and his life will be dedicated to fighting crime.

The guilt complex is an intriguing character element and a strong motivation for any hero, not just superheroes. It helps when the character's guilt is really justified. Every person has done bad things — we all feel guilty about something — so audiences can easily identify with a hero's feeling of guilt, and his desire to redeem himself. In *Drugstore Cowboy* (1989), Bob (Matt Dillon) is the ultimate egoist. An unapologetic junky, he cares only about where his next fix will come from, and he'll do anything to get it. But when Nadine (Heather Graham), an innocent young girl in his crew, kills herself in reaction to his gross insensitivity, Bob is motivated to change his life. The guilt he feels over destroying Nadine inspires Bob to redeem his own life. Though Bob is not a super-hero, his dedication to his new cause is just as powerful and inspiring.

The primary psychological themes of **sin**, **guilt**, and **redemption** are extremely resonant. Audiences will instinctively identify with characters who are experiencing this crisis, but it is not an instant formula — the crisis must be carefully structured. The heart of this structure is the hero's father figure (i.e., mentor or role model). Bob's life in *Drugstore Cowboy* is conspicuously absent of a father figure. But right after Bob decides to go straight, Father Murphy (William Burroughs) appears on the scene. Father Murphy is an elderly priest from Bob's past who is also kicking the habit. He provides a much-needed role model for Bob at the time of his metamorphosis. Though Father Murphy's part is miniscule, his presence is a necessary piece in the puzzle of Bob's character — a puzzle piece you'll need to address when writing your own guilt-ridden hero.

## CHAPTER TWO SUMMARY POINTS

- The *id* is the part of the psyche that is driven by the primal urges toward sex and aggression.
- The *superego* is the part of the psyche that represents morality and social customs... the conscience.
- The *ego* is the part of the psyche that represents a compromise between the libido (the id drives), and guilt (the restrictive power of the superego).
- The id is often represented in film as the *villain*.
- The ego is often represented in film as the *hero*.
- The superego is often represented in film as the *mentor*.
- Often times, the villain either starts out or ends as a *prisoner*. This theme represents the function of the villain as id – which must be subdued and repressed by the ego.
- The villain's *comeuppance* represents the resolution of the Oedipal complex. Hence, the villain's comeuppance should be appropriately dramatic. It also should impart a sense of justice.
- Film characters frequently face a *crisis of conscience*, in which they must overcome selfish needs by making moral decisions. The hero's character development through a crisis of conscience symbolizes the development of the ego and the triumph of the superego over the id.
- The hero's character development is typically guided or inspired by a strong *mentor figure*.
- *Cowardly characters* tend to be comical. They represent the fear or reluctance that many people experience when facing moral challenges or major life choices.
- The *antihero* is the most common type of hero in American movies. The antihero is a character who is initially controlled by his id. He eventually overcomes his self-centeredness and sacrifices himself for the good of others.
- The *fallen hero* is a tragic figure who tries to overcome the baser side of his nature, but who eventually succumbs to the dark side.
- Many heroes, especially superheroes, are driven by a *guilt complex*. They feel that they must redeem themselves for a sin or shortcoming that is haunting their consciences.

## CHAPTER TWO EXERCISES

1. The best villains are driven by their own primal desires or libido. How can you spice up your villain by addressing the sex and aggression drives? Remember, the villain can never be too despicable.

2. How can you incorporate the notion of just retribution in your villain's comeuppance?

3. Devise three forms of comeuppance that are new, exciting, or inventive.

4. Describe your hero's primary conflict in two or three sentences. If you cannot do this, then you probably do not have a solid understanding of this character's motivations. Though the hero's internal neurotic conflict may address complex psychological issues, the conflict should be crystal clear to you as the writer.

5. Identify the villain character in five of your favorite films, and explain how this character epitomizes the psychological function of the id.

6. Identify the hero character in five of your favorite films, and explain how this character epitomizes the psychological function of the ego.

7. Identify the mentor figure in five of your favorite films, and explain how this character epitomizes the psychological function of the superego.

8. Guilt is a basic element of internal conflict. Think of what your hero could feel guilty about, and consider how this guilt could be incorporated as a motivating factor for character development.

9. Is your hero a classical hero, an antihero, a fallen hero...? You do not have to limit your hero to any one of these types, but envisioning him or her as one or the other may help in delineating your hero's motivations.

10. Analyze the neurotic conflict of classic film characters such as George Bailey (James Stewart) in *It's a Wonderful Life* (1946), Matt Garth (Montgomery Clift) in *Red River* (1948), and Judah Rosenthal (Martin Landau) in *Crimes and Misdemeanors* (1989).

## ADDRESSING NEUROTIC CONFLICT IN YOUR SCRIPT

1. If your script has a villain, are his motivations clear?
2. Does your villain get his comeuppance in the end? If so, is the comeuppance equal to his crimes?
3. Is your hero's primary psychological conflict different from his external goal?
4. Does your hero have a mentor or role model? If not, consider writing one in. The role model figure can be extremely resonant, even if his or her part is nominal.
5. Is your hero motivated, at least in part, by guilt?

| NEUROTIC CONFLICT AT A GLANCE | | | |
|---|---|---|---|
| ELEMENTS | ATTRIBUTES | CHARACTERS | EXAMPLES |
| Id | Primal impulses and libido energy | Villains Monsters | *Dr. No* *Dracula* |
| Ego | The self | Heroes | *Shane* |
| Superego | Moral conscience — internal representations of social authority | Mentors Father Figures Role Models | Obi Won in *Star Wars* Father Murphy in *Drugstore Cowboy* |
| Crisis of Conscience | Internal conflict between egoism and selflessness | Coward Heroes Antiheroes Fallen Heroes | Abbott and Costello *Shane* *Scarface* |
| Guilt Complex | Persistent guilt over a perceived sin or iniquity | Superheroes Guilty Heroes | *Spider-man* Bob in *Drugstore Cowboy* |

*Chapter Three*

# THE PSYCHOSEXUAL STAGES

Freud's developmental model of the ego is based on his belief in infantile sexuality. From the moment of birth, primal drives are expressed as **libido** energy which flows toward erogenous zones in the body that are being stimulated at each specific stage of development. The stages of development are "psychosexual" because the psychological development of the ego is related directly to the satisfaction of sexually charged impulses. If a psychosexual stage is not properly **resolved** (if too little or too much pleasure is experienced), then libido energy may become **fixated** at that stage, resulting in **neurotic symptoms** that become part of the individual's personality traits and behavior patterns. A thorough knowledge of Freud's psychosexual stages will reveal new layers of psychological complexity and sexual connotations that you can instill in your characters and plots, adding depth and emotional resonance to your script.

## THE ORAL STAGE

Freud's first psychosexual stage occurs in infancy, when babies receive most of their stimulation orally. Babies satisfy their hunger by sucking on their bottle or on mother's breast, and they also express their emotions orally by crying, screaming, laughing, cooing, babbling, and smiling. Freud believed that nursing, the experience of being held up to a woman's naked breast and sucking on her nipple, is a **primal sexual experience** and the hallmark of infantile sexuality. This infantile experience of love, pleasure, and primal satisfaction is recapitulated later in life during the sexual act, when the breast and nipple once again become focal points for oral stimulation. During infancy, the primal desire for oral stimulation becomes intrinsically linked to basic needs on physical, emotional, and sexual levels. Oral personality traits can be seen in the behaviors of characters whose oral fixations represent psychological and **emotional needs** that are not being met.

## SMOKING

Cigarette smoking is perhaps the most obvious oral fixation. Sucking smoke provides physical, emotional, and psychological comfort. It is a **neurotic behavior** – a nervous habit that is unhealthy and physically addictive. Nevertheless, the act of smoking is ubiquitous in movies, especially in older movies that were made before the fear of cancer and cigarette-related health problems made tobacco less popular. In the classic Westerns and Film Noir movies, characters were always lighting, smoking, or putting out a cigarette. Reasons behind the prevalence of smoking in films are manifold. First, smoke simply *looks cool* on screen – especially in black-and-white. The famous scene in *Citizen Kane* (1941), in which the shadows of gesticulating newsreel editors are seen through a gray haze of cigarette smoke, has a strong emotional impact, not just because of the natural obscurity provided by the smoke, but also from a sense of gritty realism – the feeling of being in a tiny theater with a gang of chain-smoking, fast-talking newsmen.

A second reason for the great prevalence of smoking film characters is that the act of smoking itself looks cool on the screen. At many points in your dialogue, you may want to insert a **dramatic pause**. A few moments of silence allows for the preceding line to resonate in the ears of your audience. The dramatic pause also gives the other character time to react to the line and consider an appropriately dramatic response. Since film is a visual medium, it is hard to write dramatic pauses that are meaningful to actors. Simply adding parentheticals such as "(beat)" or "(pause)" may not be enough. One line of direction, in which a character takes out a pack of cigarettes, lights up and smokes, gives an actor more material to work with (although this device should not be overused). When Kane's butler is asked about "Rosebud," he takes a few moments to light a cigarette. The dramatic pause allows for the very important word, "Rosebud," to sink in, and it also allows Kane's butler to conjure some ominously shady expressions as he lights up.

Finally, smoking can make a character look cool. Smoking gives characters something to do with their hands and mouth, and it provides a natural fog that obscures the light around them, giving them an ethereal appearance as they are momentarily veiled behind a cloud of blue smoke. But most importantly, smoking imparts a sense of **internal conflict**, a

*Dramatic Pause: The butler (Paul Stewart) in* Citizen Kane *lights a cigarette before answering the question about "Rosebud."*

feeling that this character is soothing some kind of inner turmoil. Whenever Rick (Humphrey Bogart) in *Casablanca* (1940) is faced with a heartbreaking memory or realization, he invariably lights up a cigarette, looking stoically heroic as he stares off into the distance through a shroud of smoke. The use of smoking as a symbol of internal conflict has not gone away. In fact, the effect may even be greater, since audiences are now aware that smoking is unhealthy. Only a severely conflicted character would light up a cancer-stick and suck on it rapaciously, killing a little bit of himself with each drag.

### ORAL TYPES

Smoking, drinking, and overeating are the more obvious symptoms of **oral fixation**. However, drug use, womanizing, promiscuity, gambling, and all other addictive behaviors could also be related to the oral stage, as they reflect a behavior pattern in which internal needs are satisfied by seeking and indulging in external stimulation. For some characters, oral behavior is their primary conflict. *The Lost Weekend* (1945), for example, is a classic movie about a man trying to overcome alcoholism. The struggle against addiction has been depicted in many fine movies; yet more often, the addictive problems of the oral type are not the primary issue in the film. Rather, they are represented as subtle qualities or mannerisms within a character. Paulie (Paul Sorvino), the Mafia boss in *Goodfellas* (1990), is extremely obese, as were Jabba the Hutt in *Return of the Jedi* (1983), and the title character (Charles Laugton) in *Captain Kidd* (1945). For these characters, obesity symbolized their overwhelming avariciousness — their emotional need to have everything for themselves. When writing your script, you may want to add oral behaviors to your characters, as they provide visceral and visual elements to your characters' personalities.

## ORAL SADISM

The quality of the nursing relationship between baby and mother begins to change later on in the oral stage of development, when baby starts to teeth. Nursing can become a painful experience, as baby realizes that it has the power to physically hurt its mother. The psychosexual experience of nursing is now infused with baby's newfound power to inflict pain. In psychoanalytic literature, "oral sadism" refers to a quality of character stemming from unresolved issues at the oral stage, expressed through a perverse desire to cause others pain. The oral sadist is seen most directly in monster villains such as vampires and werewolves, who kill and torture their female victims by tearing into them with their teeth. In *Nosferatu* (1922), the link between the vampire (Max Shrek) and his victim (Greta Schröder) is through the breast, recapitulating the infant/mother link in the oral stage. The vampire must suck the maiden's blood in order to live, just as baby must suck the milk from its mother's breast. As the human version of the monster villain, serial killers produce similar fear reactions in audiences. Viewers dread the perverse nature of villains who kill and torture in order to satisfy their own libidos.

## ORAL FIXATIONS

Oral fixations exemplify the basic problem of all villains — their inability to care for others — as demonstrated through their **selfishness**, **greed**, and **cruelty**. Villains such as Jabba the Hutt and Captain Kidd have obvious oral fixations, but the device can be effectively employed in other ways. Frank Booth (Dennis Hopper) in *Blue Velvet* (1986) is at his scariest and most evil when he is sucking voraciously on his nitrous-oxide mask. Frank's nitrous use is disturbing to look at, cueing the viewer in to the perverse and disturbing nature of his character. The oral fixations you write into your villain characters will typically demonstrate the wicked, sadistic, or perverse quality of their personalities. The oral fixations of your hero figures, however, usually represent the inner demons or character flaws that the hero must overcome.

## ORAL OBSTACLES

In Westerns such as *Rio Bravo* (1959) and *El Dorado* (1967), one supporting character is often a drunk who must overcome his alcoholism in order to help the hero in his shootout against the bad guys. Heroic characters must always face obstacles in order to accomplish their goals. Overcoming an addiction is an often-used, yet still powerful, inner obstacle for movie heroes. The device remains resonant because everyone can identify with the theme of overcoming oral desires — whether it is a crippling addiction to alcohol, or just a low-calorie diet. Obstacles are a central part of the hero formula, a character element that will be addressed throughout this book. Giving your hero an oral fixation is one way to humanize your hero by infusing him with a basic human foible that everyone in the audience can relate to.

## THE ANAL STAGE

Freud's second stage of psychosexual development revolves around the toddler's struggle to master toilet training. For the first time in its life, the toddler must learn to control its basic impulse to expel feces and urine whenever it feels the urge. As such, toilet training represents the developing ego's very first neurotic conflict. The toddler must repress its id desires for immediate release, in deference to the wishes of the parental figures, who insist that the toddler hold it in and wait to release its feces in the potty. Since the power struggle between parent and toddler over toilet training is a primary conflict, the resolution of this stage has tremendous implications on both the child's relationship with its parents, and the way in which the developing ego will learn to deal with neurotic conflict in the future. The two anal personality types, **Anal Retentive** and **Anal Expulsive**, are the enduring legacies of anal fixations at the second psychosexual stage.

## SCHLEMIEL, SCHLIMAZEL

The fundamental setup in comedy is the **comic dyad**, a pairing of two opposite character types. The **straight man** is an anal retentive type. He desires control and restraint, just as the anal-retentive child deals with the conflict of potty training by retaining his feces, even to the point of frustration. The straight man can be controlling, like Abbot from Abbot & Costello, or he can be compulsively neat and neurotic, like Felix (Jack Lemmon) from *The Odd Couple* (1968), or he can be perpetually frustrated and irate, like Oliver Hardy from Laurel & Hardy. The humor of the comic dyad stems from the constant conflict between the anal retentive straight man and his zany foil, the anal expulsive **goofball**. Just as the anal expulsive toddler deals with the potty conflict by releasing feces and causing a mess (incontinence), the anal expulsive goofball instigates conflict by screwing things up and making a comical mess (incompetence).

Gilligan (Bob Denver) from the television show *Gilligan's Island* was the ultimate anal expulsive goofball. In every episode, Gilligan's incompetence always screwed up the castaways' chances of getting rescued. His antics were a constant antecedent for humorously frustrated reactions from his tightly wound straight man, the Skipper (Alan Hale Jr.). Felix's compulsive neatness and Oscar's (Walter Matthau) repulsive messiness in *The Odd Couple* provide a particularly accurate portrayal of the comical retentive-expulsive dyad. Whether the characters in the comic dyad are the central heroes in your script, or merely comic relief, the basis of this comedic device remains the same. The two character types frustrate each other because of the opposite ways in which they channel their id energy. The **conflict between retention and release** is amusing to audiences, because it plays upon the universal anxiety of neurotic conflict, which was first experienced in early childhood during toilet training.

INTERNAL CONFLICT

Unless your script has a character that transforms physically into a beast (i.e., a vampire, werewolf or Dr. Jekyll/Mr. Hyde character), the theme of the individual struggling with his inner beast or libido must be depicted in subtler forms. In most movies, there is a point where the hero's personality changes in a noticeable way — either for good or for bad. The change might be related to an external obstacle that the hero must overcome. Other times, the change could be an epiphany, in which a retentive or restrained character suddenly becomes expulsive, releasing his pent-up libido drives and acting wildly. The internal conflict between restraint and release is extremely effective in building tension and suspense, as the audience senses the pressure of id energy building higher and higher in the hero's psyche, and waits excitedly for the dam of restraint to burst.

### DESTRUCTIVENESS VERSUS NON-VIOLENCE

In Sam Peckinpah's *Straw Dogs* (1971), David Sumner (Dustin Hoffman) moves to the English countryside, ironically to escape the violence in America. But the local hoodlums harass David and his wife in increasingly vile and brutal ways. David reacts to their bullying with controlled repression and restraint, until the climax of the movie, when the hoods go too far and David experiences a radical epiphany, resulting in an orgy of vindictive rage.

The release of the inner beast as character epiphany is also epitomized in the *Popeye* cartoons. Popeye endures abuse upon abuse from the barbaric Bluto throughout each cartoon, until Popeye *"can't stands no more!"* He eats his spinach, which, like Dr. Jekyll's potion, unleashes Popeye's pent-up id in a frenzy of violence. When writing the change or development in your character, whether the change portends a fall into vice or an epiphany, keep in mind the fundamental interplay between retention and expulsion — the restraint and release of libido energy. Either force can be climactic when it is proceeded by 100 minutes of the other.

### PASSION VERSUS ABSTINENCE

In *American Beauty* (1999), Lester's (Kevin Spacey) repressed and frustrated personality changes radically after he starts smoking some extremely potent marijuana. Like Dr. Jekyll's potion, Lester's pot releases his libidinous nature, and his once restrained character becomes wild and reckless. In *The Age of Innocence* (1993), the two main characters spend a good deal of the movie restraining themselves from the act of love that they both desperately desire. When they do get together, a visceral sense of release is experienced, as massive amounts of sexual tension are finally discharged. The tension between the release of passion and the inhibition of abstinence is a central device in all romantic plot lines. When writing the romantic script, remember to practice restraint, and not give away too much, too soon. Audiences want to feel the vicarious thrill of lust, passion, and romance. These thrills are saucier when they have to wait for them, just as food tastes better after a long, hungry anticipation.

## REBELLION VERSUS OBEDIENCE

There is a rebel inside everyone of us. At different times in our lives, we've all wanted to rebel against the tyrannical authority figures we faced at home, in school, or at work. The rebel character is a ubiquitous figure in movies, as audiences immediately identify with him. The rebel formula begins with **injustice**. In *Jesse James* (1939), the evil railroad men use trickery and brutality to run the poor farmers off their land. In *Braveheart* (1995) and *The Patriot* (2000), the evil English imperialists treat their Scot and American colonists with cruelty, barbarity, and contempt. In *Spartacus* (1960), the cruel Roman slave-masters oppress and mistreat Spartacus (Kirk Douglas) and his fellow gladiator-slaves. And in *Mutiny on the Bounty* (1939), Captain Bligh (Charles Laughton) is sadistic and wicked to the men of his crew. Tension rises as the **evil deeds** of the authority figures accrue and become more vile in nature. The authority figure finally goes too far and commits an act so vile that the hero must rebel in order to defend his own **honor**. The straw that breaks the camel's back is always a deeply personal and tragic loss. The railroad men in *Jesse James* (Henry Fonda) kill Jesse's mother. The English soldiers in *Braveheart* rape and kill William's (Mel Gibson) wife, and the English soldiers in *The Patriot* kill Benjamin's (Mel Gibson) son. Fletcher Christian (Clark Gable) is finally moved to mutiny when Captain Bligh's brutal punishment of an innocent sailor leads to the poor man's death. The longer your hero remains obedient and non-violent, the more tension you will build in your plot. Tension makes the story more engaging, and it increases the excitement in the moment when the tension is finally released, and the obedient pacifist becomes a violent rebel.

## THE PHALLIC STAGE

In Freud's third psychosexual stage, libido energy is directed toward the phallus, as the young boy discovers the pleasurable experience of self-stimulation. Once again, the developing ego must learn to repress its desire for instant gratification in deference to the demands for social propriety made by the parents. The most significant conflict at this stage is the Oedipal complex. The boy's libido energy, stemming from his incestuous longing for mother, is further restricted by the parental pro-hibition against phallic self-stimulation. As the young boy learns to repress his libido, he becomes obsessed with **phallic symbols**, which supply an outlet for the boy's **repressed sexuality**. Phallic symbols are typically violent in nature, because they also serve as channels for the boy's pent-up **aggression** toward his father. Hence the ubiquitous obsession that young boys have with guns, knives, swords, cannons, rockets, bats, clubs, and other phallic instruments of destruction. Have you ever wondered why the typical children's cartoon is filled with guns, bullets, sticks of dynamite, and other ultra-violent forms of aggression? Freud would say that young children (especially boys), are obsessed with these symbols and themes because they are redirecting their sexual desire for mother and their aggressive drive toward father into phallic images of destruction.

It is ironic that television shows and movies made for children tend to be extremely violent. Blockbuster "family films" such as *Jurassic Park* (1993) and *Spy Kids* (2001) are packed with fight scenes and frightful images of death and destruction. Despite the complaints of concerned parents, child advocates, and censors, films made for child audiences continue to be extremely violent, because that is simply what children (especially boys), want to see. These themes, however, are not relegated solely to children's movies. Westerns, gangster movies, cop movies, and war movies all provide heroes and villains who handle their phallic sym-bols (their **guns**), with supreme talent and agility. In these movies, the gun is a visual representative of the character's strength and masculini-ty. The manliness of Western gunslingers like Shane (Alan Ladd) and tough cops like Dirty Harry (Clint Eastwood) are measured by the length of their gun barrels and their skill in shooting.

### THE WEAPON AS A SYMBOL OF IDENTITY

There is a close psychological link between a hero's weapon and the hero's identity. Luke's identity as a hero in the original *Star Wars* trilogy is related directly to his mastery of his light saber. Apart from being an obvious phallic symbol, the light saber represents Luke's ultimate goal of becoming a Jedi knight. It is also a symbol of his relationship with his father, as Luke's light saber once belonged to Darth Vader. Each of the *Star Wars* films, including the latter installments, *The Phantom Menace*

(1999) and *Attack of the Clones* (2002), culminates in a climactic light saber duel, just as most Westerns culminate in a big shootout. Since the hero's relationship with his weapon is linked so closely with his identity, you may want the weapon to play a significant part in the climax of your script. In *Return of the Jedi* (1983), the climactic duel between Luke and Vader is doubly significant, because Luke has been learning to master his saber throughout two films, and also because Luke is using his father's weapon against him.

The Arthurian legend (which inspired the *Star Wars* movies), illustrates a superb example of the link between the hero's weapon and his identity. In the 1st act of *Excalibur* (1981), Arthur's (Nigel Terry) identity as the heroic king is defined by his ability to draw the mythical sword from the stone. In the 2nd act, Arthur loses Excalibur and all seems lost. But then, in the 3rd act, he is reunited with Excalibur, and he can lead his army one last time into victory. Since the phallic symbol exists on a purely figurative level, the craft you use in structuring the hero's weapon should not stand out overtly in the script. The symbolism should reveal itself as a sense of psychological depth in the hero's character. In effect, the weapon or phallic symbol is *any* material aid that assists the hero on his quest. The "weapon" can be the hero's car, boat, airplane, computer, etc. By paying just a bit more attention to your hero's weapon, you can add a whole new dimension to his identity.

## Penis Envy

According to Freud, the little girl's realization that she has no penis results in "penis envy." The feeling of envy exists until sexual maturity, when the female can incorporate a penis into her body (at least temporarily), during the act of sex. Penis envy is eventually transformed into a desire to give birth to a male child, the deep psychological need to create and own a being with the physical member that she unconsciously desires. Not surprisingly, this element of Freudian theory was not appreciated by female readers, who found the notion of penis envy to be unfounded, untrue, and blatantly offensive. Nevertheless, feminist revisionists have reinterpreted Freud's original theory and embraced it as an essential part of feminine psychology. In the revisionists' interpretation, the girl does not envy the actual penis, she envies the social status and **empowerment** awarded to boys and denied to girls, by nature of the fact that boys have penises and girls do not. Women throughout

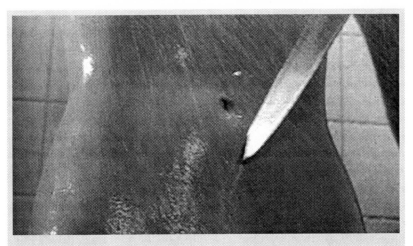

*The knife as phallic symbol: Janet Leigh in the infamous "shower scene" in* Psycho *(1960).*

history have been treated as second class citizens and forced to live as subordinates in male-dominated societies. The right to equality and social empowerment is a universal female desire that is often repressed, due to a fear of retribution from an autocratic male society. Just as women in many cultures are forced to hide their faces behind veils, women have also been forced to veil their desires for freedom and equality behind a mask of complacency.

The theme of penis envy is most literally depicted in Slasher movies, in which a girl is hunted by a male psychopath and his terrifying phallic symbol. The slasher's **knife** is phallic not only because of its shape, but also because of its function in the film — to be thrust into the female body. But most importantly, the knife represents male power and violence, the forces that men have used to subjugate women since the dawn of civilization. The goal of the female hero in these films is to overthrow their male subjugators. Typically, the heroine accomplishes this feat by using her superior intelligence to disarm the villain and catch him by surprise. The heroine then arms herself, usually with a knife, and kills the slasher. On a figurative level, penis envy is represented by the heroine's fear of the man. Penis envy is resolved when the female acquires her own phallic symbol, represented by a knife and her determination to use it.

## Girl Power

Female empowerment is the central theme in "Girl Power" movies such as *Lara Croft: Tomb Raider* (2001), *Charlie's Angels* (2000), and *Buffy the Vampire Slayer* (1992), in which women are cast in the traditionally male roles of conquering heroes. Despite their one-dimensional characters and sexually revealing outfits, the "anything you can do I can do better" credo of these heroines advances the notion that women can be just as powerful as men. The same theme is expressed in subtler ways in movies such as *Working Girl* (1988) and *Erin Brockovich* (2000), in which women display their equal power and abilities by becoming conquerors in the traditionally male realms of business and corporate law. In *G.I. Jane* (1997), O'Neil (Demi Moore) is seeking acceptance into the male dom-inated world of the Navy Seals. As the only female cadet, she suffers many insults and injuries, mostly at the hands of the sadistic chief (Viggo Mortensen). In her climactic fight scene, just before she knocks the chief out, she tells him: "*Suck my dick!*" O'Neil's penis envy is overcome with her mastery of physical violence, expressed as ownership of her own powerful phallic symbol. Apparently, she now has a "dick."

In its broadest interpretation, the theme of penis envy is almost always addressed in movies with a strong female lead role. No matter what the heroine's goal is, there is always at least one scene in which a burly male chauvinist chides the heroine and laughs at the idea of a woman trying to succeed in a man's world. The device has become tired and trite, yet it still remains resonant with many viewers. If you are writing a script with a female lead, your challenge is not necessarily to avoid the penis envy theme, but to find new and interesting ways of expressing this inherently female conflict in a manner that amplifies the complexity of the character, rather than reducing her to a hackneyed cliché.

## The Genital Stage

Following a period of "latency," in which libido urges are successfully repressed and sublimated, psychosexual conflict reemerges with a vengeance in the final stage of development. At puberty, sex hormones herald the dawn of sexual maturation, and a fully developed sex drive awakens. Young adolescents have resolved their Oedipal complexes by now, so sexual desire is directed safely away from opposite sex parents and onto other love objects. Resolution of this stage involves the search for a romantic partner who provides as much love and intimacy as mother supplied during infancy, while also being a satisfying and receptive sexual partner. First love, however, may still be tinged with **Oedipal undercurrents**. Adolescent crushes are often directed toward older adults such as teachers and counselors, who play the roles of parental figures in young people's lives. Adolescent crushes on adult father or mother figures represent a regression to Oedipal desires, and obstruct the teenager's development toward psychologically mature love relationships.

## CHARMING ELECTRA

The popular **teen temptress** genre plays upon the sexual tension that arises when a sexy teenage girl becomes infatuated with an older father figure. Films such as *The Crush* (1993) with Alicia Silverstone and *Poison Ivy* (1992) with Drew Barrymore use the sexual attraction between an underage girl and an older man as a source of danger and suspense. The girl has reached sexual maturity and is extremely appealing on a physical level; but psychologically, she is still a child and prone to dangerous obsessions and irrationality. The older man is torn between his physical desire for the girl and his awareness that acting upon this desire is immoral, unlawful, and socially unacceptable. While the father figure is typically portrayed as a good man in a state of moral conflict, the troubled teen is usually depicted as a" bad girl" – a female child who never resolved her **Electra complex** – in the body of a sexy, yet unstable, young woman.

When the father figure's superego finally takes hold and impels him to rebuff the temptress' seduction, her passionate love is transformed into an equally passionate rage – the *"fury of a woman scorned."* The teen temptress is ultimately punished for her actions, the inevitable retribution for not properly resolving her Electra complex. Though the teen temptress figure is rife with emotion, conflict, and psychological complexity, her part in films has rarely deviated from the rather simplistic formula spelled out above. Some talented filmmakers such as Stanley Kubrick *Lolita* (1962) and Francoise Ozon *Swimming Pool* (2003) have depicted teen temptresses in more intricate and interesting ways. Screenwriters should be aware of the untapped potential in this character. Teen temptresses carry the primal power of both sex and aggression, and the heroes they seduce can fall into great pits of tragedy and despair. Formulaic teen temptress thrillers are a-dime-a-dozen, but unique and original depictions have been few and far between.

## Teen Sex Movies

The *American Pie* (1999, 2001, & 2003) films have been heralded by some as the springboard for a fresh new wave of teen sex movies, though it's difficult to see how the characters, plot, and humor in these films deviate significantly from the *Porky's* movies of the 1980s, and dozens of other films just like them. The male-oriented teen sex movie typically centers around a neurotic, insecure teenager Pee Wee (Dan Monahan) in *Porky's*, Jim (Jason Biggs) in *American Pie*, whose desperate struggle to resolve his genital stage of psychosexual development is represented by the goal of losing his virginity. The **virgin hero** has a clear journey (the path of sexual conquest), a distinct goal (sex), a band of allies (his equally horny buddies), an inner flaw he must overcome (his own desperation), and a great reward (intercourse). There is even a moral lesson that the hero typically learns — that sex is an empty experience without love.

When the hero earns a beautiful girlfriend in the end, he has realized all of the essential elements of the hero formula in a way that any teenage boy can identify with. Hence, the same formula (replete with similar penis jokes, gratuitous nudity, and raunchy sex humor), can be re-tilled every decade for a new generation of teen audiences, and the characters and themes will resonate just as strongly. The basic psychosexual themes of genital development — finding and learning about first love and sex — are experienced anew by every generation of teenagers, so the same old stories seem fresh and original to teens currently experiencing these challenges. You may be the screenwriter who will write the *Porky's* or *American Pie* for the class of 2005. If so, try to use the formula to express new or interesting insights into the conflicts of adolescent sexuality, rather than abusing the formula by slapping together another teen sex comedy about a bunch of horny boys trying to score.

## CHAPTER THREE SUMMARY POINTS

- The *oral stage* of psychosexual development is related to neediness on emotional, physical, and psychological levels.
- An *oral fixation* is depicted when a person deals with an emotional, physical or psychological need by placing external objects or substances in his mouth.
- *Smoking* is the most common oral fixation seen in films.
- *Oral types* are often depicted in film as avaricious characters who are constantly seeking immediate gratification.
- *Oral sadism* is the perverse desire to dominate and inflict pain on others.
- Movie characters must often overcome oral obstacles such as addiction to drugs or alcohol in order to develop.
- The *anal stage* of psychosexual development is related to the way in which people deal with the psychological pressure of neurotic conflict.
- The *anal retentive type* deals with neurotic conflict by repressing and controlling his drives, typically to the point of frustration.
- The *anal expulsive type* deals with neurotic conflict by releasing and indulging his drives, often times inappropriately.
- The quintessential *comical dyad* is a pairing of an anal retentive type with an anal expulsive type.
- Heroes often struggle with an *internal conflict* between the desire to release a primal drive and an equally powerful need to control or repress this drive.
- The most common internal conflicts related to the anal stage are *destructiveness versus non-violence, passion versus abstinence* and *rebellion versus obedience.*
- The *phallic stage* of psychosexual development is related to the resolution of the Oedipal complex.
- When Oedipal desires are successfully repressed by the superego, sexual and aggressive urges are expressed through the use of *phallic symbols* — weapons of destruction, such as guns and knives, that embody both violent and phallic qualities.
- The hero's *weapon* is a phallic symbol that can be extremely significant and relevant to his sense of identity.

- *Penis envy* in females is typically interpreted as a woman's desire for equality, independence, and empowerment in a male-dominated society.
- *Girl power* movies typically address the issue of penis envy as a central theme.
- The *genital stage* of psychosexual development is related to the integration of mature (non-Oedipal) romantic relationships.
- The *teen temptress* figure in movies is a sexy adolescent female who is dangerous and illicit, because she has not yet resolved her Electra complex.
- The *virgin hero* figure in teen sex movies is a character who resolves his genital stage of development by losing his virginity and forming a mature romantic relationship.

## CHAPTER THREE EXERCISES

1. Come up with two or three "oral" behaviors that haven't been used before.
2. Oral obstacles in heroes are personal flaws that are related to physical, psychological, or emotional neediness. Create an oral obstacle that your hero must overcome, but stay away from hackneyed or overused obstacles, such as alcoholism or drug use.
3. The comically mismatched pair of characters is a basic formula for comedy. Do you have a comic dyad in your script? Whether the twosome are lead characters (i.e., Nick and Nora in *The Thin Man* movies), or comic relief (i.e., Jay and Silent Bob in *Clerks* and *Mallrats*), how can you use the opposing forces of retention and expulsion (restraint and release), to build humorous conflict within your dyad?
4. If you have only one comic character, consider the effect of giving him a partner or foil. What could this element add to your script?
5. The hero's weapon is typically a phallic symbol, a psychological representation of the hero's identity and power. How can you structure your hero's weapon so that it pertains to or reveals your hero's identity?

6. Brainstorm all the different kinds of weapons or material aids that characters have used in your favorite movies.
7. Now imagine how your hero might use some of these weapons in your script.
8. Come up with five different weapons or forms of material aid that have never been used before.

## ADDRESSING THE PSYCHOSEXUAL STAGES IN YOUR SCRIPT

1. Internal conflict can be depicted visually through an oral fixation. Think of how your character can portray internal conflict by smoking, drinking, eating, or other "oral" behaviors.

2. The opposing psychosexual forces also are an excellent source of internal conflict. Heroes often deal with the conflicting drives of destructiveness and non-violence, passion and abstinence, or rebellion and obedience. How can you infuse your hero with an internal conflict related to retention and release?

3. The "weapon" is any material aid that assists the hero on his or her quest. Does your hero have a "weapon?"

4. In its broadest interpretation, "penis envy" represents any fear of dominating power or authority, as well as issues of disenfranchisement and empowerment. Female heroes in films typically deal with these issues. How can your heroine resolve the issue of penis envy in a way that embodies her own weaknesses and strengths?

5. Issues of intimacy, love, and sex are ubiquitous in movies. You may be finding it difficult to address these issues without resorting to cliches and overused devices. Try analyzing the romantic relationship in your script in terms of the Oedipal themes of possessiveness, rivalry, and forbidden love. This might help you find new insights into the relationship that will lead to original conflicts and story lines in your script.

| THE PSYCHOSEXUAL STAGES AT A GLANCE | | | |
|---|---|---|---|
| STAGES | CHARACTERISTICS | CHARACTER TYPES | EXAMPLES |
| Oral Stage | Emotional Neediness | Smokers & Drinkers | Film Noir & Westerns |
| | Selfishness | Overeaters | *Goodfellas* |
| | Greed | Stealers & Cheaters | *Casino* |
| | Cruelty | Sadists | *Silence of the Lambs* |
| Anal Stage | Obsessive Control | Comic Dyads | Abbott & Costello |
| | No Self Control | Inner Demons | Werewolves |
| | Internal Conflict | Conflicted Characters | *Straw Dogs* |
| Phallic Stage | Obsession with Phallic Symbols | Destructive Characters | Westerns & War Movies |
| | | Violent Heroes & Villains | Action Movies |
| | Penis Envy | Empowered Women | "Girl Power" Movies |
| Genital Stage | Forbidden Love | Teen Temptresses | *Poison Ivy* |
| | First Love | Virgin Heroes | *American Pie* |

*Chapter Four*

# THE EGO DEFENSE MECHANISMS

*operating System "Windows"*

Like your computer's hard drive, the unconscious is an incredibly complex storehouse of knowledge and functions of which you, the user, are blissfully unaware. The split between unconscious and conscious processing of information is absolutely necessary, because it would be impossible for us to lead productive lives if we didn't focus on very specific issues, one at a time. Similarly, working on a computer would not be very productive if, rather than focusing on the single page on the screen, you were forced to pay attention to the millions of pieces of data and ongoing functions going on just behind your computer screen. And, just as the threat of viruses is a constant issue in your computer, neurotic conflict is a constant issue in the unconscious. Like virus detection software in your hard drive, the ego defense mechanisms are the silent protectors of the psyche, perpetually vigilant in their search for neurotic conflict. If unresolved unconscious issues were to break through the barrier of ego defense mechanisms and emerge into consciousness, the problem would dominate and overwhelm all of the individual's attention, in the same way that a rogue virus would overwhelm the normal functioning of your computer.

The defense mechanisms "defend" the ego by relieving it of the pressure of libido energy and neurotic conflict in a variety of ingenious ways. When the libido energy is relieved or otherwise controlled, guilt decreases and the anxiety caused by neurotic conflict is temporarily assuaged. The key word in this concept is **temporarily**. The defense mechanisms do not eliminate or resolve the neurotic conflict, they merely put a bandage on the problem. The only way to truly resolve a neurotic conflict is to analyze it, understand it consciously, and tear it out by the root. Unlike analysis, the ego defenses keep the troublesome issues completely unconscious, so that the individual is entirely unaware of them.

### THE DEFENSIVE HERO

Adding defense mechanisms to your hero's personality will add psychological depth to his character. When your hero says things he does not mean, does things he does not want to do, and acts in ways that are counterintuitive to his situation, he automatically becomes more complex. The audience wonders: "Why is he acting that way?" and "Why did he do that?" The audience intuitively senses that these characters are dealing with internal conflicts, and they are drawn into their dilemmas in the same way that readers are drawn into a mystery story. Audiences have learned from many years of film viewing to be incredibly perceptive. They scan the larger-than-life faces of the characters on screen for any trace of innuendo, and they are constantly analyzing their heroes — trying to find the hidden root to their motivations and the psychological conflicts that they know lie just beneath the surface of their cloaked demeanor.

### THE OBLIVIOUS HERO

The key to writing a defense mechanism is that the characters themselves are completely unaware that they are exhibiting defensive behaviors. The unconscious element of **defensiveness** raises tension and suspense, as the other characters in the film and the viewers in the audience watch the heroes and become frustrated with their obliviousness to their own glaring problems. The defense mechanism typically becomes a goal for heroes, a **weakness** that they must overcome. Since defense mechanisms are universal traits, audiences immediately identify with the defensive hero.

In a way, movie watching itself is a defense. Audiences escape their own problems and conflicts by shutting themselves off from their personal lives and becoming emotionally involved with the characters on screen. Like a defense mechanism, watching a good movie provides temporary relief from personal conflict and strife. And, like a defense mechanism, the psychological power of a movie is felt primarily on an unconscious level.

### REPRESSION

Repression is at once the most simple and the most sophisticated of the defense mechanisms. Neurotic conflict arises when libido energy is blocked by guilt. Repression works by apprehending the initial desire and stowing it away deep down in the unconscious. By hiding the initial urge, repression ebbs the flow of libido energy and blankets the root of the conflict. In *Remains of the Day* (1993), a stodgy British butler, Stevens

(Anthony Hopkins), represses his lust for Miss Kenton (Emma Thompson), hiding his desire so effectively that, although the viewer can sense his true feelings, we are unsure if Stevens himself is aware of his desire for Miss Kenton. However, repression, like all the defenses, is only a stopgap solution. Every time the object of desire is seen, libido energy arises once more and it must be repressed all over again. Even though Stevens is a veritable master of repression, his lust for Miss Kenton never truly dies. At the end of the film, he and Miss Kenton reunite after decades of separation. His love for Miss Kenton is still there, yet he is still unable to release his repressed feelings and express his love to her.

Repression can be an extremely powerful emotional force. In certain scenes in *Remains of the Day*, the tension between Stevens and Miss Kenton is so great that the audience wants to scream out at the screen, "*Kiss her, you fool!*" Anthony Hopkins' performance is so resonant because his character is a tragic figure, a victim of his own repression. But when feelings are repressed for a long time and then finally released, the experience of **catharsis** – the psychological purging of intense emotions – can be equally as powerful. In romance movies such as *It Happened One Night* (1934), the release felt when the two characters finally give in to their mutual lust and experience a moment of passion is no less than orgasmic.

Director Robert Altman displayed the profound power of repression in *Gosford Park* (2001), a film set in an environment much like the one in *Remains of the Day*. The guests and servants in this traditional English manor are all appropriately repressed, especially in their sense of class distinctions and propriety. Servants are expected to appear and disappear without being noticed by their lordly masters. The audience is completely immersed in this sense of social repression for the first hour of the film. When a lowly maid (Emily Watson) speaks out to her masters in the 2nd act, the audience's reaction to her breach of propriety is as extreme as if she blew someone's head off. The incredible resonance of this scene arises from the fact that an extreme reaction of shock was elicited, merely by the shot of a maid speaking a few revealing words out of turn. The drama of her impropriety overshadows the more subtle fact that her motivation for speaking was her secret affair with the lord of the manor.

When writing repressed characters in your script, remember that intense reactions and high drama can be elicited without extreme violence or melodramatic situations. By creating an extremely high level of repression in your characters, you create **tension** and **suspense** in your plot. When this tension is finally released, even a few words, a touch of the hand, or a simple kiss can be incredibly cathartic and dramatic.

## DENIAL

The epitome of the oblivious hero is seen in the character suffering from denial. Denial of a troublesome desire or an anxiety-provoking event is occasionally used as an element of **character strength**. In *The Little Princess* (1939), Sara (Shirley Temple) is confronted with the news that her beloved father died at war. Sara's reaction to this unthinkable fact is complete denial. She refuses to believe that her father is dead. Sara clings resolutely to her denial throughout the film, until she is miraculously rewarded for her constancy in the end and reunited with her father, who, as it turns out, was only injured and shell-shocked, rather than killed. Typically, denial is an element of **character weakness**. In *Jaws* (1975), the close-minded mayor of Amity Island (Murray Hamilton) refuses to believe that there is a man-eating shark stalking the shores of his town. His foolish denial raises tension and suspense in the plot, as the wary sheriff (Roy Scheider) becomes more and more frustrated with the mayor's negation of Jaws' existence.

Denial is often used as an **obstacle** for the hero, represented by a **denying authority figure** who frustrates and hinders the hero by denying the existence of danger. The real-estate developer in *Poltergeist* (1982) and the parents in *A Nightmare on Elm Street* (1984) all represent obstacles of denial that the hero must overcome. In the '50s, movies such as *Invasion of the Body Snatchers* (1956) and *The Blob* (1958) symbolized the paranoia of the McCarthy era, by placing heroes in situations in which everyone around them is in complete denial of the insidious danger invading their communities. Denial as an obstacle can also be represented as an **internal weakness** within the hero that he or she must overcome. Rosemary (Mia Farrow) in *Rosemary's Baby* must overcome her denial that her beloved husband (John Cassavetes) and benign neighbors are evil conspirators, before she can take action to defend herself and her unborn baby.

When writing denial in your script, be clear about the role you want this device to play. A character who denies the existence of danger in order to hinder the hero, but who actually knows that the danger exists, is not in denial. This character is simply lying. The distinction between denial and deceit is subtle but extremely important. The liar is purposefully deceiving the hero in order to benefit himself, making this character a bad guy or villain. The character in true denial is not purposefully deceiving anyone, this character actually believes in what he is saying. The character in denial is **oblivious** to the world and to himself. Though he is frustrating and troubling, this character is ultimately a tragic and pitiable figure. Overcoming the denial figure is merely a prelude or afterthought to the hero's primary goal of defeating the actual danger or villain.

When a character is struggling to overcome his own flaw, it is more dramatic to cue his realization of inner denial by inciting it through a **tragic loss**. In *Jaws*, the mayor only realizes his folly when more people are killed because of his obliviousness. In *Rosemary's Baby*, Rosemary only begins to suspect her husband when her beloved friend, Hutch (Maurice Evans), mysteriously dies. The device of epiphany through tragic loss pays respect to the powerful forces of the unconscious, admitting that only a dramatic jolt to the system can lift the veil of denial. It also adds drama to the plot.

## IDENTIFICATION

The resolution of the Oedipal complex is achieved through identification with the same-sex parent, making identification a capstone experience in ego development. By identifying with others and imitating their goals and behaviors, the ego relieves itself of the anxiety provoking feelings of self-doubt that arise when we act on our own initiative. How could our behaviors be wrong, if we are simply doing what Father, Mother, Brother, Sister, Teacher, Preacher, or others around us are doing? The danger of identification arises from the **loss of individuality** that occurs when we accept the comfort and safety of conforming to the crowd.

Identification is a double-edged sword, representing either a goal or an obstacle to the hero. In *High Noon* (1952), everybody in town wants Marshal Kane (Gary Cooper) to run away from the murderous outlaws who are coming to town to kill him. Even the town judge (Otto Kruger) runs away, telling Kane that he should flee, as well. Kane's challenge in *High Noon* is to resist identification with this cowardly mentor figure, and to stay true to his own code of honor. The opposite formula is played out in *Sergeant York* (1941). In this film, Gary Cooper plays a roguish character who lives according to his own rules. His challenge in the 1st act is to identify with the town preacher (Walter Brennan), and become a humble and meek member of the town congregation.

Whether your hero's challenge is to conform or to rebel, the process of identification is intrinsically linked with the hero's identity. The best way to express the process of identification is by providing your hero with a clear **mentor figure**, but this does not mean that you, as a screenwriter, must conform to a rigid structural formula. The mentor figure is an **inspiration**, not necessarily a character. The hero's mentor can be an idea, a philosophy, a memory, or even a dream. Be creative and original in the way you set up your hero's identification. The basic structure of hero identification and a mentor figure should be viewed as a springboard to creativity, rather than a cookie-cutter formula for character motivation and development.

## SUBLIMATION

Freud believed that all great individual works are products of sublimation – the process of channeling libido energy into productive and artistic activities. Sublimation in films is often portrayed through **passionate labor**, driven by sexually charged motivations behind the character. In *Like Water for Chocolate* (1992), Tita (Lumi Cavazos) sweats and moans as she rolls her tortillas, sublimating all of her sexual desire for Pedro (Marco Leonardi) into her spicy, sensuous cooking. In *Lust for Life* (1956), Van Gogh (Kirk Douglas) sublimates his sexual frustration, violent rage, and tempestuous nature into his painting. And in *Raging Bull* (1980), Jake La Motta (Robert De Niro) channels his primal carnality and fury into his fighting.

Sublimation is an unconscious process that audiences easily recognize. The primal impulses of love, hate, sex, and aggression are powerful forces that can charge characters with Herculean strength and energy, making them capable of accomplishing anything. The **power of love** is a device often called upon in the 3rd act of a film, as a nearly supernatural force that helps the hero defeat his formidable foe and rescue the maiden. Superman (Christopher Reeve) has superpowers, but nobody would believe that he could fly around the world so fast that he could reverse the orbit of the earth and turn back time, unless he was doing it to bring his beloved Lois Lane (Margot Kidder) back to life. This would seem too colossal of a task, even for Superman, unless his desperate flying was driven by his passionate love for Lois. The power of sublimation could make unbelievable feats seem believable to the audience, though the credibility of the hero's actions must be firmly grounded in his motivations. The audience has to believe that Superman really loves Lois, before they would believe that he could actually turn back time in order to bring her back to life.

REGRESSION

Childhood was a time when there were less obligations, less responsibilities, and fewer restrictions on our behavior. Regression to a childish state provides a temporary release from anxiety and the pressures of adulthood. Audiences can relate to regressive behaviors, and can enjoy them vicariously by watching movie characters regress on screen. Often times, adult characters use a **substance** to incite their regression. In a much copied scene from *The Big Chill* (1983), a group of thirty-something college buddies smoke pot and regress to behaviors more appropriate to teenagers. By regressing to adolescence, they are free to act silly, release their inhibitions, and even indulge some of their long-repressed sexual desires. In the 1980s, it was very common for movies to have a sequence in which all of the characters get high or drunk, followed by a musical montage of short scenes with the characters dancing, carousing, laughing, and otherwise acting like children. Thankfully, this device is no longer in vogue.

Regression is most often used for **comic relief** or a bit of **musical fun**. On several occasions, [i.e., *The Breakfast Club* (1985) and *Planes, Trains & Automobiles* (1987)], John Hughes used regression scenes to create a dramatic shift in the plot. Directly after the musical sequence of childish behaviors, the characters would be sitting quietly, coming down off their high, but still intoxicated. The childish fun was a moment of bonding, and now, with their lips loosened by liquor or pot, the characters can share a **moment of intimacy** by disclosing their deepest secrets. A melodramatic scene of intense emotional expression packs even more of a punch when it is juxtaposed with an extremely happy sequence of childish behavior directly preceding it. Occasionally, regression will be the theme of an entire movie, rather than one sequence of comic relief. In *Cocoon* (1985), a group of senior citizens is made magically young again by swimming in a pool infested with mysterious alien pods. They proceed to enjoy their newfound vigor by engaging in some youthful behavior, including some much appreciated sexual release.

By far, the most common theme in the regressive hero movie is an obsession with a young lover. Woody Allen made three movies that deal directly with this issue, [*Manhattan* (1979), *Alice* (1990), *Husbands and Wives* (1992)] and he made other films that address the issue as subtext. In *Blame it on Rio* (1984), the conflict within the regressive hero theme is intensified when a middle-aged man (Michael Caine) becomes infatuated with his best friend's teenage daughter. The older man/young girl formula is reversed in *How Stella Got Her Groove Back* (1998), in which Stella (Angela Bassett) indulges in a passionate relationship with a man half her age. Whether regression is used in one sequence or the entire film, the device should move the plot forward and provide more than just comic relief or libidinal release. Ideally, regression should lead to **character development**. By taking a step backwards, the characters should learn more about themselves or their situation, preparing them for a great leap forward — and bringing them that much closer to their goals.

### REACTION FORMATION

Defense mechanisms protect the ego by shielding the mind from its own desires. The reaction formation is even more crafty than the other defenses, because it reacts against the impulse, rather than avoiding it. The character exhibiting reaction formation exposes his own deepest desire by reacting strongly against it. The complexity of the reaction formation makes it one of the less used defenses in film characters, but it is, nonetheless, a powerful force and an intriguing behavior pattern. The defense can be seen in courting behaviors, especially in female characters in old movies. Mary Kate (Maureen O'Hara) in *The Quiet Man* (1952) reacts with anger and distaste when Sean (John Wayne) brashly kisses her on the lips. Her **extreme reaction** against Sean is the "good Catholic girl" part of her personality, expressing the opposite of what Mary Kate's libido truly desires. Mary Kate's lips tell Sean "no!" — but her eyes say "yes! yes!"

Extremely repressed or uptight characters often display reaction formation in their prudish behaviors and attitudes. In the ultimate reaction formation, the character is so conflicted by his inappropriate desire that he tries to destroy the thing that he loves the most. Frollo (Sir Cedric Hardwicke) in *The Hunchback of Notre Dame* (1939) is so conflicted over his inappropriate lust for the sexy gypsy girl, Esmerelda (Maureen O'Hara), that he is motivated to destroy her. And Frank Fitts (Chris Cooper) in *American Beauty* is so conflicted over his repressed homo-erotic feelings that he is motivated to destroy the object of his desire – Lester (Kevin Spacey). It is difficult to effectively portray the contradiction of characters saying and doing one thing, when inside they desire the opposite. But if you could pull this off, you can create characters with exceptional complexity and depth.

## DISPLACEMENT

William Foster (Michael Douglas) in *Falling Down* (1993) is filled with rage. Divorced from his wife, estranged from his daughter, fired from his job and stranded in an urban-sprawl wasteland, Foster cracks and goes on a violent rampage, displacing his fury on everyone he meets. Displacement is the redirection of a sexual or aggressive drive onto a **substitute outlet**. Rather than venting troublesome libido energy onto the source of neurotic conflict, the negative energy is displaced onto someone else. Displacement is a practical defense for the ego, because the source of the conflict (a spouse, a boss, etc.), may not appreciate being yelled at or abused. The substitute outlet on whom the negative energy is displaced upon is typically a **safe target** – someone who cannot strike back or cause further conflict.

Like most of the other defenses, displacement is typically used as a **character trait**, a passing behavior that is part of the hero's personality, but not a central part of the plot. Still, displacement is often used to advance the plot by creating rifts between characters. In *My Darling Clementine* (1946), Doc Holliday (Victor Mature) is a brooding, tragic figure. Once a respectable doctor, he has fallen into a state of disgrace – an alcoholic degenerate gambler and killer, dying of consumption and ashamed of his life. Chihuahua (Linda Darnell), the showgirl with a heart of gold, loves Holliday and is constantly by his side, despite the fact that she is a perpetual outlet for Holliday's abuse. Holliday displaces all of his anger and self-loathing onto Chihuahua, calling her names, ridiculing her and treating her like dirt. Finally, Holliday goes too far and Chihuahua drops him. The rift created by Holliday's displacement creates **romantic tension** in the plot, and allows for some much needed **character development**. Like any other dramatic device, displacement should be used not just as an embellishment of a character's behavior, but also as a means of inciting character development and advancing the plot.

## RATIONALIZATION

Many of the characters in Woody Allen's movies epitomize the mechanism of rationalization – in which emotions are dealt with by **intellectualizing** the issues. When emotions are rationalized and translated into intellectual terms, they lose their emotional impact, as passionate feelings become cold, rational ideas. Rationalization is the optimal form of defense for many of Allen's characters, who tend to be cerebral intellectuals who are much better at mastering complex ideas than intense emotions. In *Love and Death* (1975), *Annie Hall* (1977), *Manhattan* (1979), and many of his other films, Allen's characters discuss the riddles of love with constant references to Freudian theory, existential philosophy, and other ultra-intellectual fields, as if they were trying to solve a problem in theoretical physics rather than dealing with issues of the heart. Rationalization is an amusing character trait in Allen's movies, because the audience intuitively knows that for all of the characters' intellectual brilliance and high-brow ramblings, they are no closer to resolving their emotional problems than they would be if they had never heard of Freud, Heidegger, Neitzsche, or Sartre. As with all of the other defenses, the psychological power behind the device is that the audience is aware of this weakness in the character's personality, even though the character is not. The audience is at once frustrated with, and sympathetic to, the character's plight.

## PROJECTION

Projection occurs when a troublesome unconscious impulse is attributed to somebody else. Since projection is a defense, the unconscious impulses projected onto others are usually negative. The mechanism defends the individual's ego by giving him the sense that the negative desires or drives do not belong to himself, but rather, to the morally inferior people around him. In *The Treasure of the Sierra Madre* (1948), Dobbs (Humphrey Bogart) becomes obsessed with the paranoid notion that his gold-mining partners are planning to cheat him out of his share of the gold. Of course, Dobbs is actually the one with "gold fever" — the evil impulse to keep all the gold to himself. By projecting his gold fever onto his partners, Dobbs can retain a somewhat clear conscience, believing that he is merely defending himself against his corrupt partner, even as he kills him and takes his gold.

Projection can also make for some complicated **family dynamics**. It is natural for parents to project the hopes and dreams that they once had for themselves onto their children. Tension arises when the children reach an age at which they want to define their own identities, rather than living out the projected fantasies of their parents. In *Of Human Hearts* (1938), Reverend Wilkins (Walter Huston) projects his own religious devotion onto his son, Jason (James Stewart), whom he expects to become a minister. When Jason decides to become a man of science rather than a man of God, his father is sourly disappointed, causing a great deal of tension in their relationship that eventually escalates into an irreparable rift.

Similar dynamics play out in *Gypsy* (1962). Rose (Rosalind Russell) is a failed actress who has projected all of her stage ambitions onto her talented younger daughter, June. When June marries and escapes her mother's controlling web, Rose transfers her projected dreams onto her elder daughter, Louise (Natalie Wood). Despite the fact that Louise has no talent, Rose forces her on stage and insists that she become a success. Rose's projection is so strong that she forces her daughter into a degrading life of stripping. But Rose is still never completely satisfied, because projection never fulfills Rose's original desire to become a star herself. The tension that builds between Louise and her jealous stage-mother eventually destroys their relationship.

Unlike most of the other defenses, projection is often used as the central issue in films focusing on parent/child relationships. Audiences sympathize with both figures in these movies. It is understandable for children to want to choose their own paths. But audiences can also identify with parents who only want the best for their children, even though these parents fail to realize that their dreams for their children's futures are often their own unrealized dreams, projected outwardly onto their offspring.

## ISOLATION

Characters in isolation are fleeing from their own repressed issues, and typically hiding from memories of a **tragic past**. The goal for these characters is to come out of isolation and **reintegrate** themselves into society. In order for this to happen, the characters must deal with their conflicts in some clear way, rather than avoiding or running away from the negative feelings. In *Finding Forrester* (2000), Forrester (Sean Connery) is a reclusive Pulitzer Prize winning writer who isolates himself in his apartment in a self-enforced exile from his tragic past. In order for him to emerge from isolation, he must overcome his fear of feelings and become emotionally involved with another person. By becoming a mentor to a young writer, Forrester conquers his own defenses. With the aid of his young hero, Forrester is able to face his past and liberate himself from isolation.

Many of the great Western heroes were isolated men – loners who appear like apparitions from out of the wilderness, complete a heroic act, and then disappear again into a life of wandering isolation. *Shane* begins with the lone cowboy riding into civilization from the open range, and ends with him returning to the wild. In the famous final scene, little Joey calls out: "*Come back

The Lone Hero: John Wayne in The Searchers (1956).

*Shane!"* — but of course, the **lone hero** must return to his natural habitat, the isolated wilderness. A similar theme is seen in *The Searchers* (1956). In the opening sequence, Ethan (John Wayne) appears as a lone rider rising out of the landscape. And in the unforgettable final shot of the film, Ethan's departing figure is framed between the doorframes of a prairie house as he returns to his solitary life on the trail. The isolated character is almost always a tragic figure, a guilt-racked man perpetually on the run from memories of a distressing past. Shane and Ethan are both outlaws trying to escape the violence behind them, yet inevitably drawn by the irony of their own existences into more violence. The isolated hero can escape his tragic fate by facing his past and rejoining society; or he can remain a lone wolf, retaining the romantic air of an isolated cowboy riding off into the sunset.

## FREUDIAN SLIPS

Slips of the tongue are often referred to as "Freudian slips," because Freud was the first theorist to attach great psychological significance to this phenomenon. A slip is when a repressed or hidden feeling slips out unconsciously during speech. As my Intro to Psych. professor in college said: *"A Freudian slip is when you mean to say one thing but instead say a **mother**."* Slips are part of common usage, and nearly every sophisticated viewer knows what a slip is and why it is psychologically significant. One overused device is having a deceitful character give away his diabolical plot through a slip of the tongue. At the end of *The Bad and the Beautiful* (1952), Shields (Kirk Douglas) makes a costly slip in casual conversation with James Lee (Dick Powell), revealing that he was indirectly responsible for the death of James Lee's wife. Though slips are useful devices, they're a bit too predictable and convenient in these situations. They are better used when a character is repressing an **intense feeling** that is begging to be let out. The slip seems more realistic in these instances, as it expresses emotion rather than information, and because it provides **cathartic release** for both the character and the audience.

## JOKES

Humor is an integral part of any film, no matter how serious the subject matter. Ironically, the best place for a joke is often just before or after a moment of extreme dramatic tension — when the need for **comic relief** is the greatest. In action movies, the hero often delivers a comic one-liner just before he kills the villain. When Arnold Schwarzenegger says "*Asta La Vista, Baby,*" right before he blows someone away, the dark tragedy of death and dismemberment is lightened by a little humor, reminding the audience that the ghastly violence is all in good fun.

Freud believed that jokes serve the function of an ego defense, because laughter is a direct form of **emotional release**. The need for emotional release is at its greatest when there is tension and anxiety in the air, hence the ubiquitous phenomenon of **nervous laughter**. Comic relief relieves the anxiety at the most anxious moments in the film, allowing the audience to enjoy itself rather than getting too nervous or upset. Remember, though drama and tension are necessary parts of the film, the audience is there to be entertained, not to be put through an emotional ordeal.

Jokes also serve as defenses because subject material that is deemed **taboo** in normal conversation is perfectly acceptable in the form of a joke. The majority of jokes told in the world are either dirty or darkly satirical. Late night talk show hosts typically start their monologue with jokes about the president's stupidity, while jokes told over the water-cooler are either overtly sexual, derisive of the clergy ("a priest and a rabbi walk into a bar..."), or blatantly offensive (Polish jokes, blonde jokes, etc). All of these topics of conversation would not be socially appropriate unless they were cloaked in the form of a joke. The same liberties that people take in joke-telling are taken by moviemakers in their comedies. The **gross-out humor** popular in contemporary comedies are examples of how far you can stretch the bounds of good taste in the name of a big laugh. Drinking urine (*American Pie*), mishandling sperm (*There's Something About Mary*), and public defecation (*Me, Myself and Irene*) are scenes that would not make the cut in most movies, yet in comedies, they are all par for the course. Other taboos frequently broken in comedies are the perpetuation of racial stereotypes (*Undercover Brother*), making fun of the handicapped and mentally impaired (*There's Something About Mary*), objectifying women (*Porky's*), and cruelty to animals (*There's Something About Mary,* once again).

While comedies typically use the humor loophole to take the low road in violating taboos, some comedies take the high road. Stanley Kubrick's *Dr. Strangelove* (1964) addressed the very touchy topics of Cold War, excessive military power, and nuclear annihilation in a way that no other film could, because of the superb humor and satire he wove into it.   Similarly, Kubrick's *Lolita*, though controversial, was a popular success, because it addressed the sensitive issue of pedophilia in a humorous style.   But whether you as a screenwriter choose to take the low road or the high road, the key to good comedy is not just breaking social taboos.   You can get cheap laughs through gratuitous nudity, racist and chauvinist gibes, gross-outs, and offensive sight gags, but the best humor will always be character driven — arising from the psychological complexity of the characters themselves, rather than the randomly humorous incidents that transpire around them.

## CHAPTER FOUR SUMMARY POINTS

᠂ᠵ᠊

- The *ego defense mechanisms* are behaviors that defend the ego by releasing some of the pressure from blocked libido energy.
- Movie characters displaying defense mechanisms are intriguing because they are usually completely *oblivious* to their defensive behaviors.
- *Repression* of desire, passion, or emotion is a universal defense mechanism.
- Repressed energy is typically discharged in a dramatic scene of *catharsis* or emotional release.
- *Denial* can be used as either a character strength (constancy), or character weakness (obliviousness).
- In horror, thriller, or suspense movies, there is often a *denying authority figure* who denies the existence of danger. The hero must overcome this figure in order to defeat or conquer the danger.
- *Identification* also can be used as either a character strength or character weakness. If the hero identifies with a *positive mentor figure*, then he is on the right road for character development. If the hero is identifying with a *negative mentor figure*, then he must first overcome this *negative identification* before he can start developing in the right direction.
- *Sublimation* is the process of channeling libido energy into productive or artistic activities. In films, sublimation is often portrayed through passionate labor and the ubiquitous "power of love" theme – in which a hero overcomes great obstacles in order to defend or rescue his true love.
- *Regression* scenes in movies are typically facilitated by a substance such as alcohol, marijuana, a magic elixir, or a "fountain of youth."
- The most common type of *regressive hero* is the middle-aged character who seduces a young lover.
- *Reaction formation* is when a character exposes his own deepest desire by reacting strongly against it. For example, gay bashing may be indicative of latent homo-erotic desires, which are so disturbing to the individual, that he reacts against them through homophobia.
- *Displacement* is the redirection of a libido drive onto a safe substitute outlet.
- *Rationalization* is when a character intellectualizes his issues by discussing them coldly and objectively, rather than dealing with his issues on an emotional level.

- *Projection* is a central theme in movies dealing with family relationships. Parents often "project" their own dreams and goals onto their children, and are hurt and upset when their children express the desire to follow their own dreams.
- *Isolation* is a defense used by the "loner" character, who is typically isolating himself from others because of a traumatic or ignominious past.
- A *Freudian slip* is when a repressed feeling slips out unconsciously during speech. The slip is often used in film to reveal hidden information to the hero — typically when he needs it the most.
- Jokes allow for the expression of taboo subject material in a socially appropriate manner. The reaction to jokes — laughter — is an intense emotional release that is also socially appropriate.
- Even the most serious films can benefit from moments of "comic relief," a scene in which tension is released through laughter.
- Gross out and politically incorrect humor in comedies take advantage of the joke loophole in society to express extremely taboo subject matter in order to elicit lowbrow laughs.

## CHAPTER FOUR EXERCISES

1. Using your knowledge of film, identify three movie characters who display the defense mechanism of regression.
2. Identify three movie characters who display the defense mechanism of denial.
3. Identify three movie characters who display the defense mechanism of displacement.
4. Identify three movie characters who display the defense mechanism of rationalization.
5. Identify three movie characters who display the defense mechanism of isolation.
6. Analyze the defense mechanisms displayed by characters in movies such as *Ordinary People*, *The Big Chill*, and *American Beauty*.

## ADDRESSING THE EGO DEFENSE MECHANISMS
## IN YOUR SCRIPT

1. Both repression and denial are marked by a character's general obliviousness to his own desires, fears, and neuroses. Consider how you can use the attribute of obliviousness as either a character strength or character weakness in your hero.

2. Identification typically offers character motivation through an external mentor figure, while sublimation typically offers character motivation through internal conflict of libido drives. How can you create psychological depth in your characters' motivations by juxtaposing the contrary forces of identification and sublimation within your hero?

3. Slips are most realistic when they express emotion rather than just information. If you are using a Freudian slip in your script, think of how you can write the slip as a form of emotional release, instead of the tired old *"Oops, I can't believe I just told you my big, bad secret!"* set up.

4. Comic relief is an essential part of any movie. Do you have at least one instance in your script that is designed to elicit a laugh?

## THE EGO DEFENSE MECHANISMS AT A GLANCE

| DEFENSE MECHANISMS | FUNCTION | CHARACTERISTICS | EXAMPLES |
|---|---|---|---|
| Repression | Holding in an impulse and not allowing it to become conscious | Obliviousness Frustration Restraint | *Remains of the Day* *Gosford Park* |
| Denial | Refusing to acknowledge an impulse or troublesome information | Obliviousness Obstinacy Tenacity | *Lost Weekend* *Jaws* *Little Princess* |
| Identification | Modeling one's beliefs and behaviors after someone else | Conformity Inspiring Mentors | *Zelig* *Star Wars* |
| Sublimation | Channeling impulses into productive or artistic activities | Passionate Labor Power of Love | *Frida* *Superman* |
| Regression | Releasing impulses by engaging in immature behavior | Substance Use Young Lovers | *The Big Chill* *Manhattan* |
| Reaction Formation | Acting in opposition toward a troublesome impulse | Homophobia Fickle Women | *American Beauty* *The Quiet Man* |
| Displacement | Releasing an impulse onto a substitute outlet | Venting Rage | *Falling Down* |
| Rationalization | Dealing with emotions on an intellectual level | Intellectualizing | Woody Allen movies |
| Projection | Attributing impulses and desires to somebody else | Paranoia Parents living vicariously through their children | *Treasure of the Sierra Madre* *Of Human Hearts* *Gypsy* |
| Isolation | Running away and hiding from troublesome issues | Tragic Pasts Loner Heroes | *Finding Forrester* *Shane* |
| Freudian Slips | Releasing an issue by mistake through an inappropriate remark | Villains giving away their plans | *The Bad and the Beautiful* |
| Jokes | Expressing taboos through humor, and gaining emotional release through laughter | Comic Relief Gross-out Humor Social Satire | *There's Something About Mary* *Dr. Strangelove* |

*Chapter Five*

# DREAMWORK

Freud's "dreamwork" is the psychoanalytic process of recalling and interpreting dreams. The basic theory behind dreamwork is deceptively simple. First, the patient recalls the **manifest content** — the dream itself, as accurately as the patient can recall it. Then, the analyst and patient deconstruct the dream and analyze each element... every place, event, person, and object. The analyst draws out the patient's personal **associations** with all of these elements, in the belief that a simple figure, object, or event may symbolize a much more significant issue in the patient's unconscious. By analyzing these associations and interpreting the psychological symbolism behind them, the analyst and patient reveal the **latent content** — the hidden meaning of the dream. According to Freud, dreamwork is a *"royal road to a knowledge of the unconscious,"* because it provides direct access to the inner workings of the unconscious mind.

## WISH FULFILLMENT

In Freudian analysis, the primary root of the dream is always some form of wish fulfillment. The purpose of dreamwork is to reveal the latent content of the dream and uncover the hidden wish to conscious perception, culminating in an **epiphany** or realization in the patients about their unconscious neuroses. Just as epiphany or self-realization is the stepping stone to the patients' development in analysis, epiphany is also a crucial step in the **character's development** in a film. Before the protagonist can accomplish his goal and become a full-fledged hero, he must know himself, and develop as a person. The dual elements of wish fulfillment and epiphany in dreamwork are represented in films by the very popular plot in which the hero suddenly gets everything he wants. In *Mr. Deeds Goes to Town* (1936), Deeds (Gary Cooper) is a simple country-bumpkin whose material wishes are fulfilled when he inherits a fortune. Through a process of trials and tribulations, Deeds realizes that money will not make him happy, and that his true wishes are not for material possessions, but for the spiritual riches of love and inner peace.

Audiences enjoy this very common plot device on two levels. In the 1st act, they find **vicarious pleasure** in the notion of suddenly becoming rich and famous. Winning the lottery *It Could Happen to You* (1994), a sudden inheritance *Brewster's Millions* (1985), and identity switching *Dave* (1993) are all common ways in which the unconscious wish for money, power, or fame are suddenly fulfilled, only to reveal to the hero and his audience that these superficialities are existentially worthless. The only things that are truly worth living for are the things that cannot be bought or owned – love and a personal sense of **integrity**.

When writing the wish fulfillment plot, try to indulge the audience on both levels. Film audiences experience wish fulfillment when they become engrossed in a movie and experience it in much the same way that they experience their own fantasies and dreams. Audiences want to see their hero enjoy sudden success, because they enjoy it vicariously through him, so have some fun with the plot. If your 1st act is the setup, then the first half of the 2nd act should be filled with as much **indulgence** as possible. The audience intuitively knows that conflict will eventually rise in the 2nd act, and that the 3rd act will be devoted to fixing all the problems caused by the changes made in the 1st act — so the first half of your 2nd act should be full of fun and pleasure. Let your heroes gorge on expensive foods, buy fancy clothes, visit exotic locations, bask in the attention of gorgeous admirers, indulge every whim and fantasy, and otherwise fulfill their (and the audiences') deepest wishes.

Don't hurry the conflict, let it come naturally. But when the conflict does come, it should relate to something personal within the character. Often times, external factors such as greedy lawyers or ruthless rivals make the hero feel disenchanted with his new identity. These obstacles fulfill the function of creating conflict in the plot, but they do nothing to advance character development in the hero. When weaving together this form of plot, the central question you must answer is: "*What is it about the hero himself that conflicts with his newfound status or wealth?*" External obstacles are fine and usually necessary, but don't abandon the psychological depth of inner conflict for the easy accessibility of bad guys and foils.

## INCUBUS & SUCCUBUS

Sexual figures in films often take on the form of dark seducers and seduc-tresses. They have preternatural power over the characters they seduce. These figures embody the qualities of the mythical incubus and succubus — **sexual demons** who invade the dreams of innocent people and ravish them while they sleep. Angela (Mena Suvari), the sexy teen in *American Beauty*, is a reappearing succubus in Lester's (Kevin Spacey) fantasies, driving him on his lustful quest to recapture his youth. The Devil is a very literal incubus in *Rosemary's Baby*, as Rosemary is asleep whenever she encounters him, and he appears like a ravishing demon. Freddy Krueger (Robert Englund) in the *Nightmare on Elm Street* movies is a violent incubus whose sadistic slayings are sexually charged, as well. The incubus and succubus represent the most primal impulses, **sex** and **aggression**, and their function in their characters' dreams are typically one-dimensional. Nevertheless, these figures can provide very interesting insights into a character's psyche.

In *The Natural*, Roy (Robert Redford) is haunted by the memory of the mysterious woman from his past (Barbara Hershey), who seduced him and then destroyed his career. Though she is dead, she haunts his dreams. The appearance of the succubus in Roy's dreams cues him in to the dan-ger in his real life — that his new girlfriend (Kim Basinger) is a menacing succubus who also will ruin his career. When Roy finally dumps the new seductress, he tells her: *"I've seen you before!"* — referring to the real dark seductress from his distant past, and the menacing succubus that has been haunting his dreams.

Writing the incubus or succubus figure can be a liberating experience, because these characters are fantasy rather than reality. They can do any-thing, appear anywhere, and represent anything. They're also brimming with sexual and aggressive power. The dream demons are excellent sym-bols of **internal fears** and **desires**. However, you should not feel limited to writing dream figures who only want to kill or copulate. The incubus and succubus can represent any troubling conflict, including but not limited to: guilt, fear, shame, loneliness, anxiety, and doubt.

### ANXIETY DREAMS

Anxiety is a particularly frequent subject of dreams, both in real life and in films. The anxiety dream sequence is typically portrayed as a state of **paranoia**, in which everyone and everything is menacing and destructive, and the dreamer is confronted by his **deepest fear**. In Tim Burton' *Pee Wee's Big Adventure* (1985), Pee Wee (Paul Reubens) is plagued by terrible nightmares in which his lost bicycle is destroyed. The dreams cue the audience in to the **emotional intensity** behind Pee Wee's anxiety over his beloved bike. The over-the-top imagery of dream sequences adds a bit of whimsy and fantasy to movies that dwell in the dull world of reality. *Pee Wee's Big Adventure* didn't really need more whimsy, but the celebrated dream sequence in the early film noir, *Stranger on the Third Floor* (1940), is a fantastic anxiety dream that takes the audience out of the ordinary world for awhile and allows the imagination of the filmmakers to run wild. *Stranger on the Third Floor* is an example of a mediocre film with a marvelous dream sequence — but sometimes that's all it takes to make a movie stand out in the audience's memory.

### THE DREAM WITHIN A DREAM

Experiencing a film is, in many ways, like experiencing a dream. The dark, quiet, cavernous theater parallels the sleeping mind. The screen of symbolic images is the show that the unconscious presents for its captive audience. Many films exploit that quality by creating a **surreal atmosphere** that mirrors the whimsical or uncanny world of dreams. If film is a metaphorical dream, then dream sequences within films are dreams within a dream. There are certain visual elements often used within dream sequences to give the audience a sense of **unreality**. Fog, smoke, soft focus, eerie music, expressionistic or surrealistic set designs, odd camera angles, distorted sound, slow motion, dim lighting, and irregular costuming all impart a visual sense of the dream world.

In *Poltergeist* (1992) and other horror movies, the surreal atmosphere of a huge storm coming down upon a house at night provokes nightmarish images, such as the devilish face of a clown doll, the menacing figure of an old tree, and the terrifying flashes of lightning and crashes of thunder. These surreal elements **foreshadow** the real moments of terror, when the ghosts possess the household objects and turn them into actual monsters.

A surreal setting was a tried-and-true device for all the classic Gothic horror movies such as *Dracula* (1931), *Frankenstein* (1931), *The Mummy* (1932), and *The Wolf Man* (1941). In what is considered to be the very first feature-length horror film, the sets in *The Cabinet of Dr. Caligari* (1920) are wildly **expressionistic**, creating a surreal milieu for the characters and plot, in which nothing is quite as it seems. When a nightmarish atmosphere is established, the feeling of a scary dream is evoked in the audience, priming it for a dreamlike visual experience and heightening suspension of disbelief. In a surreal atmosphere, it is understood that anything can happen.

## DAYDREAMS

A surrealistic effect could be evoked in any film, not just horror movies. In Martin Scorcese's *The King of Comedy* (1983), expressionistically set **daydream sequences** in which Rupert (Robert De Niro) fantasizes about being the king of late night comedy are the driving force behind his character. Daydreams and fantasies provide direct insight into Rupert's deepest desires, and his unstable emotional state is expressed visually through the irrational sets. Rupert's daydreams and actual experiences become enmeshed, as he loses his ability to distinguish between fantasy and reality. The **delusional** character who is lost in a fantasy world creates an atmosphere of **personal surrealism**. Since anything can happen in the character's fantasies, the audience is more willing to believe that anything can also happen in the character's real life. When Rupert's wild ride of fantasy and felony climaxes with him becoming a world famous comedian, the denouement that doubles as wish fulfillment seems oddly appropriate.

A very different impression is set up by the fantasy/dream sequences in the Coen Brother's *The Big Lebowski* (1998). The Dude's (Jeff Bridges) marijuana and liquor inspired flights of fancy create an atmosphere of absurd playfulness that both mirrors and establishes the general feel of the entire film. The repeated jaunts into musical fantasy allow the audience to enter the whimsical, laid back, somewhat buzzed and stoned world of their hero. The fantasies help the audience to identify with the Dude, realizing that everything in his world is completely nonsensical and chaotic. Like the Dude, the audience simply sits back and take things as they come — not worrying too much about logic or reason — and not trying too hard to bring order into the increasingly absurd situations in which the Dude finds himself.

## REALISM AND UNREALITY

Since dreams and films are both products of the human imagination, they are both unreal, and therefore free from the rational constraints of other forms of expression. When audiences watch a film, they enter the dreamlike world of fantasy and imagination and they automatically suspend their disbelief. Nevertheless, audience trust and belief should never be taken for granted. While the most fantastic and unbelievable things can happen in movies, audiences intuitively know when one of the two cardinal rules of film fiction are broken. The first rule is that **the film must stay true to itself**. If a movie establishes itself as a realistic depiction of actual people in a real world environment, the movie cannot suddenly introduce fantastic plot twists and unrealistic events, just to advance the story. If a film does not stay true to itself, the fabric of the illusion tears, suspension of disbelief is revoked, and audiences will shake their heads in disillusionment.

The second rule is that **all characters must stay true to themselves**. While characters in a film should and must develop as the story progresses, sudden unexplained changes in character are never acceptable. There is even less flexibility in this rule, because while audiences willingly suspend their disbelief in accepting unrealistic or fantastic stories, **characters must always seem realistic**, at least in terms of the quality of their personalities. It doesn't matter if the character is an office clerk or a medieval wizard, if the character's personality and motivations are not realistic, the audience will not be able to identify with this character, and there will be no psychological connection between the audience and the movie. Sudden leaps or gaps in character development (unexplained changes of heart), result in unrealistic characters. Regardless of the genre or plot of the film, elements of character development must always be carefully structured and well established throughout the story. There are no exceptions to this rule.

## CHAPTER FIVE SUMMARY POINTS

+~+

- Freudian *dreamwork* is the process of dream analysis, in which a dream's hidden or "latent" meaning is derived from analyzing the symbolic imagery or "manifest content" that the dreamer experienced.
- Freud believed that virtually all dreams function as *wish fulfillment*, in which a repressed or blocked libido desire is experienced, enjoyed, or expressed.
- Movie viewers experience wish fulfillment when they become engrossed in a film and experience it in much the same way that they experience their own dreams. A very basic element of the film experience is living through and enjoying *vicariously* the exciting and wonderful experiences of the characters on the screen. *Indulging* viewers with these pleasures should not be avoided.
- The wish-fulfillment plot structure involves a common character who suddenly gets everything he ever dreamed of having. *Conflict* arises when his newfound wealth or status causes problems with his life or sense of identity.
- The *incubus* is a male sexual or sexualized demon who ravishes or torments a female victim in her dreams.
- The *succubus* is a female version of the dream demon who usually tempts and seduces her victims rather than ravishing or tormenting them. Nevertheless, the succubus is just as dangerous, if not more so, than the incubus.
- *Anxiety dreams* provide insight into a character's neurotic conflict.
- Standard elements of dream sequences include a *surreal atmosphere*, *expressionistic sets*, *overt symbolism*, and other unrealistic or fantastic qualities.
- The elements of dream imagery can be used in non-dream sequences to create eerie atmospheres, as in horror movies and sci-fi or fantasy films.
- *Daydreams* and *fantasies* serve the same purpose as sleeping dreams — they are windows into the character's unconscious mind.
- Though film itself is an unreal fantasy — a dream world unto itself — there are *two cardinal rules* that should never be broken.
  1. The film must stay true to itself.
  2. Characters must stay true to themselves.

## CHAPTER FIVE EXERCISES

1. The traditional happy ending is the most overt element of wish fulfillment in film structure. Does your script have a happy ending?
   Come up with several different happy endings to your script... each
   one being more and more indulgent.
2. Is there a plot twist in your script in which a character's wish is fulfilled,
   leading to a moral or existential lesson?
3. Is there a deep fear or anxiety that your hero has addressed or
   extinguished within the course of your script?
4. Try to conceive of all the different ways in which the wishes of your
   hero can be fulfilled in your script.
5. Do you have a dark seducer or seductress figure in your script? How
   can you evoke the primal forces of the incubus or succubus within
   these figures, to make them seem more powerful and psychologically
   resonant?
6. Using Freudian dreamwork, analyze the dreams in films such as *The
   Wizard of Oz, Jacob's Ladder*, and *Vanilla Sky*.
7. Identify and analyze dream, daydream, or fantasy sequences from
   five of your favorite films.
8. Write a dream sequence for every character in your script. Fill these
   dreams with wishes, anxieties, and meaningful symbols. Creating
   dreams for your characters will give you insight into their
   unconscious minds and internal conflicts.

## ADDRESSING DREAMWORK IN YOUR SCRIPT

+~+

1. Freud believed that at the core of every dream is an element of wish fulfillment. Though wish fulfillment may not be at the core of the film you are writing, is there an element of wish fulfillment addressed somewhere in your script?

2. Does your script have a dream sequence? How can you create an atmosphere of "unreality" in this sequence?

3. An element of surrealism is a common device in horror and fantasy movies, as they prime the audience to suspend disbelief. Whether you want to create this impression for the entire film or for just one scene, how can you use surrealism to build suspension of disbelief in your audience?

4. Daydreams can provide insight into your character's deepest fears and desires. They also can be used to reveal the character's psychological and emotional state. Think of how you can use a daydream sequence to add depth to your character.

### DREAMWORK AT A GLANCE

| Elements of Dreamwork | Symbolism | Plot Device | Examples |
| --- | --- | --- | --- |
| Wish Fulfillment | Unconscious desire behind the dream | Sudden wealth or success | *Mr. Deeds Goes to Town* |
| Incubus & Succubus | Taboo sexual desires & impulses | Dark Seducers & Seductresses | *Rosemary's Baby* *The Natural* |
| Surrealism | An environment of "unreality" | Expressionistic Sets Illusionary Atmosphere | *The Cabinet of Dr. Caligari* |
| Fantasizing | Daydreaming | Insight into the character's deepest desires & emotional state | *The King of Comedy* *American Beauty* *The Big Lebowski* |

# PART TWO

~

*Erik Erikson*

*Chapter Six*

# NORMATIVE CONFLICT

While Freudian analysis tends to focus on the internal sources of conflict – the diverging unconscious drives clashing against each other – Eriksonian analysis focuses on the ego's struggle to adjust to a conflicting environment. The difference between Erik Erikson's perspective and Sigmund Freud's is evident in the names that they gave to their theories. Freud's theory is psychosexual, maintaining that conflict arises from one's own sexual impulses and drives. Erikson's theory is **"psychosocial,"** maintaining that conflict arises when one's own needs and desires come into conflict with the expectations of society. When the inner life of the ego conflicts with the outer life of society, "normative conflict" occurs. The developing ego is struggling to normalize itself; it is struggling to fit in with the social expectations being imposed upon it, while also trying to remain true to itself.

Each stage of life presents different normative conflicts that must be resolved. The central normative conflict at each stage has an extremely significant impact on the developing ego identity, raising each of these normative conflicts to the level of **"identity crisis."** An identity crisis is a period of extreme change and transition in one's sense of self, a time of metamorphosis for the ego identity. Each stage of identity crisis is centered on a specific normative conflict, and the resolution of each identity crisis has a crucial effect on the individual's identity.

Erikson's eight stages of identity crisis present an outline for the basic elements of identity development. As a writer, your central concern is the **identity development** (or character development), of your heroes. While the plot and action of a story represent the outer world of a film, the identity of the hero represents the inner world of the film – the inner conflict or crisis that the hero must resolve in order for his character to develop.

## TRUST VERSUS MISTRUST

Erikson's psychosocial stages of identity crisis were directly inspired by Freud's psychosexual stages of ego development — though it is clear that Erikson adopted the main lines of Freud's model, and then freely improvised upon each theme with the confidence and assurance of a theoretical virtuoso no less brilliant than his mentor. The first stage of identity crisis, "Trust versus Mistrust," corresponds to Freud's oral stage. Rather than focusing on the physical aspects of oral nourishment via breast-feeding, Erikson focused on the emotional relationship between mother and child.

At the very first stage of life, the child is completely helpless and vulnerable. With its survival entirely dependent on the nurturing of a caregiver, the child's sense of **trust** that it will be fed, protected, sheltered, and not abandoned is a fundamental belief. If the child is abandoned, neglected, or mistreated, the primary identity crisis results in a sense of **mistrust**, a general sense that others cannot be trusted, that people are innately selfish and unkind, and that life is inherently cruel and unfair.

## THE DUBIOUS HERO

Mistrust can be seen in the character who is reluctant to commit himself to a heroic cause, because he is unable to trust the good people who need his help. The dubious hero is typically a somewhat shady character, an anti-hero with a sordid past. He has been around the block a few times and has the scars to prove it. He's been burned before, and he's learned from experience not to trust anyone. Jack Nicholson's characterization of Jake in *Chinatown* (1972) is a classic example of the dubious hero type. As a street-smart gumshoe detective, Jake personified the conflict of mistrust. He trusts no one, and for good reason… his world is a world of shady characters, a world of back stabbing, corruption, and deceit. The dubious hero's challenge is to resolve his identity crisis by overcoming his mistrust. He must believe in someone else and allow himself to trust in another person or an unselfish cause.

## THE LEAP OF FAITH

The resolution of the mistrust conflict is achieved through a leap of faith, a scene in which the dubious hero lets his guard down and gives himself over to someone else. In *The African Queen* (1951), Charlie (Humphrey Bogart) starts out as a completely self-interested steamboat captain. He cares about nobody and nothing except for his boat, his booze, and himself. But on his arduous journey down the Congo, he learns to love and admire his passenger, Rose (Katharine Hepburn). Charlie's love for Rose changes his identity, giving him the ability to trust someone else and to put his faith in something outside of himself. This newfound ability to trust and care for others is a transformative spell that inspires Charlie to make a leap of faith, in which he sacrifices his beloved boat and risks his own life to fight for Rose's cause against the evil Germans.

The leap of faith does not have to be a monumental transformation of character. The leap can be a simple step for a character, in which he or she moves from an inert state of reluctance to a more proactive state of dedication to another person and/or cause. In *Raiders of the Lost Ark* (1981), Marion (Karen Allen) is reluctant to help Indiana Jones (Harrison Ford), because she has been burned by him in the past. But when the evil Germans attack her and burn down her bar, she overcomes her mistrust and joins forces with Indiana. The fact that she was forced to trust Indiana lends a forced quality to their relationship. Though there is love between them, there is also anger and resentment. The resolution of mistrust between these two principal characters (the leap of faith), occurs in steps throughout the film, as Indiana and Marion gradually earn each other's trust and respect.

## CHARACTER IS ACTION

Mistrust and the leap of faith are important elements in your script because they address the reality of the world. Real people are usually quite unwilling to risk their necks for other people's causes. Real people's allegiance and trust must be earned. When structuring your character's leap of faith, be sure to address this theme realistically, rather than just paying lip service to the device. An example of what not to do can be seen in *The Mothman Prophecies* (2002). In the film, John (Richard Gere) is trying to solve the mystery of his wife's death. He hunts down a mentor-like figure who has been studying the strange alien sightings that John is investigating. John knocks on his door, asking for help. The mentor refuses to help two times, but when John asks a third time, the mentor says "Okay," opens the door, and lets him in. The entire process of mistrust, refusal, reluctance, and leap of faith is covered in about 15 seconds. That's just way too easy. The effect of the scene is laughable (which is not a good effect for a horror movie).

The leap of faith symbolizes a significant resolution of a deeply personal internal conflict. It is not just a hackneyed little game of words that two characters must play before they join forces and move on with the plot. Addressing the leap of faith flippantly is an example of the most common error in screenwriting — the error of placing plot before character. As a writer, you must remember that the plot revolves around the characters. You should never sacrifice character complexity in the name of keeping the plot moving quickly with lots of action. As F. Scott Fitzgerald said, "Character IS Action!"

## THE POLLYANNA

The antithesis of the dubious hero figure is **the gullible hero**, the character who is too trusting. Rather than learning how to trust, this character's challenge is to learn how to say "no." The gullible hero must acquire the strength of character it takes to stand up for herself and not allow others to take advantage of her. In *Romancing the Stone* (1984), Joan Wilder (Kathleen Turner) is a Pollyanna figure. She starts out as an insecure and unconfident woman who is not even able to fend off the intrusive sidewalk merchants who flock to her on the streets. Joan's challenge is to become stronger and (as her name suggests), a little bit "wilder." Strength of character for Joan does not mean trusting others less; rather, it means trusting *herself* more, and allowing herself to express her will without self doubt.

Joan's character development is initiated by a journey to save her sister, and driven forward by Jack (Michael Douglas), a character who is everything that Joan is not. Jack is wild, adventurous, shady, and inherently mistrustful. Like Bogart in *The African Queen*, Jack is a lone adventurer in a foreign land. He is interested only in himself. He has learned to trust nobody, as he suspects that all other people are as egoistic as himself. *Romancing the Stone* is a character driven action movie, because both of the principal characters are heroes with internal conflicts, and each character functions as a mentor for the other. Jack must teach Joan how to be strong, independent, wild, and assured. And Joan must teach Jack how to trust, love, and care for somebody else. The resolution of both of their trust-related conflicts creates a romantic union that is psychologically complementary. In the end, Joan walks confidently down the streets of New York, calmly eschewing the pesky peddlers with a wave of her hand. And Jack returns to civilization to be with Joan.

The denouement of this film relates a valuable lesson to screenwriters. Characters can learn much from role models and mentors, but their final stage of development should illustrate that they have integrated their new-found strengths within their own identities. While the relationship between the characters can certainly go on and flourish, they should not need each other to be psychologically complete. Each individual character, when fully developed, should represent a complete and balanced psychological identity in-and-of-itself.

## AUTONOMY VERSUS DOUBT AND SHAME

Just as Freud's second psychosexual stage (the anal stage), centers around the power struggle between parent and child over toilet training, Erikson's second stage of identity crisis focuses on the child's struggle for autonomy from his parent. Autonomy, for Erikson, is the individual's basic sense of identity, the child's *"will to be oneself."* In film, the theme of autonomy is typically played out by characters who rebel against tyrannical forces in their environment. **Rebel heroes** usually start out in a state of subjugation, in which they are not free to express their own autonomy. *Spartacus* begins with the title character (Kirk Douglas) working as a slave in the salt mines. When Spartacus defends a fellow slave against a brutal slave driver, we immediately see that he is struggling outright with the issue of autonomy.

As we follow Spartacus' journey into a gladiator academy, we see him sub-jugated by tyrannical authority figures and wallowing in the shame of his lowly state. He is treated like an animal, trained to fight to the death for the amusement of the ruling class... even a moment of intimacy with a slave girl is used as a form of perverse entertainment by his owners. Shame of his lowly condition and the doubt that he can ever rise above it are what hold Spartacus back. But once he overcomes his shame and doubt, the titanic force of his own sense of autonomy inspires Spartacus to rebel. His rebellion inspires the other slaves, and a massive slave rebellion ensues. Though Spartacus is crucified in the end, he is still a victorious hero. He is no longer ashamed of himself — he is proud of what he did and what he has accomplished. Though he dies, his identity as a free and autonomous man lives on, both in his legend, and in the life of his son, who is a free citizen of Rome.

All civilized people carry the burden of society. Laws, rules, taxes, govern-ment officials... all the confining aspects of society restrict our individual autonomy and frustrate our natural instinct to be free. Heroes like Spartacus are inspiring because they play out powerful internal conflicts through external battles. Rebel heroes embody the universal struggle for autonomy. It doesn't matter whether the hero in your script is fighting the Roman army or arguing a parking ticket, the conflict is exactly the same. By fighting the good fight against authority, rebel heroes express their autonomy in ways that ordinary people typically cannot. As a result, film audiences experience a vicarious sense of pleasure when the character they are identifying with spits in the eye of authority.

## INITIATIVE VERSUS GUILT

In Freudian theory, the phallic stage of development marks the resolution of the Oedipal complex, when the superego becomes a governing force in the unconscious. Erikson's third stage of identity crisis focuses on guilt (the product of the superego), and the counter-force of initiative (a desex-ualized version of the libido). While Erikson poised initiative and guilt as opposing forces in the unconscious, they are commonly used as comple-mentary forces of character motivation in film. The **misdirected hero** needs a healthy dose of guilt to set him on the healthy path of righteous-ness. Ebenezer Scrooge's (Reginald Owen) initiative is misdirected in *A Christmas Carol* (1938). Scrooge's energy is dedicated to money, greed, and selfishness rather than meaningful relationships with other people. When the Christmas ghosts show Scrooge how his personality became demented, and how his miserly ways affect the life of his poor employee, Bob Cratchit (Gene Lockhart), Scrooge experiences a wave of guilt. But in Scrooge's case, guilt is a positive, motivating force. Guilt incites Scrooge into action, motivating him to change his life and to realign himself with the youthful initiatives of love and caring that he became dis-associated with over the years. For Scrooge, the twin forces of guilt and initiative work together as the principal motivations behind his character.

Guilt, however, can also be depicted as a neurotic complex in the classical psychoanalytic sense, which the hero must overcome in order to realize his true initiative. Conrad (Timothy Hutton) in *Ordinary People* (1980) must rise above his guilt over surviving the accident that killed his brother, before he can understand himself and his problems with his mother. In

Conrad's case, guilt is holding him back from a return to "ordinary" life, and it stands as a psychological barrier between himself and other people. Whether you use initiative and guilt as complementary or opposing forces in your script, the thing to remember is that they are always interrelated. Your character's development will, in some way, hinge on one or both of these crucial motivations.

## INDUSTRY VERSUS INFERIORITY

In Freudian theory, the "latency" period between the phallic and genital stages of development is not a real stage, but rather, a time in which psychosexual impulses are repressed and sublimated by the developing ego. In Erikson's model, the art of sublimation is seen as a crucial skill that is intrinsically linked with the individual's sense of identity. By sublimating our psychological energy into our work, we are actively defining ourselves, because who we are is determined in large part by what we do. The basic desire to feel successful, productive, and industrious can be thwarted by feelings of inadequacy and inferiority. In film, the internal conflict between a positive sense of industry and a negative sense of inferiority is depicted in the classic **underdog** theme. The triumph of the diminutive underdog over the massive rival or foe (i.e., the David and Goliath plot), is a staple of sports and action movies. *Rocky* (1976), *The Karate Kid* (1984), *The Bad News Bears* (1979), *Hoosiers* (1986), and *The Mighty Ducks* (1992) are just a few of the many examples of successful underdog themes in sports movies. *The Dirty Dozen* (1967), *The Magnificent Seven* (1960), and *The Devil's Brigade* (1968) are some examples of the underdog band of heroes (i.e., "ragtag band of misfits"), theme in action movies.

The underdog plot device will always be popular in films, because audiences readily identify with the theme of triumph over insurmountable odds. The external battle between small hero and massive rival represents the internal conflict between industry and inferiority. The underdog theme, however, is not relegated only to sports and action movies. The theme can be equally effective in personal stories of triumph over adversity. *My Left Foot* (1989), *Shine* (1996), *A Beautiful Mind* (2001), and *The Elephant Man* (1980) are great examples of the industry over inferiority motif, in which remarkable individuals overcome extremely personal hardships.

Whether the underdog theme in your script is about the little team facing the big team, the humble contender facing the imperious champion, or the earnest individual overcoming his own impediments, the emotional effectiveness of your plot will always hinge on the basics — your character's motivation. The underdog theme is not original. It has been enacted a million times, and it will be reenacted a million times more. What can be original is the motivation behind the plot. Ask yourself, *"Why must my hero overcome adversity?" "Why must he triumph over this particular opponent or obstacle?"* and *"How does this goal relate to my hero's personal sense of identity?"* The underdog theme provides a simple structure, but the structure itself has no substance without strong motivations… the supports that hold up the structure.

# CHAPTER SIX SUMMARY POINTS

- *Normative conflict* is when the inner life of the ego conflicts with the outer life of society.
- An *identity crisis* is a period of extreme change and transition in one's sense of self. Erikson's model of identity development posits eight stages of identity crisis.
- Identity development and the stages of identity crisis are analogous to the movie character's process of *character development* and the *crisis of character* that he struggles through in the film.
- *Trust versus mistrust* is the first identity crisis.
- The *dubious hero* must overcome his identity crisis of mistrust by taking a *leap of faith* and trusting another character... typically his love interest.
- The *gullible hero* must acquire a healthy sense of mistrust as an element of character strength.
- *Autonomy versus doubt and shame* is the second identity crisis.
- The *rebel hero* starts out in a state of subjugation. This hero's rebellion against tyranny symbolizes the universal human need for freedom and autonomy.
- *Initiative versus guilt* is the third identity crisis.
- The *guilty hero* (i.e., Conrad in *Ordinary People*), must overcome his crippling sense of guilt in order to develop as a character.
- The *misdirected hero* (i.e., Scrooge in *A Christmas Carol*), must acquire a sense of guilt in order for his initiative to be guided in the right direction.
- *Industry versus inferiority* is the fourth identity crisis.
- The *underdog hero* theme represents the basic need to overcome a sense of inferiority by establishing a sense of industry or positive self-worth.

## CHAPTER SIX EXERCISES

✛✛

1. Using your knowledge of film, identity five movie characters who could be labeled "dubious heroes."
2. Identity three movie characters who could be labeled "gullible heroes."
3. Identity seven movie characters who could be labeled "rebel heroes."
4. Identity three movie characters who could be labeled "guilty heroes."
5. Identity three movie characters who could be labeled "misdirected heroes."
6. Identity five movie characters who could be labeled "underdog heroes."
7. Identify three films in which there is an "underdog band of heroes."

## ADDRESSING NORMATIVE CONFLICT IN YOUR SCRIPT

✛✛

1. The issues of trust and mistrust may be represented within your script by your hero's initial reluctance to commit himself to other people and their heroic causes. Identify a moment in your script when your hero may be required to make a "leap of faith." How can this conflict be a significant source of suspense and/or tension in your plot?
2. Part of the charm of heroic figures is their inclination toward iconoclasm and rebellion. If your hero has these qualities, how does his or her behavior reflect an inner sense of autonomy that audiences can relate to?
3. Guilt is a powerful psychological force that can be used as a means of character motivation, or as an inner obstacle that a character must overcome. How can you infuse the force of guilt in the motivations or obstacles of one or more of your characters?
4. Are you writing an underdog hero or underdog band of heroes plot? If so, what is your hero's motivation to succeed over his rival? Think of how this motivation can relate to more than just a general desire to win. How can you tie your hero's motivation in with some personal identity issues?

## NORMATIVE CONFLICT AT A GLANCE

| IDENTITY CRISIS | PLOT DEVICE | EXAMPLES IN FILM |
| --- | --- | --- |
| Trust vs. | Cynicism & Incredulity | Jaded Film Noir Heroes |
| Mistrust | Reluctance to Commit | Reclusive Mentors |
| | Leaps of Faith | Bogart in *The African Queen* |
| | Gullibility & Naiveté | Kathleen Turner in *Romancing the Stone* |
| Autonomy vs. | Rebelliousness | Kirk Douglas in *Spartacus* |
| Doubt & Shame | Non-conformity | Harold in *Harold and Maude* |
| Guilt vs. | Motivating Guilt | Ebenezer Scrooge in *A Christmas Carol* |
| Initiative | Debilitating Guilt | Conrad in *Ordinary People* |
| Industry vs. | Underdog Heroes | *Rocky* |
| Inferiority | Underdog Band of Heroes | *The Bad News Bears* |

*Chapter Seven*

# IDENTITY CRISIS AND BEYOND

Sigmund Freud summed up the endpoint of ego development in the expression, **"lieben und arbeiten**," the ability to love and to work. Upon completion of the genital stage of development, the individual has learned to project his desire for both emotional and physical intimacy onto an appropriate love object ("lieben"); and he has learned to sublimate his primal drives into socially appropriate and personally rewarding work, ("arbeiten"). Inappropriate sexual desire for the mother has become appropriate love and desire for the wife; and inappropriate feelings of aggression toward the father have become an appropriate identification with a role model and a healthy ego.

Erikson's model divides the struggle of "lieben und arbeiten" into two separate identity crises: the crisis of identity formation and the crisis of forming a long-term intimate relationship. Erikson then went beyond Freudian theory, postulating stages of identity development that occur long past adolescence — identity crises that are particular to the stages of midlife and old age. Erikson pioneered the "life course" approach to human development, and his expansions on Freudian theory went beyond interpretation, making his theories as groundbreaking and influential as those of "the Master's."

## IDENTITY VERSUS IDENTITY DIFFUSION

The fifth stage of identity crisis is the centerpiece of Eriksonian theory. While Erikson focused on the young person's need to find a personally meaningful career or life's work, the search for identity in film is most often depicted in the struggle to find a meaningful cause with which to identify. The 1st act of a film is usually the time when the hero's identity is established, so that the 2nd act can deal with the struggles against obstacles and foes, and the 3rd act covers the resolution of the struggle and final bits of character development. Within this type of structure, the 1st act is devoted mainly to character development — that is, establishing the hero's identity.

## BACKSTORY

In *Superman*, there is an extremely lengthy 1st act in which we witness the infancy, childhood, adolescence, and emerging adulthood of Clark Kent and his superhero alter ego. By the time we get to the real plot of the film – the 2nd act, when Lex Luthor enters the story – we are already about an hour-and-a-half into the film. However, the backstory about Superman's identity is so engaging that the audience is not bored or wondering when the action will begin. Audiences love to hear about the emergence of their hero's identity, and as long as this story is told with style, the identity development part of the 1st act could be extremely long.

## To Voice Over or Not to Voice Over

Often times, the backstory is so complicated that it would take too long to display it in real scenes, (unless you don't mind writing a film that's over 150 minutes long, like *Superman*). For this reason, voiceover narration is often used in the first act to deliver the backstory and bring the audience up to speed. Some writers disapprove of voiceover narration, claiming that it's a lazy man's approach to telling a story. This opinion is very often true, as the device of voice over accompanying short exemplary scenes has become almost a standard format in the 1st act of comedies, which tend to be rather formulaic to begin with. Nevertheless, it is unfair to discredit an entire writing style, merely because it is very often abused. When used correctly, the voiceover backstory delivery can reel the audience in and engage it in the story with alacrity and style.

A case in point is Wes Anderson's *The Royal Tennenbaums* (2001). Anderson's film has such a complex and elaborate backstory, that voiceover narration is really the only way to deliver all the necessary information the audience needs to know about the characters within a reasonable period of time. The quick pacing, amusing short scenes, juxtaposition of dialogue with voice over, and inventive use of titles and props makes the voiceover portion of the 1st act as engaging and entertaining as any sequence of real scenes within the film. A particularly interesting device was to make many of the characters in the film authors of books. By showing a quick shot of the book a character wrote, the audience gets a very real sense of the character's identity and personality, summarized neatly in a book title and dust jacket.

## HIDDEN BACKSTORIES

Backstory imparts crucial aspects of the character's identity and it also provides essential elements of conflict in the plot. How you choose to deliver the backstory within your film will, in many ways, determine the structure of the entire script. Whether you choose to deliver all of the backstory in the 1st act, or weave it throughout the course of the story, the relationship between a character's backstory and identity development should always be closely linked. Often times, it is useful to hold back a crucial nugget of backstory, so that the unveiling of this juicy bit of information coincides with a development in the plot or a development within the character himself. In *One Hour Photo* (2002), we follow uneasily as Sy (Robin Williams) becomes more and more obsessed with the photographs of a family to whom he has become very inappropriately attached. We do not learn until the very end of the film that Sy himself was abused as a child, and that this abuse was linked with photography. The choice to keep this crucial bit of backstory hidden until the very end increases the general creepiness of Sy's character. The audience is kept in the dark throughout the film about Sy's motivation and the root of his depravity.

## PERSONAL DISCLOSURE OF BACKSTORY

The revealing of backstory can be particularly effective on an emotional level when the character himself discloses the personal information. Though most of the backstory in *The Royal Tennenbaums* is delivered through voice over in the long, opening sequence, we do not learn about Royal's (Gene Hackman) special relationship with his loyal sidekick (Kumar Pallana) until he tells the story of their meeting to his grandsons. The heart of the film revolves around Royal's desire to win back his family, so when he shares a moment of intimacy and disclosure with his grandsons, we see Royal becoming a central figure in their young lives.

A quiet, sincere moment of disclosure and self-reflection can be extremely powerful. While the disclosing character creates intimacy with the person he is speaking to, he also creates an intimate emotional bond with the audience, as well. Just as an actor's soliloquy in a Shakespearean play offers the audience direct insight into the thoughts and feelings of the character onstage, the film actor's moment of disclosure allows the audience to enter the mind and motivations of the character on screen. The most memorable scene in *Your Friends & Neighbors* (1998) occurs when a mean-spirited, ultra-macho womanizer (Jason Patric) discloses to his two buddies that the best sex he ever had was when he and his high school buddies raped a male classmate. Suddenly, the audience gains insight to this character. Where as before the audience was appalled by his savage cruelty to women, the audience is now enthralled with the conflicted sexuality within this character's behaviors and backstory.

## IDENTITY DIFFUSION

Some films, especially biographic subjects, are all about backstory. Every single scene in Spike Lee's *Malcolm X* (1992) deals directly with Malcolm's (Denzel Washington) developing identity and its relation to his backstory. For these films, action truly is character, as every bit of plot and story is purposefully designed to add another dimension to the portrait of the character whose story the film is telling. But even non-biographic films can be character driven to the point where the plot is secondary to character development.

Though he had major parts in only three feature films, James Dean epitomized the adolescent character struggling through an identity crisis. Dean's character in *Rebel Without a Cause* (1955) is a troubled teen whose main struggle is to somehow understand himself. The film is relatively "plot light," focusing mainly on the characters and their sense of identity diffusion – the search for a personal and meaningful sense of self.

## MORATORIUM AND FORECLOSURE

When structuring your character's identity crisis, keep in mind the element of "moratorium" – the stage of active searching that precedes identity achievement. *Malcolm X* is the story of one man's moratorium, a life-long search for a meaningful sense of personal identity, which, in turn, inspired a new sense of identity for an entire nation of African Americans. Another important element in Erikson's model is "foreclosure" – the danger of ending the search too early, and settling on an identity supplied by others rather than a personally meaningful identity achieved through self-discovery.

At one point in *Malcolm X*, Malcolm submits himself completely to the Nation of Islam. Malcolm identifies himself to the core with the Nation's leader, Elijah Muhammad. He aligns himself with the tenets of his leader and his religion, even when the tenets of these role models conflict directly with his own sense of morality. The conflict that ensues is another identity crisis, in which Malcolm must realize that the identity he adopted from Elijah Muhammad and the Nation of Islam is a foreclosed identity — an identity originating from without rather than from within. In order to achieve a true sense of identity, Malcolm must dig within his own soul and find a religion and philosophy that is personally meaningful to him as an individual, rather than as a faceless follower of a false father figure. Malcolm's search for a personal sense of identity is represented by his spiritual pilgrimage to Mecca.

## REBELLION

The juvenile delinquents in *Rebel Without a Cause* and other films like it, such as *The Wild One* (1953) with Marlon Brando, are conspicuously devoid of any strong role models in their lives. Erikson believed that rebellion is common among teenagers because they have reached a stage of life in which they are ready to reject the role models they identified with as children. The parents and authority figures whom the individual looked up to as a child now seem rigid, hypocritical, old fashioned, restrictive, and hopelessly square in the hyper-critical eyes of the teenager. The intense conflict of identity diffusion arises from the fact that these teenagers have unilaterally rejected all of the adult role models in their lives, while not yet accepting new role models to fill that void. Hence, the troubled teen is lost. He has no true sense of identity, and no one to show him the way. This internal conflict, which Erikson believed is ubiquitous in teenagers, is typically displayed through external conflict between adolescents and adults in teen movies.

Even in teen movies that do not deal directly with identity issues, there are typically no competent adult figures to serve as role models for the confused teens. In teen movies such as *Animal House* (1978), *American Pie*, and *Porky's*, all of the adults are either laughable, moronic characters, or blatantly anti-adolescent figures who are openly hostile to the teen heroes. The message in these movies is that adults are either hopelessly out of touch, or they are the mortal enemy of teens everywhere. In either case, adults cannot serve as proper role models. The teens themselves must somehow figure out how to solve their own problems — and in doing so — they resolve their own identity crises.

## FINDING ONE'S SELF

The problem of identity is an inherently personal problem. Though your hero could, and often should, receive help and guidance from friends and mentors, the final resolution of the crisis must always be self-driven. The character must discover himself. His identity should not be handed to him on a plate by someone else. The first *Star Wars* trilogy presents a very complete example of identity development. At each stage of his journey, Luke Skywalker comes into contact with another element of his identity, as he learns more and more about his complicated backstory and the true identity of his father. Though he has two wise mentors (Obi Wan and Yoda), and several loyal allies (Han Solo, Princess Leia, etc.), Luke always tackles each milestone of his identity development on his own.

There is a striking scene in *The Empire Strikes Back* (1980) in which Luke enters a dark cave, encounters a vision of Darth Vader, and then beheads him, only to see his own face within Vader's mask. The search for identity is a dark, confusing path that is often scary and disturbing. Though Yoda easily could have told Luke about his true identity, the wise Jedi master sent Luke alone into the dark cave of his own psyche – knowing that true self-knowledge must come from within. Like Yoda, you must also send your hero into the dark cave alone. Don't be afraid to let your hero suffer the pain, anguish, and confusion of identity crisis. The harder your hero struggles, the more your viewers will identify with his conflict, and the more they will root for him to succeed in the end.

## INTIMACY VERSUS ISOLATION

Erikson's sixth stage of identity crisis deals specifically with the challenge of love. Romantic intimacy in life and on film exists on two levels. The physical level, sex, was traditionally only alluded to on screen. Now, the sex scene has become almost a mandatory fixture of any romantic film. Sex scenes are relatively easy to write. As a primal drive, sex requires little-to-no motivation. It is extremely visual and it easily captures and holds the attention of viewers, as it keys into the basic voyeuristic appeal of motion pictures. Emotional intimacy, on the other hand, is a bit harder to achieve on film. One thing to remember when trying to build emotional intimacy between characters is that the Latin root of the word intimacy in *"intimare"* – which means, "to let the innermost be known." Personal disclosure is the key to creating intimacy between romantic characters.

## TRUST AND INTIMACY

In many ways, the identity crisis of intimacy versus isolation recapitulates the primary identity crisis of trust versus mistrust. On a Freudian level, the feelings first experienced in the psychosexual relationship between baby and mother are later projected onto the psychosexual relationship between lovers. According to Freud, the feelings are essentially the same, only the object of love is changed. And, on an Eriksonian level, the basis of trust – the bedrock of the relationship between baby and mother – is similarly the bedrock of the relationship between adult lovers. A couple in a love relationship must trust each other before they are willing "to let the innermost be known." Personal disclosure, revealing one's deepest feelings and secrets, places a person in a situation of extreme emotional vulnerability, a situation that no one would willingly enter unless he or she had complete trust in the other person. Without trust, there can be no intimacy.

## THE GAME OF LOVE

In romance movies, the two would-be lovers play the game of courtship in which they approach and disengage like birds during mating season. Each approach offers a bit of either physical or emotional intimacy. In *It Happened One Night* (1934), the blockbuster mega-hit which became the veritable blueprint for romantic comedies, each scene is another play in the game. Tiny little gestures: Peter (Clark Gable) picking a straw out of Ellie's (Claudette Colbert) teeth, a discussion about donut dunking over breakfast, Ellie catching an eyeful of Peter with his shirt off, Peter catching an eyeful of Ellie's leg as they hitchhike – all take on monumental significance as the audience observes the two stars patiently, waiting for the moment when they will both give into their mutual attraction and growing love. While other movies tend to have big scenes full of action or plot, romantic comedies are filled with small scenes, in which the couple spend most of their time exchanging gibes, flirting, and chatting. In essence, these characters are getting to know each other. They are building intimacy and establishing trust, so that when love finally does develop, it feels ripened and real.

## MARS AND VENUS

Romantic comedies such as *It Happened One Night* often feature an antagonistic couple paired together by fate. Comedy, whether romantic or otherwise, arises from conflict. The "comic dyad" is a pairing of opposites that results in humorous conflict. Nature itself supplies the most basic comic dyad through the pairing of opposite sexes. Masculine and feminine, macho and sensitive, Mars and Venus... there are limitless ways in which basic conflicts between men and women can be scripted into comedic shtick that could fill most of the scenes of a 100-minute romantic comedy. But while the small scenes can and often do take up the majority of the film, you still need a basic plot structure with real conflict. So, while Peter and Ellie discuss the finer points of donut dunking, hitchhiking, and carrot eating, these scenes are intercut with segments that progress the main plot, (which centers around Ellie's father's quest to find Ellie, after she runs away from her gold-digging fiancé). If you are writing a romantic comedy, it is generally accepted that the story will be "plot light," in order to allow for plenty of lighthearted scenes in which the principal characters engage in witty banter, flirting, and provocative teasing.

### CRISIS OF INTIMACY IN THE 2ND ACT

As romantic couples becomes more and more intimate, they approach a moment of maximum intimacy – usually at the end of the 2nd act. Ideally, this moment should be emotional rather than just physical. In other words, the characters should pour their hearts out to each other, rather than just jumping into the sack. On the night before Ellie is to be returned to her father and fiancé, Peter tells Ellie about his secret dream – to run away to a tropical island. The scene stands out, because it is the first time in the film that Peter lets go of his tough-guy façade and talks sensitively about love, personal loss, and his sentimental dreams. Ellie responds in turn. She breaks down and tells Peter that she loves him and doesn't want to live without him. After these truly intimate disclosures, it seems that the couple is finally going to get together. But – in typical 2nd act fashion – just at the moment when you think the heroes are going to succeed, everything suddenly falls apart, and all of a sudden they are farther away from each other than ever before.

### COMMUNICATION BREAKDOWN

Just as communication brings the two lovers together, it is a lack of communication that tears them apart. The prevailing device used to create the 2nd act crisis is a communication breakdown leading to a tragic misunderstanding. In *It Happened One Night*, Ellie's declaration of love stymies

Peter. He suggests that Ellie return to her bed. Heartbroken, Ellie returns to her side of the room. A moment later, Peter undergoes a sudden change of heart, but when he calls out to Ellie, she has inexplicably fallen asleep, though she was crying hysterically a second earlier. You'd think that Peter would tell Ellie the rather important news that he loves her and wants to marry her; but rather than waking her, he inexplicably sneaks out and drives to New York, so he could sell his story and have money in his pocket when he proposes to her.

Of course, when Ellie wakes to find Peter gone, she assumes he abandoned her, so she returns to her father's house, resigned to the fate of marrying the man she doesn't love. Upon driving back to Ellie, Peter sees her in her father's car in the arms of another man. He, of course, assumes that she has changed her mind and wants nothing to do with him. So, directly after both characters reach their moment of maximum intimacy, their communication breaks down completely, leading to a **tragic misunderstanding** in which both characters feel abandoned, rejected, and betrayed.

## THE COMPASSIONATE MEDIATOR

One final device is necessary for the plot to resolve in love and reconnection. A compassionate mediator realizes the confusion and reunites the two lovers, explaining the misunderstanding and bringing them back together. In dramatic terms, the compassionate mediator in romantic comedies represents a **"deus ex machina"** — a "god from the machine" that flies in when all seems lost and saves the day. ("Deus ex machina" is a stage term, referring to the fact that this supernatural character was typically introduced onto the stage with the use of a machine, such as a suspended wire, trap door, or elaborate special effect.) In *It Happened One Night*, Ellie's father sees that both characters harbor false assumptions. He redirects his daughter back to the man she truly loves.

Though these devices (communication breakdown — tragic misunderstanding — compassionate mediator), are standard format in formulaic romantic comedies, there are some obvious problems in this structure. First of all, it rarely makes sense that at the moment of greatest intimacy and communication, there should be a complete communication breakdown. It does not make sense that at the moment in which both characters finally love and trust each other the most, that they should suddenly lose every bit of trust for each other, and believe that love between them no longer exists. But the biggest problem with the formula described above lies in the device of the compassionate mediator. The resolution of the intimacy crisis represents a resolution of a deeply personal identity crisis for both characters. This resolution is the completion of the heroes' ultimate goal, and it should ideally be self-resolved. By suddenly handing over the reigns of the plot to a third party mediator, this formula takes power and action away from the heroes at the moment when they should be the most proactive. The heroes must rise to the occasion in the 3rd act. They must show their true mettle and prove that they are worthy of heroism by resolving the crisis by themselves.

### SILLY LOVE FILMS

Despite these significant script problems, *It Happened One Night* is still considered a classic. Romantic comedies using the same basic formula are regularly successful. Because romantic comedies are expected to be "plot light," audiences tend to be very forgiving about holes in the story line, continuity problems in character and story development, and uninspired crisis resolutions. For good or for ill, *It Happened One Night* established the fact that what makes a really good romantic comedy are two extremely attractive and charismatic principal characters. As long as there is witty banter, sexual tension, and lots of chemistry – plot and character development are relatively unimportant.

As a counterpoint to this notion is the realization that modern audiences are much more sophisticated. The critical and box office failures of romantic comedies such as *Gigli* (2003) and *The Mexican* (2001) prove that audiences are less willing to blindly accept any romantic comedy regardless of how empty the plot is, as long as there are two gorgeous and charismatic stars on the screen. Modern audiences want beautiful and charismatic stars, on-screen chemistry, witty banter – and they want realistic character development and engaging stories, as well. If you can supply all of these elements in one script, you'll be way ahead of the game.

### GENERATIVITY VERSUS STAGNATION

Erikson's seventh stage of identity crisis occurs in midlife. Consequently, the terms "generativity versus stagnation" are typically used interchangeably with the more popular term – **"Midlife Crisis."** The individual undergoing a midlife crisis has experienced the realization that his life is half over. He realizes that he is not satisfied with what he has done, he does not appreciate what he is doing, nor does he look forward to the things he sees himself doing in the future. He finds that he is "stagnating." He's going nowhere. He has no meaningful goals and no perceivable purpose in life. The resolution of this crisis is found in "generativity" — the creation of new goals, a personal rededication to meaningful causes, and a commitment to supporting future generations. While stagnation is a state of lifeless resignation, generativity is a rebirth... a resurrection into a new life.

### THE STAGNATING MENTOR

Part of the despondency of the midlife crisis arises from a realization of lost youth. On a dramatic level, the middle-aged character can no longer see himself in the role of the hero, and consequently he feels lost and out of place. He is an actor who has outgrown his part. The goal at this stage is to find a new part. The middle-aged character already played the lead role of the young hero, so now he must adapt himself to the supporting role of the older mentor. Often times, the would-be mentor must be coaxed into generativity by an eager young apprentice. Mr. Miyagi (Pat Morita) in *The Karate Kid* (1984) must be convinced by Daniel (Ralph Macchio) to become his karate instructor. The intricate relationship between apprentice and mentor is symbiotic. The would-be hero inspires the would-be mentor out of stagnation and into generativity by convincing him to take on an apprentice. In turn, the mentor guides the apprentice and gives him the inspiration to become a hero.

### THE MENTOR HERO

It is very common, especially in war and sports movies, for the middle-aged mentor character to play the lead role in the film. While the younger soldiers and athletes perform the action on the field, it is the older mentor who inspires the young heroes. More importantly, the mentor is the central figure of the squad or team. He is the character that connects all of the heroes' separate plot lines. Major Reisman (Lee Marvin) is the central figure in *The Dirty Dozen*, the inspiring mentor who leads his men on their mission. Similarly, Coach Buttermaker (Walter Matthau) is the central figure in *The Bad News Bears*. The mentor hero can also play the role of teacher, as seen in *Goodbye Mr. Chips* (1939) and *Dead Poets Society* (1989).

The hero-mentor relationship is both complementary and reciprocal. The hero draws the *stagnating mentor* into a state of generativity, helping him to resolve his midlife crisis. The mentor then inspires and guides the hero on his journey, helping him resolve his adolescent identity crisis. The setting is relatively flexible. Wherever there are young heroes waiting to be inspired, there is the need for an experienced role model to rise out of stagnation and dedicate himself to the generative task of mentorship.

## BEYOND GENRE

Occasionally, films are made that depict everyday people going through everyday crises. In *American Beauty*, Lester Burnham's (Kevin Spacey) desire for a young lover, his disenchantment with his job and wife, his realization of personal stagnation, and his longing for a lost youth are all classic symptoms of the midlife crisis. The same symptoms are displayed by Mrs. Robinson (Anne Bancroft) in *The Graduate* and Gabe Roth (Woody Allen) in *Husbands and Wives* (1992). These realistic characters are tragic rather than inspiring. The quality of tragedy arises from their own obliviousness and the consequential depravity of their actions. As older adults, these characters should care for the young people in their lives by wanting to guide and inspire them as generative mentors. But when the older adults, in a desperate attempt to re-experience their own youth, use the young people's vulnerability to possess them, they transform themselves into self-centered, avaricious sexual predators. The midlife crisis is an emotionally charged conflict. When resolved in the direction of generativity, the individual becomes an inspiring mentor. When resolved in the direction of stagnation or self-indulgence, the individual becomes a tragic figure.

## INTEGRITY VERSUS DESPAIR

Erikson's eighth and last stage of identity crisis is an inherently **existential conflict**. In the final stage of life, when death is no longer an abstract eventuality in the distant future, but an imminent inevitability, the individual is forced to look back at his life in retrospect, in search of a sense of meaning. If he perceives his life story as essentially meaningful and worthwhile, then a sense of "integrity" is achieved. However, if no meaning or purpose is found, if the individual sees his life as an empty, meaningless, pointless string of random events, then the individual will regret his mistakes rather than feel proud of his accomplishments. This sense of autobiographical regret is most profound at the final stage of life, because along with the realization of a meaningless existence, comes the awareness that it is too late to do anything about it. The poignant combination of meaninglessness and hopelessness intensifies regret into an overall sense of "despair."

## SELF DETERMINATION

A central issue at the final stage is self-determination — whether the individual can credit himself with making his own choices and living his own life. Though we all make mistakes, a basic sense of integrity still can be achieved if we can look back and say to ourselves: "*at least...*" (as Elvis sang), "*I did it my way!*" To conjure a much used literary metaphor, existential meaning is found in the realization that life is a story, and that, regardless of the quality of my story, I, as an individual, was the sole author and hero of my own life story. My major life choices were not made by someone else, and the plot and story lines were not determined by characters other than me.

## THE POWER OF ONE

A sense of existential despair invoked by the realization of imminent death is a common motivation in **"life affirming"** movies such as *About Schmidt* (2002), *My Life* (1993), and *Ikiru* (1952). In these films, characters are forced to reappraise the meaning of their lives when they realize that they only have a short amount of time to change the final acts of their life stories. The motivation to change is real and believable, and the viewer is willing to follow these driven characters through their inspiring journeys of self-redemption.

*Ikiru* (1952), Akira Kurosawa's often overlooked masterpiece, stands out as one of the most resonant of the "life affirming" movies. Kanji Watanabe (Takashi Shimura) is the quintessential bureaucrat. Called "the mummy" by his coworkers, the main character in *Ikiru* is lifeless, abject, morally empty, and spiritually dead. Though he has the opportunity to do good things each day, he chooses to keep a low profile like a good government worker, and simply passes the buck whenever a civil need falls onto his desk. But when Watanabe discovers that he has cancer and that he only has three months to live, he embarks on a spiritual journey in search of his true self. For Watanabe, existential meaning is found

*Integrity: Watanabe's last scene in* Ikiru.

in the opportunity to help his community. He completely changes his personality, shedding his bureaucratic skin and becoming a whirlwind of positive social action. In the end, he sits in the playground that he brought into being, thinking that his life's work was not for naught — that he did something worthwhile that will live on after him.

Kurosawa advances his life-affirming premise even further by continuing his film after his hero's death, showing the funeral banquet, in which Watanabe's once soulless co-workers eulogize "the mummy," remarking on the remarkable change he displayed in his last days, and the inspirational effect he had on everyone around him. Kurosawa demonstrates that the power of one person, vitalized by a crisis of identity and motivated to change himself, can, in fact, inspire an entire community and even change the world.

## ERIKSON'S STAGES OF IDENTITY CRISIS

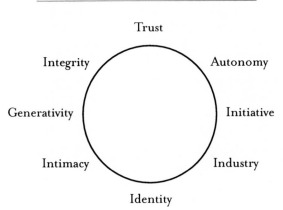

Trust

Integrity

Autonomy

Generativity

Initiative

Intimacy

Industry

Identity

## CHAPTER SEVEN SUMMARY POINTS

- *Identity versus identity diffusion* is the fifth stage of identity crisis.
- The hero's *backstory* typically provides crucial information about his identity and the crisis of identity that he is struggling with in the film.
- Backstory can be revealed through biographical opening sequences, voiceover narration, personal disclosure, and flashbacks — or it can be woven into the plot through action and dialogue.
- Most films address the issue of *identity diffusion* in some way, as the hero must struggle in order to establish a meaningful sense of personal identity.
- *Moratorium* is the stage of active searching that precedes "identity achievement."
- *Foreclosure* is when someone settles on an identity provided by outside sources, rather than searching to achieve a true sense of personal identity.
- *Teen heroes* often engage in rebellion against authority figures as a way of establishing their own sense of identity.
- In teen movies, adult authority figures are typically portrayed as moronic, hostile, or hopelessly out of touch. The teen hero has no recourse but to solve his own problems, thus discovering his own personal sense of identity.
- *Intimacy versus isolation* is the sixth stage of identity crisis.
- The search for an intimate love relationship is the central theme in romance movies and *romantic comedies*.
- The key to developing intimacy between characters is to build a sense of trust through progressively personal scenes of *open communication* and *mutual disclosure*.
- The crisis at the end of the 2nd Act in romantic comedies is typically brought on by a *communication breakdown*, which leads to a *tragic misunderstanding*.
- The crisis of intimacy most often is resolved by a third party figure… the *compassionate mediator*.
- *Generativity versus stagnation* is the seventh stage of identity crisis. It is more commonly referred to as the "*midlife crisis*."

- *Mentor figures* are typically dealing with the crisis of generativity. They must venture out of their stagnant ruts in order to become generative guides to the future generation of heroes.
- The hero-mentor relationship is both complementary and reciprocal. The hero draws the *stagnating mentor* into a state of generativity, the mentor then guides the hero on his journey.
- *Integrity versus despair* is the last stage of identity crisis.
- *Life affirming movies* often revolve around a character who realizes that death is imminent. The final struggle to establish existential integrity — a sense of meaning in one's life — inspires the hero to change his identity and accomplish great feats.

## CHAPTER SEVEN EXERCISES

1. Using your knowledge of film, identify two films in which the hero's backstory is revealed through biographical opening scenes and/or voiceover narration.
2. Identify three films in which the hero's backstory is revealed through personal disclosure.
3. Identify two films in which the hero's backstory is revealed through flashbacks or dream sequences.
4. Write a comprehensive biography or backstory for every character in your script. Come up with all the details, such as their dates and locations of birth, their major subjects in school, hobbies, dreams... even when and where they lost their virginity. Creating these biographical details of your characters' backstories may help you add depth to their roles.
5. Watch some classic romantic comedies such as *It Happened One Night*, *The Shop Around the Corner*, *When Harry Met Sally*, and *Sleepless in Seattle*. Analyze how intimacy is built between the two principal characters. Pay special attention to the crisis of intimacy at the end of the 2nd act, and how this crisis is resolved in the 3rd act.
6. Identity five "stagnating mentor figures" from your favorite movies. How does the hero draw the mentor into a state of generativity?
7. Identify three films that deal with the crisis of integrity versus despair. How does the hero establish a sense of identity integrity?

## ADDRESSING IDENTITY CRISIS IN YOUR SCRIPT

1. Your characters' identities are intimately related to their backstories. How are the backstories of your principal characters revealed? Think about how you can juxtapose the revelation of their backstories with events in the plot in ways that can add tension, suspense, conflict, or drama to your script.

2. The challenge of intimacy is an issue addressed in nearly every movie, not just romances. However, the love motif is often the weakest part of the plot – frequently thrown in just to fulfill the "love interest" requirement. Whether you are writing a script with a romantic main plot, or a non-romance with a romantic sub-plot, your love interest theme will be stronger if your characters' need for intimacy is tied in directly with their identities. How can you write a unique love interest plot that relates to deeply personal identity issues in your principal characters?

3. The "Baby Boomers" are an audience of lifelong filmgoers who have created (for the first time in history), a glut in the market for films about middle-aged people facing middle-aged issues. The idea that a major motion picture must have a young star in a lead role in order to be successful is no longer true. If you are writing a script with middle-aged characters, consider how you can address the issues of "generativity" and/or "stagnation" in your characters' motivations and conflicts.

4. Rumor has it that "DreamWorks" is planning a remake of Akira Kurosawa's *Ikiru* – possibly starring Tom Hanks, with Steven Speilberg as either producer or director. Watch the original *Ikiru* and consider how it addresses the identity crisis of integrity versus despair. Then think about a remake script that will appeal to contemporary American audiences, while retaining the existential message of the original film.

## IDENTITY CRISIS AT A GLANCE

| IDENTITY CRISIS | PLOT DEVICE | EXAMPLES IN FILM |
| --- | --- | --- |
| Identity vs. Identity Diffusion | Revelation of Backstories | *The Royal Tennenbaums* |
| | Hidden Backstories | *One Hour Photo* |
| | Personal Disclosure of Backstory | *Your Friends & Neighbors* |
| | Identity Diffusion | *Rebel Without a Cause* |
| | Moratorium & Foreclosure | *Malcolm X* |
| | Rebellion & Identity Achievement | *The Empire Strikes Back* |
| Intimacy vs. Isolation | Courtship | All Romantic Comedies |
| | Communication Breakdown | *It Happened One Night* |
| | Tragic Misunderstandings | *The Wedding Singer* |
| | Compassionate Mediators | *The Parent Trap* |
| Generativity vs. Stagnation | Stagnating Mentors | Mr. Miyagi in *The Karate Kid* |
| | Mentor Heroes | Lee Marvin in *The Dirty Dozen* |
| | Midlife Crises | Kevin Spacey in *American Beauty* |
| Integrity vs. Despair | Realization of Imminent Death | *My Life* |
| | Search for Self Determination | *Ikiru* |

# PART THREE

*Carl Jung*

*Chapter Eight*

# ARCHETYPES OF CHARACTER

Unlike Erikson, Carl Gustav Jung was never really one of Freud's students or disciples. Though Jung was inspired and guided by Freud's theories, they first met as professional colleagues, and throughout their lengthy correspondence, Jung always maintained a sense of individuality and independence in his concepts of neurotic conflict and the human psyche. Freud mistook Jung's independence and creativity as theoretical subversion, leading to a fundamental rift between the two that would never be breached. The Freudians' loss was Psychology's gain, as Jung — unencumbered by the limits of Freud's paradigm — went on to develop a theory of the human psyche which was as original, unique, and beautiful as "the Master's."

## THE COLLECTIVE UNCONSCIOUS

Jung's most significant digression from Freudian theory was his belief that there is an inherently spiritual element within the human psyche. Though he did not claim to any specific deity or spiritual force, he believed that all humanity is linked on a metaphysical level, and that this metaphysical link is the psychological force behind the universal need for religion, faith, spirituality, and the belief in a higher power. Freud, a devout atheist, rejected all non-biological bases to human drives, making Jung's unscientific assertion of a spiritual drive seem somewhat blasphemous. Jung called the metaphysical link between all humans the "collective unconscious" — as the material within this realm of consciousness is shared collectively by all humans.

## ARCHETYPES

The collective unconscious differs from the Freudian model of the unconscious (which Jung labeled the "personal unconscious"), in that the material within it is not related to strictly personal memories and emotions. The collective unconscious is composed of universally **shared associations** and images called "archetypes." The archetypes are "elemental ideas" – "primordial images" – significant unconscious figures to which all people can relate. For example, every human being has a mother. In some cultures, the universally resonant figure of a powerful, nurturing, and comforting mother figure is represented by the "**Earth Goddess**." In other cultures she is the "Madonna." In others she is "Mother Nature," in others she is the embodiment of love and sex, and in others she symbolizes growth and fertility. Though she is called by a thousand different names and depicted in a thousand different forms, the elemental idea behind all of these different representations is the same – it is the **archetype of the mother**.

Though Freud was uncomfortable with the unscientific elements of Jung's theory, the basic idea behind archetypes and the collective unconscious is not necessarily spiritual. Jung's claim was simply that all human beings, regardless of their personal experiences, share common associations related to universal human issues. All people have mothers and fathers, all people face conflicts within their own personality, and all people face crises of identity as they develop and adjust into society. The archetypes expressed in legend, myth, literature, art, and film represent these universal issues, and the collective unconscious is merely the basic human "**predisposition**" to share and understand these archetypes on an unconscious level. Archetypes in film are character types and themes that transcend the actors and plots that portray them. The archetypes are representations of psychological issues and figures that are universally resonant. Though the physical appearance of the archetypes will change, the symbolism behind the archetypes has been the same for thousands of years, and will always remain the same.

### THE HERO

The mythological hero is the primary symbol of the self. The hero is not just an archetype – it is the **central archetype**. The hero archetype is too broad to be narrowed down into one concept, because while all of the other archetypes represent different parts of the self, the hero *is* the self. It is all of the archetypes put together. As Joseph Campbell pointed out, the hero has "a thousand faces," because the hero is the archetypal representation of the self, which is constantly changing. The message delivered by any particular hero will be determined by the journey which that particular hero undertakes. The different elements of **the hero's journey** are covered in Chapters 10 and 11. The different **elements of the self** that the hero may represent – the **archetypes of the self** that the hero encounters – are the subjects of this chapter.

### PERSONA

The outer faces that we show to the world, the part of ourselves that we let others see, is our "persona." Referring to the masks that the ancient Greek actors wore, the persona is the **mask** of our personalities that we reveal to others. It is the costume covering the side of ourselves that we hide. On a physical level, actors themselves are personas. Their faces carry the stories and personalities of the heroes they portray on the screen.

Movie and television stars often complain about being "**typecast.**" When an actor's persona or screen image becomes strongly associated with his identity as an actor, audiences and filmmakers become unwilling to see this actor in a different role. For example, it is difficult to imagine Arnold Schwarzenegger in the role of a sensitive, fragile type – just as it is difficult to imagine Dustin Hoffman in the role of a typical macho action hero. Schwarzenegger has become so closely associated with his role as "the Terminator," that it was difficult for many people to accept him as the governor of California in 2003, referring to him instead as "the Governator."

Though actors bristle under the creative restraints of typecasting, being typecast is actually a statement about the effectiveness of their performances. The typecast actor is so believable as the character he portrays, that he actually becomes that character type. In terms of the archetypal function of the film, the actor who becomes typecast is fulfilling his role as the persona. The performance is so perfect that the mask separating actor and character becomes transparent, and viewers cannot see that the two identities are separate.

### STAR QUALITY

Supremely talented "**character actors**" such as Louis Calhern, Donald Crisp, George Sanders, and dozens of others are now relatively obscure. These actors were just as talented as their cohorts, John Wayne, Gary Cooper, and Cary Grant, but while the character actor has talent and range, the movie star has "star quality" – the physical presence which allows him to become the character type he plays in the mind of the audience.

Even the term "star" refers to an archetypal quality, a figure that is omnipresent, infinite, and universal. Star power never can be underestimated. In the eyes of the viewer, the star is not just a part of the movie — the star *is* the movie.

Alfred Hitchcock preferred to use big movie stars when casting lead roles in his films, because their personas were already well established. Hitch did not have to spend time in the 1st act developing his hero's character. He'd just cast James Stewart in the lead role. Before the movie even begins, the audience knows that the character played by Jimmy Stewart will be a scrupulous hero who is independent though conventional, individualistic though conservative, and strong-minded though compassionate.

When writing the characters in your script, pay close attention to the **physical descriptions** you give them. As in life, first impressions are the strongest. Envision the face and body of your characters. It's a good idea to spend some time **brainstorming** through famous movie stars until you come upon the one actor who best represents your internal image of each character. Even if you are writing a script for a low-budget film that could never cast a famous A-list actor, or even if the star who best represents your character is dead or retired, use that movie star as you are developing the script and building your characters' personalities. By invoking the persona of a famous movie star, you establish your internal mental image of that character in the mind of the script reader.

Shadow

Jung's theories were heavily influenced by Eastern philosophies, which tend to espouse the importance of natural balances created by opposing forces. Jungian psychology embraces the **psychology of opposites**, an innate **duality** in which each part of the self is complemented by an opposing or conjoining part. The Yin and the Yang, the feminine and masculine, dark and light... every psychological power has its opposing force. In Jung's model, the shadow is the opposing force to the persona. Just as our body casts a shadow on the ground in the light of day, our ego casts a shadow in the light of consciousness. The shadow is the repressed **alter ego**, the dim reflection of our unconscious selves. It is the dark side that is always with us but often unnoticed. The shadow is the hidden presence behind the mask of the persona.

### Shadow as Villain

As opposing archetypes, the villain is typically the shadow, while the hero is usually the persona. Classical heroes often have classical villains. In *Shane*, Shane (Alan Ladd) plays the part of the White Knight hero, and Wilson (Jack Palance) plays the part of the Black Knight villain. **Masked villains** such as Jason in the *Friday the 13th* films, Hannibal in *Silence of the Lambs* and Michael in the *Halloween* movies are literal depictions of Jung's shadow archetype. The madman behind the mask depicts a universal fear – the propensity toward madness and violence in all human beings.

### Contrasting Duality

The concept of duality is based on the hero/persona's goals of **encounter** and **integration**. In the dream or myth, the persona must encounter the shadow and integrate him into his Self before the conflict can be resolved. It is often useful to contrast the hero and villain in a way that elicits a sense of Jungian duality. The two characters are as different as day and night, yet in some strange way, they seem to complement each other. The contrasting hero-villain duality in *Cape Fear* (1962) is a perfect example. Sam Bowden (Gregory Peck) is moral, upright, kind, calm, and gentle. Max Cady (Robert Mitchum) is immoral, depraved, cruel, psychopathic, and violent. Pacifistic heroes like Sam must integrate some of the violent and passionate qualities of their shadows in order to defeat them.

### The Meek Hero

The theme of the meek hero becoming violent is a ubiquitous theme in Westerns and other typically violent genres. The meek hero is pushed farther and farther by the violent villain until he finally must defend his honor, his family, and himself by evoking the violent side of his own nature. The persona's integration of the violent nature of the shadow is represented in the climax of these plots, when the hero and villain duke it out in the big fight scene. Possibly the most resonant and disturbing rendition of this theme can be seen in Sam Peckinpah's *Straw Dogs*, in which a meek professor and his wife are harassed by a band of toughs to the point where he must resort to extreme violence in order to live with himself as a man. At the end of *Cape Fear*, Sam becomes as violent, enraged, and vindictive as Max in his fight to save his family. And in slasher movies, the meek girl must become violent in order to slay the psycho killer.

In order for the theme of contrasting duality to work, the hero-persona must encounter and defeat the villain-shadow *personally*. If someone else defeats the villain, such as the police or another character, then the persona has not integrated his shadow, and the psychological conflict is not resolved.

### Shadow as Alter Ego

Villains can also symbolize the dark side of good characters. In *Dr. Jekyll and Mr. Hyde*, hero and villain are combined into one man, portraying the split in the unconscious between persona and shadow. Jekyll plays the role of the socially respectable persona, while Hyde embodies the villainous shadow. In *Spider-man*, Norman Osborn (Willem Dafoe) is a gentleman researcher and caring father, but his alter ego is the Green Goblin, a dark and violent figure who is the shadow to Norman's persona. When the persona and shadow sides of one person are split into two separate identities, it depicts a clear **psychotic split** that adds an element of psychopathology to the character. Psychopathology, in turn, elicits an immediate fear response from audiences.

Norman Bates (Anthony Perkins) in *Psycho* was both himself (persona) and his evil mother (shadow). Dracula masquerades as a civilized human (persona), though behind his subterfuge he is a vampire (shadow). And serial killers such as Jack the Ripper walk the streets as regular people, though inside their minds they are evil psychopaths. Contrasting duality is an effective devise in these characters, as well. By making the persona gentle, compassionate, or dignified (i.e., a doctor, a count, or a meek motel clerk), the contrast with the sadistic, homicidal side of the character is even more striking. Extreme contrast results in extreme surprise, extreme suspense or extreme conflict – elements that all elicit fear responses in audiences.

### Dark Heroes

Sometimes, the shadow is an element of the hero's character. Heroes motivated by dark forces are conflicted. Their internal mixture of good traits and bad traits adds psychological complexity to their roles. **Vigilante heroes** such as Batman, Paul Kersey (Charles Bronson) in the *Death Wish* movies, Harry (Clint Eastwood) in the *Dirty Harry* movies, and Popeye Doyle (Gene Hackman) in *The French Connection* (1971) are all dark heroes – complex and conflicted combinations of good and evil. As crime fighters, they wear the persona of good men championing a righteous cause. But their methods (violence) and their motivations (vengeance) are the shadows behind their personas.

**Outlaw Heroes** such as Robin Hood, Zorro, and Jesse James also represent persona-shadow combinations. These types of heroes are very appealing to viewers, because they represent the psychological complexity and internal conflict that exist in real people. No one is completely good, and no one in completely evil. We are all just compromises between our personas and our shadows. The realistic hero is someone who is searching for an equilibrium between his two basic natures. This hero's quest represents the universal quest for **psychological balance**. Regardless of the type of script you are writing, always keep in mind that your hero or main characters are searching for a sense of internal balance. Whether this balance is achieved by destroying a villain, overcoming an obstacle, winning a goal, or seducing a love interest, the symbolism behind the hero's quest is to encounter and integrate a disconnected or conflicted part of the self.

## SHADOWY PASTS

A character's shadow also can be represented by a mysterious, tragic, traumatic, or disreputable past. Jake (Jack Nicholson) in *Chinatown* (1974) is haunted by memories of his days on the police force in the shadowy district of Chinatown. Elsa (Rita Hayworth) in *The Lady from Shanghai* (1947) is tortured by her shadowy history in Shanghai. In both movies, we never learn the details of what really happened in Chinatown or Shanghai, we are only given a few hazy references to the traumas in their distant pasts, mixed with wistful expressions and teary eyes. The fact that they do not want to talk about their shadowy pasts actually gives more weight to the tragic quality of their characters.

The trick to this screenwriting device is the use of **restraint**. The screenwriter does not tell us exactly what happened in the past, they leave it up to the viewer's imagination. Since we can only imagine what happened, the extent of the shadiness, savagery, and degeneracy is limitless. Furthermore, the **vagueness** of this essential element of their backstory adds a quality of **mystery** to their character. In turn, this sense of mystery is often the central quality within the character.

If you add a shadowy past to your hero's backstory, your hero should face his past at some point in the script — (otherwise, why was the shadowy past written in the first place?) Even though we never know what really happened to Jake when he was working in Chinatown, the movie resolves on a street in Chinatown. After the shocking and disturbing climax, Jake is disgusted by the world, but his disgust seems appropriate when his old police buddy tells him: *"It's just Chinatown, Jake... It's just Chinatown."* Though the details of Jake's backstory are never revealed, we get the sense that he encountered the symbol of his Chinatown shadow through his journey, which led him back to Chinatown in the end. This sense of integration is not achieved in *The Lady from Shanghai*. Not only is Elsa's backstory never revealed, but the film never addresses the Shanghai symbolism again after the 1st act. While there is a brief return to a Chinese theater in the 3rd act, the climax of the film actually occurs in a carnival house of mirrors. This lack of integration leaves the viewer feeling incomplete and confused in the end, as the central symbol of the movie was not even remotely revealed.

### RUNNING FROM THE SHADOW

Sometimes, the hero is trying to escape from his shadowy past. The hero who is running from his shadow must invariably face his shadow in order to become whole. Shane is running away from his ignominious past as a gunfighter. The symbol of Shane's shadowy past as a gunfighter is perfectly depicted as an **external figure** in the character of Wilson, a psychopathic, homicidal gunfighter who is appropriately dressed in black. In *Star Wars*, Luke's shadow is his father, the dark lord of the evil emperor. Darth Vader is a huge, fearsome, and incredibly resonant shadow presence. Through the course of Luke's three separate journeys, the primary goal of Luke's character is to encounter, overcome, and integrate the shadow of his destructive father. The *Star Wars* trilogy is an especially good example of the shadow archetype, because it drives home the point that the shadow is not really an evil villain, but a disconnected part of the self. Luke is at his most confused when he is denying his relationship to Darth Vader and not accepting the truth about his identity. The key to Luke's development is **understanding his identity** and himself. Similarly, the key to the hero's development in your script should be directly related to a deeper understanding and integration of the disconnected parts of his Self.

### THE ETERNAL SHADOW

In *Unforgiven* (1992), Will's shadow is his past as an outlaw gunslinger. Will (Clint Eastwood) ran away from his past and started a new life, but he faces the shadow of his old self again when he becomes a hired killer. *Unforgiven* is a particularly disturbing study of the shadow archetype. At the climax of Will's story, he faces Little Bill (Gene Hackman), the sadistic sheriff who killed his friend. Bill and Will are mirror reflections of each other, both murderers, both guilty of grave sins, and both unforgiven for their lives of violence. They even share a common name. In a final act of violence, Will kills Bill in cold blood, encountering and integrating his own shadow, even as he becomes his shadow once again. The dark message of the film is that no matter how far we run, our shadows will always be right there behind us.

### VISUAL REPRESENTATION OF THE SHADOW

The use of an actual character as a symbol of the hero's shadow, either as a villain, rival, or evil ally, is particularly useful in film, since film is a visual medium. Conflict with an external figure can be displayed through action – which is obviously easier to see on the screen than internal conflict. Whether your characters face their shadows through internal conflict or external action, don't make the mistake of assuming that one form of confrontation is more sophisticated than the other. The archetypal symbolism in *Shane* and *Star Wars* is sophisticated and powerful, and the visual symbolism makes it all the more resonant. Never underestimate the power of visual representation in your script. A picture is more powerful than a thousand words.

### THE GODDESS

Like Freud, Jung believed that children retain internalized images of their parents within their psyches. But unlike Freud, Jung also believed that the internalized parental figure is revealed in dreams and myth in archetypal form. The **parental archetype** carries with it the cultural associations related to the parental figures. Hence, the mother figure in myth is represented as a divine mother – i.e., earth goddess, fertility goddess, mother nature, mother Madonna, etc. The goddess archetype is the collective, universal mother who is comforting, nurturing, gentle, and kind. The Blue Fairy in *Pinocchio* (1940), Glinda the Good Witch (Billie Burke) in *The Wizard of Oz* (1939), and the Fairy Godmothers in *Cinderella* (1950) and *Sleeping Beauty* (1959) are all lucid examples of the goddess archetype. They are all comforting, nurturing, divine mother figures. More recently, the goddess appeared as Galadriel (Cate Blanchett) in *The Fellowship of the Ring* (2001). The goddess-as-mother archetype serves essentially the same function that the actual mother serves in childhood. When encountering the goddess, the hero integrates the emotional strength, intuitive wisdom, and sensitivity associated with a positive mother figure.

### THE SHADOW GODDESS

In keeping with Jung's psychology of opposites, the positive maternal archetype – the goddess – is balanced by the existence of a **negative maternal archetype** – the evil sorceress or wicked witch. In a sense, the wicked witch is the shadow of the goddess. As the goddess is the idealized mother carrying all of her positive attributes, the witch is the vilified mother carrying all of her negative attributes. The witch is often portrayed as an **evil stepmother**, recapitulating the fundamental evil stepmother/wicked witch archetype from mythology... Medea. The combined archetype of evil stepmother and wicked witch became engrained in the American collective unconscious through Disney's *Snow White* (1937) and *Sleeping Beauty* (1958).

In non-fantasy films, the witch is often a mean or menacing maternal figure, as seen in *Mommie Dearest* (1981) and *Flowers in the Attic* (1987). In *East of Eden* (1955), the long-absent mother (Jo Van Fleet) appears to Cal (James Dean) as a shadow figure dressed in black. For Cal, his mother is a shadow – a mother who abandoned him long ago, and who now runs a brothel in the seedy red light district of Monterey. Long repressed and conflicted memories from childhood, issues of abandonment, cruelty, abuse, shame, and neglect, are all represented through the shadow goddess archetype.

### REAL LIFE GODDESSES

Any comforting, nurturing female figure who offers emotional wisdom, intuitive guidance, and love (but not romantic love), fulfills the function of the goddess archetype. Realistic maternal figures are neither idealized nor vilified. A well-developed maternal figure may have qualities of both the goddess and the witch. The difference between idealized, vilified, and real maternal figures is exhibited in *East of Eden*. Cal's mother (Jo Van Fleet) is a real person. She loves Cal, but she also abandoned him. She cannot be the mother he wants her to be, but she helps Cal by giving him the money he needs to realize his ambitious goals. Real life goddesses are helpful, nurturing, even healing... but they are not always superlatively good, nor must they be completely evil.

## THE WISE OLD MAN

The male parent, the father, is represented by the wise old man archetype. Other versions of the paternal archetype are the god, the prophet, the wizard, the healer, or any older male figure who offers wisdom, advice, or guidance. In films, the wise old man fulfills the nebulous function of the **mentor figure** for the hero. (The goddess could likewise be described as a **female mentor figure** for the heroine.) As mentor, the wise old man appears in many roles: father, older brother, teacher, preacher, doctor, therapist, coach, captain, president, king, wizard, etc. And, in keeping with Jungian duality, the shadow father figure often is represented in the role of the **false mentor** or **negative father figure**. Darth Vader in *Star Wars* epitomizes the shadow version of the father archetype, (Darth Vader literally means "Dark Father"). Obi Won, on the other hand, epitomizes the wise old man in his pure, positive form. In *The Wizard of Oz*, the menacing apparition of the wizard is the shadow father figure, while the kindly old man (Frank Morgan) behind the veil of the apparition is the positive father figure. The wise old man represents the hero's need to integrate the father figure or mentor, which is often the central relationship in a film.

## ANIMA

A balanced self incorporates both masculine and feminine traits. The male self carries the embodiment of the feminine in the form of the female archetype — the anima. The qualities personified by the anima are stereotypically feminine strengths such as sensitivity, emotional wisdom, intuition, empathy, and care. The anima is not the same archetype as the goddess, as the anima is often a romantic or erotic figure. The goddess, in her function as a mother figure, is divine and therefore asexual. The goddess offers a mother's love, while the anima offers sexual or romantic love. In traditional hero stories, the anima is typically cast as the "**maiden in distress**," the female figure that the hero must find and rescue. Princess Leia in *Star Wars* plays the role of the maiden in distress whom

Luke must rescue from the Death Star. By rescuing the maiden, the hero incorporates his anima and integrates an essential part of his self.

The anima in films is usually the "**love interest.**" The love theme is considered a crucial part of the film, even if the love interest plot is ancillary to the main story of the movie. Just as love is a necessary part of each person's life, audiences intuitively feel that love is a necessary part of every movie. When a film is over, audiences need to feel that the hero's character is now fully developed and that he is somehow "complete." Getting the girl in the end, integrating the anima, addresses this need for completeness in the hero's character. Not only has he conquered his shadow and developed as a person, he has also found love. The integration of the anima completes the hero's self. She is also a reward for the hero. Once he accomplishes his goal, he is rewarded with love, and his life is now complete. He and his maiden can marry and live happily ever after.

## Femme Fatale

Every positive archetype has an opposing negative archetype... its archetypal "shadow." The **Shadow Anima** in movies is the infamous "femme fatale." The shadowy seductress offers sexual love rather than pure love. She is also typically a dangerous figure for the hero. Like the Sirens in Homer's *Odyssey*, the femme fatale lures the hero away from his quest and into her lair with her sexual siren song. She then threatens his mortality when his guard is down. As false anima, the femme fatale is either a "**vamp**" – luring the hero away from his "good girl" love interest. Or she is a true femme "fatale" – in that she poses a physical threat to the hero's life. Alex (Glenn Close) in *Fatal Attraction* (1987) and Catherine (Sharon Stone) in *Basic Instinct* both fulfill the archetypal functions of the femme fatale. In *Fatal Attraction*, Alex's obsession with Dan (Michael Douglas) threatens his relationship with his wife (Anne Archer), and also endangers his life. The shadow anima is an extremely powerful archetypal figure because she combines the two most primal drives – sex and aggression – into one character. The femme fatale's power arises from her sexuality. Her danger lies in the hero's helplessness in the face of her alluring sexuality. Though he can fight monsters and armies, the hero is defenseless against the femme fatale.

## ANIMUS

The masculine archetype in the female psyche is the animus. The archetype represents the stereotypically masculine traits of courage, leadership, intellectual wisdom, and physical strength. Clearly, the anima/animus duality is a product of traditional Western mythology, in which the male carrying the traits listed above is the hero, and the female is the maiden whom the hero must rescue. There are very few (if any) female heroes in traditional Western mythology. Nevertheless, the modern mythology of film is the product of a modern age of liberated women, so there are many movies with female heroes, especially in contemporary cinema. In these modern myths, the animus figure plays a similar function as the anima in traditional male hero stories — the function of the love interest. So, in movies with both male and female heroes such as *Romancing the Stone*, the hero and heroine play the respective functions of animus and anima for each other. As Joan Wilder's animus, Jack inspires Joan to be brave, tough, adventurous, and strong. And as Jack Colton's anima, Joan inspires Jack to be loving, sensitive, caring, and faithful.

Since the hero archetype is traditionally masculine, when a woman is cast as the sole hero in a film, such as the title character (Angelina Jolie) in *Lara Croft: Tombraider* (2001), the heroine is usually imbued with the masculine qualities normally required of male heroes. Consequently, male love interests in female hero movies take on the functions normally required of the anima, and are often rescued by heroines, as seen when Lara Croft goes back in time somehow to rescue her love interest, Alex (Daniel Craig). Male love interests also tend to be sensitive, loving, and supportive rather than strong and brave. In these stories, the heroines are strong and brave, and their male love interests are "males in distress."

## THE SHADOW ANIMUS

The monster, serial killer, or psycho fulfills the function of the shadow animus in "slasher" movies such as *Halloween*, *Friday the 13th* and *A Nightmare on Elm Street*. Shadow animus figures such as Freddie Krueger (Robert Englund) and Red (Robert Downey Jr.) in *In Dreams* (2003) are particularly Jungian figures, because they haunt their female victims in their nightmares and dreams. The heroine in these films plays the traditional feminine role as a "maiden in distress." In the end, the heroine develops her character by encountering her shadow animus rather than running from him. At this final climactic encounter, she integrates his violent power by destroying him in a typically gruesome manner.

## THE TRICKSTER

Many of the ancient mythological gods were deceptive deities who played tricks on mortals to confuse them and mess with their heads. In *The Greatest Story Ever Told* (1965), Satan (Donald Pleasance) confounds Jesus (Max von Sydow) by tempting him with earthly pleasures and testing his faith in God. When trickster gods offer wisdom, the wisdom is most often delivered in the form of a riddle. The hero must prove his intelligence by solving the riddle before being rewarded with the god's wisdom or guidance. In *Excalibur* (1981), the immortal guardian of the Holy Grail does not reward Percival (Paul Geoffrey) with the Grail until he answers his cryptic question.

*Trickster Heroes: Gene Wilder & Cleavon Little in* Blazing Saddles *(1974).*

When the trickster archetype appears in movies, it is usually in the form of a comedian. Charlie Chaplin, Buster Keaton, and Harold Lloyd played archetypal **trickster heroes**. They encountered and defeated their shadows using trickery, chicanery, and deceit. Though trickster heroes may also display the traditional heroic qualities of physical strength, bravery, and determination, their principal strengths are intelligence, alacrity, and ingenuity. When Mel Brooks made a Western farce in *Blazing Saddles* (1974), he transfigured the traditional Western hero into trickster heroes. Though Bart (Cleavon Little) and the Waco Kid (Gene Wilder) are brave and strong, they defeat the bad guys by tricking them in a succession of comical pranks.

When the trickster figure is not the hero, he probably plays the part of a **comic-relief sidekick**. In the Marx Brothers and Abbott & Costello movies, the box office draw was not the hero of the films – the young man who fought the bad guy, won the girl's heart and saved the day – the draw was the comic-relief sidekicks, the trickster characters who helped the hero at every step of the way by hoaxing the villains and running them around in circles. Whether your trickster character is a comical sidekick or the hero of your story, remember that the key to this archetype is **intelligence**. Heroes, especially action heroes, gain most of their victories through physical strength, skill, and courage. In the mask of the trickster, the hero must succeed through intelligence – a crucial, yet often overlooked, archetypal quality of the heroic character.

## THE SHAPESHIFTER

Jung believed that shapeshifters are symbolic of the Self, which is always growing, changing, and developing. In a sense, all principal characters are shapeshifters. Principal characters should develop through the course of the story, and development means that the characters change in some significant way. The slick big-city reporter (Jean Arthur) in *Mr. Deeds Goes to Town* (1936) becomes less jaded when she falls in love with the innocent and wholesome Deeds (Gary Cooper). The egoistic, womanizing airforce cadet (Richard Gere) in *An Officer and a Gentleman* (1982) is transformed into a caring soul by his love for a town girl (Debra Winger). And Bud (Charlie Sheen), the eager young stockbroker in *Wall Street* (1987), is corrupted by a crooked financial fat-cat (Michael Douglas) and turned into a back-stabbing, greedy scoundrel. In the 3rd act, Bud shifts shape once again and is reborn as a man with integrity and honor.

## SHAPESHIFTING TRICKERY

The mythological gods were often shapeshifters, as well as tricksters. The two archetypes are similar both in function and symbolism. Zeus, for example, would shapeshift into the form of an eagle, so he could fly down from Mount Olympus and shapeshift once again into human form and trick a beautiful mortal into sleeping with him. Similarly, shapeshifting is an archetypal form of trickery in movies. Bugs Bunny would regularly disguise himself as a woman to evade Elmer Fudd. Luke and Han in *Star Wars* disguised themselves as Stormtroopers to gain entry into the Death Star. And Bart and the Waco Kid in *Blazing Saddles* disguise themselves as Klu Klux Klansmen in order to infiltrate the gang of marauders. The shapeshifting-as-trickery plot line is as ancient as myth itself, and it still continues to be an effective device in stories told today. Like all of the archetypal characters and plots, though they are ancient and formulaic, they still can be very powerful and engaging if they are pulled off with originality and wit.

## PHYSICAL SHAPESHIFTERS

Vampires and werewolves are terrifying and awesome archetypal figures because they represent the supernatural power of the gods. In mythology, only divine beings could physically shift into the shape of animals or other non-human forms. Count Dracula is possibly the most frequently depicted shapeshifter in film history. The shapeshifting villainous robot (Robert Patrick) in *Terminator 2* (1991) represents a modern version of the ancient supernatural archetype. Whether shapeshifting is accomplished through physical transfigurations in shape or critical transformations in character, the shapeshifter archetype is a universal feature in stories and film, and an extremely resonant symbol of the human potential for personal change, transformation, and rebirth.

## CHAPTER EIGHT SUMMARY POINTS

+~+

- The *collective unconscious* is composed of universally shared images and associations called *archetypes*.
- *Archetypes* represent the basic human predisposition to share and understand common psychological issues such as the experience of having a mother and father, the desire for love, or the need for spiritual healing and rebirth.
- The *hero* figure in myth, legend, literature, and film is the primary archetype of the self.
- The *persona* is the "mask" of our personalities that we reveal to others.
- *Actors* are the physical embodiment of the persona — they are the body and face of the characters they play.
- *Typecasting* arises from the psychological connection that audiences make between actors and their on-screen personas.
- The hero character usually fulfills the function of the persona archetype in the myth or dream of his own story. As his own persona, the hero must *encounter and integrate* the other parts of his self — represented by the other archetypes.
- The *shadow* archetype is the dark side of our personalities that we hide from others.
- The *villain* figure in films usually fulfills the function of the shadow archetype.
- The *goddess* archetype represents the mother archetype in positive form.
- The evil stepmother or wicked witch are archetypal representations of the *shadow goddess* — the negative or dark qualities associated with the mother figure.
- The *wise old man* archetype represents the father figure in positive form. This figure typically fulfills the function of the mentor character.
- *Darth Vader* in *Star Wars* epitomizes the false mentor archetype... the negative father figure.
- The *anima* archetype represents the feminine character traits in positive form.
- The anima is typically depicted as the *maiden in distress* and/or *love interest* in traditional hero stories.

- The *femme fatale* archetype is the shadow anima. She is a dark temptress who seduces the hero away from his journey or true love and into the realm of danger.
- The *animus* archetype represents the masculine character traits in positive form.
- *Freddie Krueger* in the *Nightmare on Elm Street* movies epitomizes the shadow animus — the dark, perverse, sadistic, and destructive side of the masculine character.
- The *trickster* archetype uses humor and intelligence to trick his way through his journey. Tricksters are typically cast in the role of the comic relief sidekick.
- The *shapeshifter* archetype is symbolic of the self, which is perpetually developing and changing in nature. Shapeshifting also represents spiritual or divine power.

## CHAPTER EIGHT EXERCISES

1. List your top 10 film heroes.
2. List your top 10 film villains.
3. List your top 10 film mentors.
4. Using your knowledge of film, identify five movie characters who fulfill the function of the goddess archetype.
5. Identify five movie characters who fulfill the function of the shadow goddess archetype.
6. Identify five movie characters who fulfill the function of the anima archetype.
7. Identify five movie characters who fulfill the function of the femme fatale archetype.
8. Identify five movie characters who fulfill the function of the trickster archetype.
9. Identify five movie characters who fulfill the function of the shapeshifter archetype.

# ADDRESSING ARCHETYPAL CHARACTERS IN YOUR SCRIPT

1. In order for your hero to develop in the mind of your audience, he must have a clear weakness or lacking in his character. In a Jungian sense, what element of the Self does your hero need to develop in order to be psychologically complete?

2. The physical presence of your hero is a big part of the hero's persona. Try to conjure a mental image of your hero, and then brainstorm through famous movie stars. Pick a movie star that best fits the physical and psychological identity of the character you want to write, and use that star as a guide when describing your hero in your script.

3. The duality of persona and shadow in the Self is typically represented in movies by the hero/villain duality. This duality is most effective when the hero and villain contrast greatly, and are therefore psychologically complementary. If your script has a hero and villain, how can you structure their characters so that the hero must acquire a trait inherent to the villain in order to overcome him.

4. Often times, the hero has a shadowy backstory – a skeleton in his closet that he must face. Does you hero have a shadowy past? If not, how would including a shadowy past add to his character? If he has a shadowy past, does he deal with it and integrate it in a satisfactory way?

5. The Goddess and Wise Old Man archetypes represent mentor figures for both male and female heroes respectively. Does your hero encounter and integrate wisdom or guidance from a mentor figure? If not, think about how including this ancient archetypal element may add depth to your characters and plot.

6. Similarly, the Anima and Animus archetypes often play the role of love interest for the hero. Does your hero encounter and integrate a love interest? If not, think about how including this archetypal element may add romance or "heart" to your script.

7. The Trickster and Shapeshifter archetypes frequently embody the heroic attribute of intelligence, either by posing the hero with intellectual challenges that he must overcome, or by the hero using trickery or shapeshifting himself to outsmart his enemies. How can you use trickery or shapeshifting in your script to imbue the crucial element of intelligence in your hero?

## ARCHETYPAL CHARACTERS AT A GLANCE

| ARCHETYPE | FUNCTION | CHARACTER | EXAMPLES |
|---|---|---|---|
| Hero | The primary symbol of the self | The Hero<br>The Band of Heroes | Luke in *Star Wars*<br>*The Fellowship of the Ring* |
| Persona | The public "mask" of the self | Movie Stars<br>The Public Self | John Wayne, Clark Gable<br>Clark Kent in *Superman* |
| Shadow | The hidden, secret or dark side of the self | The Villain<br>The Alter-ego | Darth Vader in *Star Wars*<br>Green Goblin in *Spider-man* |
| Goddess | Mother and/or the feminine mentor | Positive Mother Figure<br>Negative Mother Figure | Fairy God Mothers<br>Wicked Witches |
| Wise Old Man | Father and/or the masculine mentor | Positive Mentor<br>False/Negative Mentor | Obi Won in *Star Wars*<br>Darth Vader in *Star Wars* |
| Anima | The feminine side of the male self | Female Love Interests<br>The Maiden in Distress | Lois Lane in *Superman*<br>Princess Leia in *Star Wars* |
| Shadow Anima | The embodiment of dark femininity | The Femme Fatale | Alex in *Fatal Attraction* |
| Animus | The masculine side of the female self | Male Love Interests<br>The "Male" in Distress | Jack in *Romancing the Stone*<br>Alex in *Lara Croft: Tombraider* |
| Shadow Animus | The embodiment of dark masculinity | Psychopaths, Slashers<br>Monsters | Robert Downey Jr. in *In Dreams*<br>*Dracula* |
| Trickster | Challenging the hero's intelligence | Trickster Gods<br>Threshold Guardians<br>Trickster Heroes | Satan in *The Greatest Story...*<br>The Grail Keeper in *Excalibur*<br>Charlie Chaplin, Bugs Bunny |
| Shapeshifter | Personal and physical transformation | Transforming Heroes<br>Shapeshifting Tricksters<br>Physical Shapeshifters | Bud Fox in *Wall Street*<br>Burt & Jim in *Blazing Saddles*<br>*Dracula, The Wolf Man* |

*Chapter Nine*

# ARCHETYPES OF PLOT

As with the archetypal figures, archetypal themes are collectively shared by all humans. They represent universal life transitions such as birth, marriage, and death, and they also represent the universal need to develop, change, and grow through the archetypal themes of rebirth and transformation. By realizing the archetypal themes, we connect with other people through the **"transpersonal"** realm of the collective unconscious and become "whole." Mythology allows us to **transcend** and resolve our personal conflicts. It is an essential element of both individual psychological health and collective social adjustment. Whereas mythology historically has been transmitted through stories, legends, religion, and art — all of these methods are now integrated in the modern mass medium of film. In contemporary society, people get their myths on the movie screen. Film, the communal dream, has become a primary process for expressing, transmitting, and integrating the archetypes of our time.

## ENCOUNTER AND INTEGRATION: THE TRANSCENDENT FUNCTION

Archetypes symbolize different parts of the self. When the different parts encounter each other and integrate themselves into the Self, they complement one another and create balance where there was conflict. The function of dreams (the personal myth), and the function of myths (the collective dream), is a "transcendent function." By integrating the conflicting parts of the self, we become psychologically **"whole."**

In *East of Eden*, Cal's journey of self-discovery begins when he encounters his mother, who represents the shadow of his past and the conflict between good and bad within himself. After integrating the shadow goddess, Cal's journey to become whole leads him to integrate his anima figure — represented by the romantic love of Abra (Julie Harris). In the final scene, Cal makes amends with the wise old man — his father. By encountering and integrating his shadow, anima, and wise old man, Cal transcends the singularity of his own conflicted persona and becomes psychologically and emotionally whole.

## QUATERNITY

An archetypal theme in Jung's model is the complete whole comprised of four parts — the "quaternity" — which represents a balance between two opposing dualities. In the psyche, the integration of the four primary archetypes of the Self represents a complete quaternity. The persona and shadow are the opposing dualities of the internal Self, and the opposite sex archetype, along with the same sex parent archetype, are the opposing dualities related to external figures. So, the complete quaternity in the male psyche consists of the persona, shadow, anima, and wise old man. And the complete quaternity in the female psyche consists of the persona, shadow, animus, and goddess. If we translate these figures into archetypal character roles in film, we have the **hero, villain, love interest**, and **mentor**.

According to this Jungian model, the hero must encounter and integrate some elements of the villain, mentor, and love interest figures into his character through the course of his story. More specifically, the hero must address his own shadow (i.e., problems, conflicts, challenges or weaknesses), he must learn something from his mentor (spiritual or existential wisdom), and he must win the heart of his love interest (romance). If these archetypes are encountered and integrated in ways that are significant to the hero's identity, then a sense of psychological completeness should be achieved by the end of the film. Quaternal completeness in the hero's story translates into a feeling of complete character development.

## TRANSFORMATION

Each archetype within the quaternity has the ability to completely transform the hero's character. An evil and menacing shadow–villain, such as the degenerate SS commandant (Ralph Feines) in *Schindler's List* (1993), can inspire a very unlikely hero such as Oskar Schindler (Liam Neeson) to heroic action. Similarly, a wise mentor such as Gandalf the Wizard (Ian McKellen) in *Lord of the Rings* (2001) can inspire a tiny hobbit (Elijah Wood) to great heroism. And, of course, the love of a beautiful maiden such as Mary (Cameron Diaz) in *There's Something About Mary* (1998) has inspired many regular guys such as Ted (Ben Stiller) to enter the adventurous realm of heroism. Transformation is an archetype in-and-of-itself, as it represents the universal propensity and need for personal change and development.

**Tragic transformation** occurs when characters are corrupted by their sudden changes in identity. Willy Starks (Broderick Crawford) in *All the King's Men* (1949), Lonesome Rhodes (Andy Griffith) in *A Face in the Crowd* (1957), and Dirk Diggler (Mark Whalberg) in *Boogie Nights* (1997) are all naïve characters who experience a tragic fall as a result of their personal transformations.

Often times, the crux of the plot turns on the transformation of a supporting character rather than the hero's character. In *Mr. Smith Goes to Washington* (1939) Smith (James Stewart) starts out as a patriotic idealist and remains so throughout the film. Smith's own idealism leads to his downfall, but he is rescued in the end, not by his own transformation – but by the transformation of Joe Payne (Claude Rains), the senator whom he inspired. Similarly, Calloway (Ben Johnson) in *Shane* (1953) starts out as an ornery cowboy who finds pleasure in ridiculing and harassing Shane and his homesteader friends. Shane stands up to Calloway, earning his respect. This seemingly tangential plot line becomes central when Calloway transforms himself in the 3rd act, just in time to warn Shane of the ambush awaiting his friend Joe (Van Heflin) at the saloon.

Transformation in your script can be upward toward heroism or downward toward tragedy. It can occur as a reaction to evil, as inspiration through wisdom, or as motivation for love. And it can occur within the hero, or within the supporting characters who affect the hero. In any case, transformation is a vital part of any story, and a critical element of character development. If one or more of the characters is not different by the end of the film, if a character does not change, then the story will feel incomplete.

## LUCKY COINCIDENCES

Jung described "**synchronicity**" as a phenomenon that connects all people and all events through the collective unconscious. As a transpersonal "acausal connecting principle" that functions on a fourth dimension of human experience, synchronicity is as elusive and esoteric an idea as Albert Einstein's "Unified Field" theory. But as mysterious as synchronicity may be as an intellectual idea, the archetypal phenomenon of synchronicity is a thematic mainstay in stories and films.

The plot of *Changing Lanes* (2002) is driven forward when two men (Samuel Jackson & Ben Affleck) happen to have a car accident on the exact morning in which both of their lives depend on being somewhere on time. And in *Back to the Future* (1985), Marty McFly (Michael J. Fox) can only return to his future existence if he can recharge his time machine with a massive amount of electricity. Fortunately, Marty was given a flyer before he traveled back in time. The flyer told the story of how the town clock tower was struck by lightning – providing the exact time and date. Marty coincidentally kept the flyer in his pocket, so he could realize later on that the lightning could help him get back to the future. The preposterous preponderance of lucky coincidences stretches even the wildest of imaginations, yet the synchronicity in the plot line hardly even tugs at the audience's suspension of disbelief.

Though dubious as a psychological theory, synchronicity is a tried-and-true archetypal plot line in movies. It is accepted by audiences without a second's thought. When the hero needs it most, a lucky coincidence comes into play to save the day. Though synchronicity should not be overused or invoked willy-nilly, when adopted with wit and style, the extremely lucky coincidence is a perfectly acceptable way to advance your plot.

### HEALING

Healing is a universal human issue. At some point in all of our lives, we suffer wounds or traumas. **Wounded hero** plot lines typically involve the death of the hero's wife and/or child. For Kersey (Charles Bronson), murder becomes motivation for revenge when his wife is killed and his daughter raped by a gang of burglars in *Death Wish*. Wounded heroes are driven by grief and vengeance. Mel Gibson is extremely adept at playing the vengeful wounded hero, having done so as Max Rockatansky in the *Mad Max* films (1979, 1981, 1985, and 2004) and Sgt. Martin Riggs in the *Lethal Weapon* movies (1987, 1989, 1992, and 1998). Gibson's character is also motivated by tragedy and vengeance in *Hamlet* (1990), *Braveheart* (1995), *Ransom* (1996), *Payback* (1999), and *The Patriot* (2000). Healing for this brand of hero is almost always achieved through violence.

Heroes in need of healing are also frequently wounded in battle. Sean Thornton (John Wayne) in *The Quiet Man* (1952) and 'Prew' (Montgomery Clift) in *From Here to Eternity* (1953) are ex-prizefighters who are racked with guilt for destroying other men in the ring. For these heroes, being wounded is a motivation against violence.

In essence, the wounded hero is missing a part of his soul. He is looking to become whole again. The wounded hero's challenge is to overcome the shadow of pain, betrayal, or tragedy in his past. By facing his shadow and dealing with the past, he integrates this part of his Self into his character and becomes whole again. In *Casablanca* (1941), Rick (Humphrey Bogart) heals his own wound by encountering his shadow of lost love. He allows himself to care for Ilsa (Ingrid Bergman) once again, an act of integration of both shadow and anima that erases his loss and makes Rick's character complete.

## FATE

Rick's infamous line in Casablanca: "*Of all the gin joints in all the towns in all the world, she had to walk into mine*" − epitomizes the "**love as fate**" theme in movies. Belief in ideas such as "love at first sight" and the existence of "soul mates" presupposes the notion that love is a force controlled by destiny, perhaps in that same transpersonal fourth dimension in which synchronicity exists. The ultra-romantic notion of "fated lovers" is an ancient archetypal theme that is still extremely popular in fairy tales, myths, and movies. But the archetype of fate or destiny is not just relegated to love.

Death is another existential force that many people believe is controlled by fate. In *The Time Machine* (2002), Professor Hartdegen's sweetheart, Emma (Sienna Guillory), is killed the moment after he proposes marriage to her. Hartdegen (Guy Pearce) goes back in time to change this unfortunate coincidence, but every time he goes back, Emma is somehow killed on that same night. Fate had deemed that Emma should die that night, and no mere mortal, no matter how ingenious, could alter that fate. Similarly, in *Artificial Intelligence: AI* (2001), even super-aliens from thousands of years in the future cannot help David (Haley Joel Osment) resurrect his mother (Frances O'Connor), because every life takes up an individual "time/space pathway" − another sci-fi interpretation of kismet, karma, or fate.

As a plot device, fate should be used sparingly. Unlike the lucky coincidence, fateful occurrences carry an existential gravity that should be reserved for the most meaningful aspects of life: **love**, **death**, **birth**, and **rebirth**.

## THE LOVE SCENE

The final union of the hero and his anima (love interest) represents a unification of the opposite sex archetypes. **"Hieros Gamos"** is a sacred copulation or holy marriage. It is a consummation of the love between the hero and his love interest, and it is a physical embodiment of psychological unity, (i.e., Shakespeare's "beast with two backs"). In the sex scene or love scene, the two archetypes become one. The product of Hieros Gamos is the **"birth of the divine child"** – a being that embodies the unification of the opposing sex archetypes. The hero is reborn as a psychologically androgynous being. In Jung's model, **androgyny** is the epitome of mental health, because the androgynous individual retains the strengths of both the masculine and feminine archetypes.

In terms of the hero's character development, the love scene infuses the traditional male hero with the emotional power of the anima. This new-found power symbolizes a moment of **spiritual rebirth**. The hero is 10 times stronger after the love scene, imbued with the awesome power of love. In *The Royal Tennenbaums*, one forbidden kiss from Margot, the love of Richie's life, heals Richie's suicidal wound and motivates him to reconnect with his estranged father (Gene Hackman), and rescue his best friend (Owen Wilson) from drug addiction.

The love scene is also commonly used as a reward for the hero after over-coming some major obstacles... an act of sexual or romantic compensation for a job well done. When it appears at the end of the film, the love scene helps to add a sense of resolution to the story by resolving all the sexual tension that has been building throughout the film. The love scene can be an emotional catharsis, a psychological unification, an archetypal integration, and a romantic consummation. Through the magic of film, all of these complex issues can be portrayed through just one little kiss.

## ARCHETYPAL QUATERNITIES

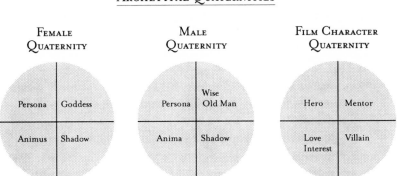

FEMALE
QUATERNITY

| Persona | Goddess |
| Animus | Shadow |

MALE
QUATERNITY

| Persona | Wise Old Man |
| Anima | Shadow |

FILM CHARACTER
QUATERNITY

| Hero | Mentor |
| Love Interest | Villain |

## CHAPTER NINE SUMMARY POINTS

- According to Jung, the lessons we learn from the archetypes encountered in both myth and dreams serve a *transcendent function*. By revealing the wisdom from the realm of the collective unconscious and applying it to the issues and conflicts we are experiencing in our personal unconscious, we transcend our personal discord and become psychologically "whole."
- The transcendent function is achieved by *encountering* and *integrating* the different conflicting parts of the Self — which are symbolically represented by the archetypes.
- The *quaternity* represents a complete whole comprised of four parts. The quaternity of archetypes is a balance between two opposing archetypal dualities.
- The quaternity of archetypes in the male psyche is composed of the persona, shadow, anima, and wise old man archetypes. The quaternity of archetypes in the female psyche is composed of the persona, shadow, animus, and goddess archetypes.
- If we apply Jung's theory of quaternity to film, the movie character's archetypal quaternity is seen to be composed of the *hero*, *villain*, *mentor*, and *love interest*.

- The hero's ultimate goal in terms of character development is *trans-formation* — becoming a better or healthier person by integrating his different archetypes.
- *Synchronicity* in Jungian theory is an "acausal connecting principle" that links all people and all events on a metaphysical level.
- Synchronicity is represented in film by plot lines involving extremely *lucky coincidences*, as well as plot lines involving *destiny*, *fate*, and *dramatic irony*.
- *Hieros gamos* is an archetypal theme that means "sacred copulation" or holy marriage.  It is typically represented in film by the love scene.
- Another common archetypal theme is *spiritual healing* or *spiritual rebirth*.  Often times, this rebirth occurs as a result of the hero integrating the love of his anima.
- The *divine child* archetype represents rebirth.
- The divine child is the hero, reborn after integrating his primary archetypes and vitalized by the divine power of spiritual wisdom and psychological balance.

## CHAPTER NINE EXERCISES

1. Analyze your favorite male film character and identify the four archetypes within that character's "quaternity."
2. Do the same for your favorite female film character.
3. Watch a movie you've never seen before and analyze it from a Jungian perspective.  What archetypes can you recognize in this film?  How does the hero transform as a result of encountering these archetypes?
4. Identify the theme of synchronicity, as interpreted in this chapter, in five of your favorite films.

## ADDRESSING ARCHETYPAL PLOTS IN YOUR SCRIPT

1. The quaternal whole of the hero character consists of hero (persona), villain (or rival), mentor, and love interest. Does your hero encounter and integrate all three of these figures? If not, do you think that incorporating this idea in your script could add an element of wholeness or completion in your hero's character?
2. Character development can occur through a variety of transformations. How do your main characters develop or transform? If you cannot see a transformation in their characters, think of how you can create a wound or fault in your character that must be healed.
3. As an archetypal function, the love scene should provide more than just a physical reward, gratuitous nudity, or sex. The love scene should "complete" the hero in some way. Does your love scene help to complete the hero? If not, how could your love scene provide a symbolic completion or healing of your hero's character? In other words, how is the love interest complementary to the hero?

### ARCHETYPAL PLOTS AT A GLANCE

| ARCHETYPES | FUNCTION | PLOT DEVICES | EXAMPLES |
| --- | --- | --- | --- |
| Quaternity | Integrating the villain, mentor & love interest | Resolution & Denouement | Luke Skywalker integrating Vader, Obi Won & Leia |
| Transformation | Spiritual Rebirth | Character Development | Oskar Schindler transforming from egoist to savior hero |
| Synchronicity | Advancing the Plot | Lucky Coincidences | Marty in *Back to the Future* keeping the lightning bolt flyer |
| Healing | Becoming "Whole" | Wounded Heroes | Parry in *The Fisher King* being healed by the Holy Grail |
| Fate | Love as Fate Death as Fate | Soul Mates Destiny | Dr. Hartdegen & Emma in *The Time Machine* |
| Hieros Gamos | Integrating the opposite sex archetype | Love Interests Love Scenes | Richie & Margot's kiss in *The Royal Tennenbaums* |

# PART FOUR

*Joseph Campbell*

*Chapter Ten*

# THE HERO WITH A THOUSAND FACES

Joseph Campbell was not a psychologist. He was a scholar of humanities, the classics, and world myth. Yet his vast knowledge of the psychoanalytic models of theorists such as Freud, Jung, Erikson, and Otto Rank gave him the background to apply psychological theories to his studies of world myth. Of his many books, *The Hero with a Thousand Faces* (1949) endures as his most popular and influential. It is a psychological analysis of the classical myth formula that breaks down the myth into a basic structure. By revealing the structure of myth, Campbell uncovers the vast psychological power of the hero archetype and the archetypal "Hero's Journey."

The hero "ventures forth" into the world and encounters various figures and characters. Though he embarks on an external journey, the myth symbolizes an **inner journey** – a journey on which the hero must encounter and integrate different parts of his own Self. No matter where the hero goes and what his adventure entails, his journey is always an inner journey of self-discovery, and his goal is always that of character development. The hero is seeking to become psychologically complete.

## THE MYTHICAL HERO

William Wallace (Mel Gibson) in *Braveheart* (1995) and Maximus (Russell Crowe) in *Gladiator* are both traditional heroes who traveled traditional mythical journeys. Both films were tremendous box office and critical successes, selling millions of tickets and garnering numerous Academy Awards. *Braveheart* won the Oscar for Best Picture and Best Director (Mel Gibson) and was nominated for best Screenplay (Randall Wallace). *Gladiator* won for Best Picture and Best Actor and was nominated for Best Director (Ridley Scott) and Best Screenplay (David Franzoni, John Logan & William Nicholson). Obviously, the filmmakers involved with these incredibly successful productions did a lot of things correctly. The one we'll focus on is their choice of a classical hero's journey as a template for their screenstories. By using the archetypes of the hero's journey, the filmmakers adopted a story structure that has proven its ability to communicate to billions of people across the world for thousands and thousands of years. The structure is a rock solid foundation for heroic tales.

## ACT ONE: DEPARTURE

The first stage of the hero's journey is a departure from his "**world of the common day.**" Wallace's world was his childhood world of political violence in 11th Century Scotland, a world in which his father was a leader in the Scottish rebellion against the brutal English imperialists. Maximus' world was the world of warfare as a Roman general under the command of his emperor, Marcus Aurelius (Richard Harris). The world of the common day represents home, the starting point and ending point of human development. The hero "ventures forth" in the first stage of his journey, and he returns home in the latter stages. Venturing forth and returning is a universal symbol for identity development. Just as a teenager leaves home for army service or college, the hero figure leaves his home as an undeveloped character and returns as a full-blown hero.

In the world of the common day, the hero typically encounters and integrates his **primary mentor figure** – the archetype of his father. Wallace's primary mentor was his own father, a martyred Scottish rebel. Maximus' primary mentor was his Emperor, a wise old man who calls Maximus "*the son I should have had.*" The hero may find a **secondary mentor figure** in his world of adventure, but the primary mentor is the most significant. While the secondary mentor may offer wisdom, guidance, and inspiration to the hero, the journey ends with the hero symbolically *becoming* the primary mentor. This is why the primary mentor typically dies in the 1st act. As a deceased figure, the primary mentor is a spiritual inspiration that the hero carries with him throughout his adventure – an inner compass leading him home and guiding his journey.

There is also an element of **fulfillment** in the hero's return, as the hero fulfills a quest bequeathed to him by a father figure or mentor. Wallace's father dies in his childhood world, a martyr to the cause of rebellion against the English. In Wallace's final stage, he also will become a martyr to the same cause. Similarly, Emperor Marcus is killed shortly after charging Maximus with the task of making Rome a republic once again. In his final stage, Maximus kills the Emperor's murderer and fulfills his promise of returning democracy to Rome. Writing the hero's world of the common day takes a lot of forethought and planning. The common-day world sets up the hero's primary tasks and goals, and provides both a beginning and endpoint to the hero's journey. If the hero's return does not fulfill some integral prophecy, quest, or need — then the entire journey will feel unresolved and incomplete.

## STAGE ONE: THE CALL TO ADVENTURE

Though heroes are natural adventure seekers, they usually require several "calls to adventure" in order for their inner natures to be revealed. The call lures the hero out of his inert state of inactivity and launches him into the realm of heroism. Sometimes evil forces enter the hero's world and confront him in his home. Wallace, for example, is home in Scotland when an English soldier rapes and kills his wife. Other times the hero wanders into the world of adventure by mistake. And other times, the hero is thrust unwillingly into the world of adventure and forced to fight his way back home. Alfred Hitchcock often used the latter device. In *North by Northwest* (1959), Roger Thornhill (Cary Grant) is an "ordinary fellow" in a typical Hitchcock plot. Mistaken by villains as a spy, Thornhill is thrust suddenly and unwillingly into a world of danger and intrigue.

## THE HERALD

Herald figures bring news to the hero of the terrible foe or impending evil that must be fought. They call upon his honor to enter the fight. Maximus is called upon by his Emperor to become the liberator of Rome in *Gladiator*. Wallace's father's former allies call upon him to rebel against the English in *Braveheart*.

Joseph Campbell noted that in Celtic myth, the hero's journey typically begins when he follows a mystical fawn into the woods while hunting. The herald fawn lures the hero into a mythical realm. The herald then transforms or "shapeshifts" into another archetype, such as the "Queen of the Fairy Hills," and the hero finds himself "in full career of an adventure." The herald in fairy tales is often a friendly talking animal such as a rabbit. The rabbit, though harmless, is a force of nature and a bearer of natural wisdom. Animals have a sense of intuition that transcends human knowledge. They can foretell changes in the weather and disturbances in their natural environment.

The **rabbit herald** appears most notably in *Alice in Wonderland* (1951), as the mystical White Rabbit who lures Alice into the magical parallel dimension of Wonderland.   In *East of Eden*, an old drunk named "Rabbit" sets Cal on his journey, when he tells him that his mother is alive and living as a madam in Monterey.   No matter how it comes, the call to adventure is typically made early in the film.   It creates the first element of conflict in the hero's character and draws the audience into his story.   If the film is more than 20 minutes into the 1st act and the call has not been made, you run the risk of losing your audience.   They'll start asking themselves: "What's going on?" "What's the conflict?" "What is this movie about?"

STAGE TWO: REFUSAL OF THE CALL

The archetypal hero is typically a **Reluctant Hero**, a character who has the inner nature of heroism but who needs to be drawn out.   The hero's reluctance represents the inner reluctance that all people have when faced with great challenges or adventures.   It is always easier to do nothing.   To stay at home.   To avoid danger and hardship and let others heed the call.   At this stage of reluctance, an **upping of the ante** is needed to push the hero out of his nest of unwillingness and into the risky world of heroism.

Wallace refuses the call of his father's old allies to aid in their rebellion against the English.   Wallace is moved to rebellion only after his wife is raped and murdered by English soldiers.   Maximus initially refuses his Emperor's call to liberate Rome.   But after the Emperor is murdered by his degenerate son, Commodus (Joaquin Phoenix), Maximus is perceived by Commodus as an enemy.   He escapes his own execution and returns home, only to find his wife and kids murdered by Commodus' assassins.   Though Maximus is captured and sold into slavery, the goal of his journey is now directed squarely at returning to Rome and destroying Commodus and his dictatorial regime.

Movies work primarily on an emotional level.   Effective films manipulate the audiences' emotions, making them feel what the hero feels and making them **identify** with his motivations.   Vogler (1998) notes in his book, *The Writer's Journey*, that a "raising of the stakes" is often needed to pull the hero into action.   The function of upping the ante or raising the stakes is to direct anger at the bad guys, and to make the audience identify with the hero's motivations to fight them.   **Vengeance** for the murder of a loved one, **freedom** from tyranny, and the eradication of **evil** are the classic motivations behind the hero's journey. One of the main reasons why films like *Braveheart* and *Gladiator* do so well is because these mythical themes build intense emotions in the audience, and create powerful motivations for their heroes that their audiences can identify with. Nothing creates more tension, builds more emotion, or produces more motivation than the slaying of the hero's wife and kids. Not only is vengeance and extreme violence justified, it is emotionally necessary. Furthermore, the hero becomes a man with nothing to lose, a dangerous force of vengeance that cannot be stopped. The extreme emotions created by these movies testifies to the critical importance of setting up strong and clear character motivation early on in your script.

STAGE THREE: SUPERNATURAL AID

Before the hero plunges forth into the wild, he is usually provided with some necessary **weapons of power**. The classical heroes were sons of gods who were fittingly suited with supernatural aid in the form of powerful weapons. Perseus was provided with an unbreakable sword, an invisibility helmet, and a flying horse. Arthur was provided with Excalibur, and in the modern version of the knight's tale, Luke in *Star Wars* was provided with a light saber. At this stage of the journey, the would-be-hero also may go through **training** with a mentor figure. Wallace inherits a **secondary mentor** in the figure of a fiery old Scottish rebel, the father of his best friend and a former comrade of Wallace's own father. Maximus finds a secondary mentor in his new master, Proximo (Oliver Reed), the owner of the gladiator academy. Proximo also happens to be a former gladiator who was freed by Maximus' primary mentor, Emperor Marcus. Proximo teaches Maximus his most valuable lesson as a gladiator: *"Win the crowd, and you will win your freedom!"*

Wallace and Maximus also are provided with symbolic objects that empower them with spiritual, if not supernatural, strength. Wallace holds onto his deceased wife's handkerchief, a memento that gives him strength and motivation in his moments of weakness. Similarly, Maximus holds onto a pair of clay figurines, the only physical remembrances that he has of his crucified wife and son. The figurines are a symbolic link between Maximus and the spiritual forces that drive him. Each of these symbols is a **leitmotif** – a recurring theme and central symbol in the film. Every time we see the handkerchief in *Braveheart* or the figurines in *Gladiator*, we know that we are looking at the symbol of the hero's identity and soul. Though overt symbolism in films should not be overused, it can be an effective tool for expressing subtle emotional and psychological themes that cannot be depicted well through action, dialogue, or voice over.

### STAGE FOUR: THE CROSSING OF THE FIRST THRESHOLD
When the hero has finally accepted the call to adventure and is ready to embark on his journey, his first task is to pass the **"threshold guardian"** that blocks the entrance to the road of adventure. In movies, the threshold guardian is usually a character who tries to stop the hero from starting his journey. The irate captain in "buddy cop" movies is a threshold guardian who tries to stop the renegade cops from pursuing the underworld crime lord. The stuffy doctor in sports movies is the threshold guardian who tells the athlete hero that he's not fit to fight or compete in the big match. The frightened villager in horror movies is the threshold guardian who warns the young hero against venturing up to the haunted mansion or vampire's castle. And the stalwart studio sentry who stands post at the cross-barrier to the Hollywood studio gates is the archetypal threshold guardian for the hero with dreams of movie stardom.

In *Braveheart*, Wallace must confront his own Scottish comrades and rouse them to fight in the first major battle scene. In *Gladiator*, Maximus must organize his fellow gladiators into a cohesive fighting unit so they can battle their Roman competitors in the coliseum. The gathering of **allies** is a common threshold barrier that the hero must deal with in order to embark on his journey. Without allies, the battle cannot be won. In gathering allies, the hero proves his **leadership** abilities. And in inspiring the ragtag band of misfits to fight, the hero inspires the audience, as well.

### STAGE FIVE: THE BELLY OF THE WHALE
Upon entering completely the world of adventure, the hero is now in the *"sphere of rebirth... symbolized in the worldwide womb image of the belly of the whale."* The hero is fully immersed in the journey that will transform him. He entered the whale in one form, and he will emerge in another. Wallace enters the world of adventure as an angry man just out for vengeance. He will emerge a leader and mentor for his people. Maximus' transformation will follow the identical path. At a certain level of abstraction, all hero transformations follow the same path. They start out being inspired by a mentor, and they end up becoming that mentor. The journey is a **"mythological round"** – a character arc that begins in one spot and ends in the same place.

## ACT TWO: INITIATION

In the 2nd act, the hero becomes fully initiated into the realm of heroism. The "initiation" is similar in function to the puberty rituals common in just about every culture around the world. The puberty ritual (such as the Confirmation, Bar Mitzvah, Vision Quest, etc.), is a ceremony in which the adolescent male undergoes an **ordeal**, passes a **test**, or progresses through a **gauntlet** in order to prove his worth. After completing the ritual, the adolescent is initiated into the world of manhood as a full member of adult society. In the hero's initiation, the hero must prove his worthiness by passing through various trials and ordeals along his path to heroism.

## STAGE SIX: THE ROAD OF TRIALS

The "succession of trials" at this stage of the journey is a series of tests. They are meant to harden the hero, rather than wound or destroy him. The tests passed along the road of trials are also the **great deeds** that the hero must perform in order to establish his reputation as a hero and leader of men. Wallace establishes himself as a great warrior and leader on his road of trials by leading his army of rebels into successive victorious battles against the English. Maximus also establishes himself as a great warrior and captain by leading his gang of gladiators into successive victories in the coliseum. In a typical action or war movie, the action-packed road of trials fills most of the scenes in the 2nd act.

## STAGE SEVEN: MEETING WITH THE GODDESS

In Campbell's model, the Goddess archetype represents both mother and wife. She is the divine figure who provides nurturing and caring, and she is also the feminine part of the psyche with whom the hero must unite, vis-á-vis the "**sacred marriage**." By uniting with the holy mother, the hero-son replaces the father and usurps his position as master, thus becoming one with his own mentor. Hence, the Goddess archetype is best represented as a **ghostly** or **spiritual figure**. The deceased wives in *Braveheart* and *Gladiator* provide perfect examples of the Goddess archetype. Though she was once romantic, she is now a spiritual apparition, and therefore asexual. Because she was killed by the enemy, she also provides motivation toward victory, as well as spiritual comfort. And because she is a ghost, she is pure spirit, existing entirely in the hero's own psyche.

The Meeting with the Goddess is a spiritual encounter that provides the hero with emotional strength and resilience at his weakest moments.

Maximus meets his Goddess at various times on his journey, through memories, flashbacks, and visions. These meetings always occur when Maximus needs the love and inspiration of his wife the most. The Meeting with the Goddess provides the same power as the "Hieros Gamos" or sacred marriage. By integrating the Goddess, the hero is born again as the "divine child," who retains the power of both the masculine and feminine archetypes. Wallace's goddess, his wife's ghost, appears to him in a dream to provide him with strength and courage. His meeting with the goddess is strategically placed right before his encounter with a different feminine figure... the Temptress.

### STAGE EIGHT: WOMAN AS THE TEMPTRESS

The temptress figure plays the function of **anima**, acting as a sexual and romantic interest for the hero. Princess Isabelle (Sophie Marceau), the king of England's stepdaughter, is the anima/temptress in Wallace's journey. Lucilla (Connie Nielsen), Emperor Aurelius' daughter, is the anima/temptress on Maximus' journey. Both characters are conflicted. They are both officially allied to the hero's tyrannical enemies, but they are also both emotionally and sexually drawn to the heroes. In a sense, the temptresses are also **shapeshifters** — turncoats who betray their masters in order to help the rebel heroes. The challenge of the hero at this stage is to **trust** the temptress. He must overcome his well-earned pessimism and take a **leap of faith** by believing the temptress and joining her to defeat the tyrants whom they both despise. These sexy princesses play the part of desirable love interests for the heroes, as well.

### STAGE NINE: ATONEMENT WITH THE FATHER

At the apex of his journey, the hero "atones" with the father by following in his footsteps and becoming what he once was. By the middle of Act Two, Wallace has become a great rebel hero like his father. He is respected by the same men and reviled by the same enemies. At the same stage in *Gladiator*, Maximus arises as a gladiator hero, respected by the people of Rome but hated by Commodus. The heroes in both films have succeeded where their mentors have succeeded; but now they are at the most dangerous stages of their journeys — the place where they may fall in the same way that their mentors fell. The atonement is a moment of "at-one-ment" with the father — the point of his journey when the hero fulfills his destiny by becoming "at one" with his father and living up to his legacy.

## STAGE TEN: APOTHEOSIS

At the end of the 2nd act, the hero faces his greatest challenge. This moment of **crisis** is realized through the hero's "**supreme ordeal**" – in which the hero encounters his shadow. While undergoing his ordeal, the hero either literally or figuratively dies (like his father), but he is reborn with the power and spirit of the divine. This **symbolic death** and **spiritual rebirth** is the "apotheosis." Through ordeal and apotheosis, the hero encounters his greatest peril and fear, the threat that killed his father. But where his father failed and died, the hero succeeds and endures.

Wallace is betrayed by his fellow Scotsmen at the fateful battle of Falkirk. Though Wallace is struck down by an arrow to the heart, his symbolic death is a death of his spirit, when he is crushed by the treachery of his most noble comrade, Robert the Bruce (Angus MacFadyen). Wallace's secondary mentor is killed, his soldiers are beaten, and even his supernatural aid (his wife's handkerchief), is lost in the battle. But Wallace himself lives, his ferocity and rage multiplied by his ordeal. He emerges from his crisis and is reborn as a demonic force of vengeance, haunting the dreams of his betrayers and hunting them down, one by one.

Maximus undergoes his ordeal in the coliseum. By order of Commodus, Maximus is pitted against the greatest gladiator who ever lived. While he fights for his life, wild tigers are also set against him. Maximus is repeatedly mauled by tigers. He is wounded and nearly dies, but ultimately he overcomes and is victorious. Though the hero at this stage does not have to actually die, he should at least be touched by death in the form of a flesh wound and/or near death experience. By being brought to the brink of death in the ordeal, the hero encounters the world of the gods. Through apotheosis, the hero gains the psychological power of the gods, and is symbolically reborn with divine power.

## STAGE ELEVEN: THE ULTIMATE BOON

The hero is rewarded for surviving his ordeal. The **reward** is a moment of victory and fulfillment. The hero has fulfilled the prophecy of his birth. He has met his destiny and he has avenged, or atoned with, his father. The boon is also accompanied by a moment of **epiphany**. The hero realizes what he has accomplished, and he gains insight into his purpose and significance in the universe. He sees through himself and his own actions and into the eternal myth. For one moment, the hero does not see himself as one man, but as a symbol of man. In a sense, the hero sees himself as we, the audience, see him. The reward is not just a boon for the hero; it is a symbol of divine grace, a "magic elixir" that could save his people. Like the sword Excalibur, the Holy Grail or Prometheus' flame, the boon is the divine gift that the hero must return to human kind in the final act.

When Wallace reemerges after his apotheosis, his legend grows and he becomes an even greater inspiration to the Scots. He is rewarded with the epiphany that he is a legendary figure – a liberator of Scotland who will live on forever, no matter when he dies. He is also rewarded with a **love scene**, in which he receives some tenderness and passion from his temptress, Princess Isabelle. When Maximus emerges from his ordeal in the coliseum, he is rewarded with the love and adulation of the citizens of Rome. He also realizes that he still has devoted soldiers who are willing to fight for him. Finally, he realizes that he is on his way toward fulfilling his destiny as the liberator of Rome. The ultimate boon for both Wallace and Maximus is their destiny as liberators, a boon that they must deliver to their people in the final act of their journeys.

### ACT THREE: RETURN

The final stages of the journey depict the hero's return to his spiritual birthplace. Wallace returns to his role as leader of the Scottish rebellion, the birthright he inherited from his father. Likewise, Maximus returns to his role as liberator of Rome, the charge he was given by his emperor.

### STAGE TWELVE: REFUSAL OF THE RETURN

Just as the hero is reluctant to leave his common-day world for the world of adventure, he may now be reluctant to leave his world of adventure to return home. The hero has changed through apotheosis. He is no longer the man he used to be, and he is not sure if he can return to the place he once was. The hero may also be reluctant to trust the threshold guardians inviting him back into his old world. He's been burnt by trickery and deception before, and he's wary to put his faith in others. At first, Wallace refuses the Scottish nobles' petition for him to return as the leader of their rebellion. Similarly, Maximus at first refuses Lucilla's request to escape Rome and return as the general of a liberating army. However, both heroes quickly accept the inevitability of their roles. They have learned through their own epiphanies that they were destined to free the world of tyranny, and they are ready to accept their fate.

## STAGE THIRTEEN: THE MAGIC FLIGHT

The return home is a "magic flight" because the hero is now a semi-divine figure. The magic flight in movies is often depicted as a hectic and suspenseful chase, with the hero flying at full speed to save the maiden or kill the villain or complete his quest in whatever way it must be completed. In *Braveheart* and *Gladiator*, the magic flight is more solemn. Each hero knows he must return. Each hero knows he will probably face his own death. But each hero has the courage to make a **"willing sacrifice"** of himself, because he carries the strength of his integrated archetypes, and the divine power of his own identity.

## CATHARSIS

Though Campbell did not include it as a distinct stage in his model, it is important to mention that at some point in the 3rd act, there must be a **catharsis** – an emotional release of the hero's pent-up feelings. This catharsis typically occurs at the emotional **climax** of the film. If the hero is feeling hatred, anger, and a need for vengeance toward the villain, then the hero achieves catharsis by killing the villain. Maximus achieves this catharsis when he kills Commodus at the climax of their final battle in the coliseum. Wallace achieves catharsis throughout the film in numerous scenes of violence and vengeance against both the English and the Scottish nobles who betrayed him. His final catharsis is accomplished through a final act of defiance, in which he screams out the word *"freedom,"* even as he is being tortured to death. In romance movies, **catharsis** is achieved when the sexual tension or conflict between the two principal characters is resolved, and they share a passionate kiss. In sports movies, catharsis is achieved when the athlete hero achieves his great victory on the field. In any case, the catharsis is a crucial element of resolution in the 3rd act. Catharsis must happen, and it must be directly related to the hero's primary conflict.

## STAGE FOURTEEN: RESCUE FROM WITHOUT

The hero is often carried home on the arms of others. Campbell's model focuses on a "rescue from without," a stage in which the hero is rescued from his world of adventure and brought back home by his allies. For example, in *The Empire Strikes Back*, Luke is rescued by his allies in the Millennium Falcon after his climactic duel with Darth Vader. In *Braveheart* and *Gladiator*, the heroes are captured rather than rescued, and they are brought back to their point of origin on the shoulders of their enemies. Whether the return is accomplished via "magic flight," "rescue from without," or enemy capture, the hero is brought back to face his shadow in a final showdown, in which the hero's destiny will be determined.

### STAGE FIFTEEN: THE CROSSING OF THE RETURN THRESHOLD

*"At the return threshold the transcendental powers must remain behind."* When the hero returns to the common-day world, he leaves behind his godly status in the world of adventure, and reenters the common-day world just as he left it... as a mere mortal. By returning as a mortal, the hero sets up the possibility for a real death, not just a symbolic death, allowing the hero to finally become truly one with the father by repeating the identical act of martyrdom. The crucial symbolism at the crossing of the return threshold is the hero's relinquishment of his holds on the material world. He gives himself up completely to his father's cause, his people's cause, and his own cause.

### STAGE SIXTEEN: MASTER OF THE TWO WORLDS

Back in the world of the common-day, the hero's great deeds, his fame, his wisdom, his experience, and his encounter with the divine make him an awesome and inspiring figure. The hero is now the master of the common-day world from which he came, and also the master of the adventure world in which he journeyed. As Master of the Two Worlds, he is no longer just a hero, he is a **mentor**, as well. In this sense, he is also the master of the two archetypal worlds of heroism and mentorship. Now that he is a mentor, the hero must inspire another young hero, just as his primary mentor inspired him. The hero-mentor's role at this stage is a "**generative**" function. He must inspire a new hero to take his place, now that his journey has just about reached its end. I refer to the emerging hero that our primary hero-mentor must inspire as the "**sub-hero.**" In *Star Wars*, for example, Han Solo is the sub-hero — the character who is inspired by the primary hero... Luke. Every great hero must become an inspiring mentor by the end of his journey, thus completing his character arc by becoming the kind of man he identified with in the beginning.

In *Braveheart*, Wallace starts out as a boy inspired by his mentor, his father. By the end of his journey, Wallace has become a mentor who inspires a sub-hero, Robert the Bruce. Wallace inspires Robert to carry on the cause of rebellion after he dies. Though Wallace never brings independence and freedom to Scotland, his sub-hero, Robert the Bruce, does. Maximus also becomes a mentor in his final stages to Proximo (Oliver Reed), the man who taught him what it means to be a gladiator. Maximus inspires Proximo to sacrifice his own selfish needs and join in the fight to overthrow Commodus. He does so by telling Proximo that it was Commodus who killed Emperor Marcus, their mutual mentor figure. Hence, in a very reciprocal fashion, Maximus becomes a mentor to his own secondary mentor figure by invoking the name of their mutual mentor. The key point is, the hero at this stage must become an inspiring mentor to an emerging sub-hero.

STAGE SEVENTEEN: FREEDOM TO LIVE
In the final stage of his journey, the hero completes the mythological character arc by developing from hero to mentor, and then finally from mentor to **legend**. As a legend, the hero becomes an eternal inspiration to all people for all times. In films that are true to the ancient mythological structure, the hero almost always dies in the end. There is no greater legend or inspiration than a **martyr**. A courageous, valiant, and **climactic death** is the most dramatic and fitting end to the hero's journey, serving a variety of purposes:

1. The climactic death cements the hero's story as an inspirational legend for all time.
2. It fulfills the hero's destiny by making him spiritually one with his father.
3. It returns the hero back to the world of the divine, the world where he obviously belongs.
4. The climactic death itself creates a moment of solemn reflection that crystallizes the symbol of the hero's legend in the mind of the audience.

Perhaps the most famous and influential myth of the hero, the story of Jesus, ends in death. However, the symbol of the life of Jesus and his message live on in his legend forever. The same symbolism is seen in the legendary death of all heroes.

William Wallace dies, but in his courageous death he inspires his fellow Scots to carry on the rebellion. The handkerchief, the symbol of Wallace's soul, passes on to his sub-hero, Robert, after Wallace's death. In the final scene, Robert wields the handkerchief as he leads the Scots into a final battle that wins Scotland its freedom. Maximus also dies, but only after he kills Commodus, assuring that Rome will become a republic once again. The figurines, the symbol of Maximus' soul, pass on to one of his sub-hero's — a fellow gladiator — who plants the figurines in the ground as if they were seeds, saying: "Now we are free." By bringing freedom to their people, heroes symbolize the "freedom to live" that all people desire and cherish. Whether it is freedom from tyranny or simply the freedom to live our own lives the way we want to, the ultimate symbol of the hero is the symbol of freedom. While the hero dies, his symbolic **rebirth** is accomplished through the telling of his story. The inspiration of his legend lives on in the minds of his audience.

### Final Reward

In film, the mythological hero often receives a final reward at the end of his journey. Aside from bringing freedom to his people and being acknowledged as a legendary hero and mentor, the hero is usually rewarded with the ultimate gift — the **gift of love**. It is standard structure for the hero to get the girl in the end. Though Wallace and Maximus both die, they both are rewarded with a spiritual **return to the goddess**. In their moments of death, they both see their deceased wives, and they both return to them. The final reward lets the audience walk out on a happy, rather than somber, note. Though their hero dies a bloody and painful death, the audience can rest assured that their hero is happy in his afterlife, reunited once again with his cherished wife. The **"happy ever afterlife"** theme is standard structure for movies in which the hero dies. Though it seems rather hokey, it is a relatively sensible compromise between the classical structure of the mythological hero saga — in which the hero typically dies — and the modern structure of the Hollywood movie — in which the audience expects a happy ending.

### Caveat Lector

Let the reader be aware... since the stages represent structural elements and not a formula or program, do not expect every hero movie to include all or even most of the stages in Campbell's model. However, films that are successful in capturing the imagination of their audiences tend to represent the majority of these elements in some essential way. Even when films tell a story that isn't overtly mythological in setting or theme, they still tend to express the common archetypal elements that have the power to completely captivate audiences — even though they've been seen a million times.

## THE HERO'S JOURNEY
From Joseph Campbell's *The Hero with a Thousand Faces* (1949)

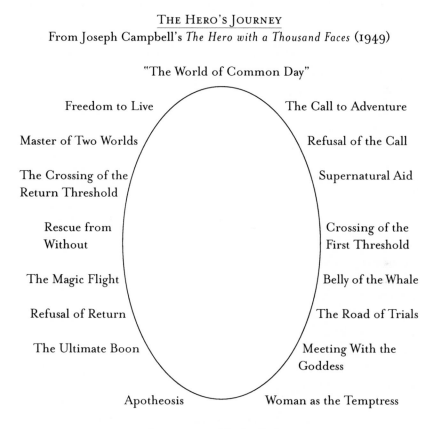

"The World of Common Day"

Freedom to Live — The Call to Adventure

Master of Two Worlds — Refusal of the Call

The Crossing of the Return Threshold — Supernatural Aid

Rescue from Without — Crossing of the First Threshold

The Magic Flight — Belly of the Whale

Refusal of Return — The Road of Trials

The Ultimate Boon — Meeting With the Goddess

Apotheosis — Woman as the Temptress

Atonement with the Father

## CHAPTER TEN SUMMARY POINTS

・ Campbell's stages of the hero's journey are a key to unlocking the symbolic code of the hero myth. Though heroes invariably venture out into the world to face external obstacles, the symbolic quest is always an inner journey. Ultimately, the hero is seeking the true nature of his Self. The symbolism of the *inner journey* is what makes the hero's journey universally resonant and engaging.

・ The three "Acts" of the hero's journey are: *Departure*, *Initiation*, and *Return*. The boy will depart from his home, he will go off on an adventure and grow up into a mature hero, and he will return home to become an inspiring mentor to others.

・ The hero's journey begins in his *World of the Common Day* — his home. It is both the starting and ending point of the hero's journey.

・ The world of the common day is also the place where the hero first encounters his *primary mentor figure* — the figurative or literal representation of the hero's father.

・ Stage one of the hero's journey is *the call to adventure*. A conflict of some kind calls the hero out of his common day world and into the world of adventure.

・ The calls to adventure are typically made by *herald* figures. Common herald figures may be figures connected to the mentors, the mentors themselves, divine figures, or messengers from the gods.

・ Stage two of the hero's journey is the *refusal of the call*. The hero's reluctance to commit himself to the cause represents the universal fears that all people have when they are faced with major life choices and transitions.

・ Often times, an *upping of the ante* or "raising of the stakes" is necessary to spur the reluctant hero into action.

・ In stage three of the hero's journey, the hero gains *supernatural aid*. The weapon or source of power is supernatural because it is linked closely with the hero's identity and motivation. The supernatural aid offers the hero spiritual, emotional, or psychological power.

・ Stage four of the hero's journey is the *crossing of the first threshold*. The hero enters the world of adventure.

・ Often times, the hero must face a *"threshold guardian"* archetype before crossing the first threshold. The guardian tests the hero's intelligence, courage, and resolve, to see if he is worthy of heroism.

- Frequently, the threshold guardian does not have to be defeated –
  the hero must use his wits to navigate around the guardian. He must
  answer his riddle or pass his test.
- In stage five of the hero's journey, the hero enters *the belly of the
  whale*. He is deep in the heart of the world of adventure, the realm
  of transformation in which he will become reborn.
- Stage six of the hero's journey is the *road of trials* – the arduous tasks
  that the protagonist must perform and the obstacles he must overcome in order to become a hero.
- Stage seven of the hero's journey is the *meeting with the goddess*, when
  the hero encounters and integrates his goddess archetype.
- Stage eight of the hero's journey is called *woman as the temptress*,
  when the hero encounters and integrates his anima archetype.
- Stage nine of the hero's journey is the *atonement with the father*. The
  hero integrates the lessons of his wise old man archetype – his primary mentor – by becoming "at-one" with his spirit. Typically, this
  is when the hero fulfills some type of quest or legacy bequeathed to
  him by his father.
- Stage 10 of the hero's journey is *apotheosis*. The hero undergoes a
  *crisis* or *supreme ordeal*, he is wounded and symbolically dies, and he
  is reborn a new man. Though he is mortal, his brush with the gods
  gives him divine power.
- Stage 11 of the hero's journey is the *ultimate boon*. The hero is now
  worthy of the prize at the end of his quest. He seizes the "sword,"
  grail, magic elixir or maiden in distress that he has been seeking. He
  may also kill the villain, beast, or enemy who has been tormenting
  him. These external representations of saving grace symbolize the
  inner boon of self-knowledge, which is the core symbol of the hero's
  inner journey.
- At this point, the hero is often *rewarded* with love or sex from his
  love interest – who may also be the maiden whom he just rescued.
- Stage 12 of the hero's journey is the *refusal of the return*. Just as the
  hero was reluctant to leave the common day world for the world of
  adventure, he may now be reluctant to return home. This stage is
  quickly overcome, as the hero knows that he must complete his journey and bring the "magic elixir" home to save his people.
- Stage 13 of the hero's journey is the *magic flight*. While the hero's
  journey up to this point was long and arduous, the return trip is
  often supercharged by his divine powers.

- The magic flight is depicted in movies by a standard "quickening of the pace" in the 3rd act, represented by the ubiquitous "hectic chase sequence."
- Stage 14 of the hero's journey is the *rescue from without*. The hero is often returned to his home on the shoulders of others. Sometimes he is rescued from the adventure world by his allies, other times he is a *"willing sacrifice"* – brought back as a prisoner by his enemies.
- Stage 15 of the hero's journey is the *crossing of the return threshold*. When he returns to his common-day world, he loses his divine power and becomes a regular mortal again.
- The hero's return to mortality in the final scenes sets up the final act of heroism, in which the hero dies and becomes a martyr to his cause.
- In stage 16 of the hero's journey, the hero is *master of the two worlds*. As a respected and honored hero, he is master of both the common-day world of mortals and the adventure world of gods and heroes.
- On a figurative level, the hero is the master of the world of heroism, and also the master of the world of mentorship – because in his final act, he will become an inspiring mentor to others and a legend for all times.
- The final stage is *freedom to live*. In sacrificing himself willingly to his cause, the hero delivers a message to his people... the message of independence, courage, and self-determination. Ultimately, the hero's story itself is the magic elixir – it is the symbol that inspires others to fight tyranny and live their lives freely and openly without fear.

## CHAPTER TEN EXERCISES

1. Identify the world of the common day for Frodo in *The Lord of the Rings*.
2. Identify the call to adventure in *Rocky*.
3. Identify the refusal of the call in *Star Wars*.
4. Identify the supernatural aid in *The Wizard of Oz*.
5. Identify the crossing of the first threshold in *Lawrence of Arabia*.
6. Identify the belly of the whale in *Raiders of the Lost Ark*.
7. Identify the road of trials in *The Lion King*.
8. Identify the meeting with the goddess in *The Elephant Man*.
9. Identify the woman as the temptress stage in *Basic Instinct*.
10. Identify the atonement with the father in *Pinocchio*.
11. Identify the apotheosis in *Indiana Jones and the Last Crusade*.
12. Identify the ultimate boon in *Excalibur*.
13. Identify the refusal of the return in *Dances with Wolves*.
14. Identify the magic flight in *The Blues Brothers*.
15. Identify the rescue from without in *The Empire Strikes Back*.
16. Identify the crossing of the return threshold in *The Greatest Story Ever Told*.
17. Identify the master of the two worlds stage in *Return of the Jedi*.
18. Identify the freedom to live in *Indiana Jones and the Temple of Doom*.

## ADDRESSING THE HERO'S JOURNEY IN YOUR SCRIPT

1. Does your script incorporate a mythological three-act structure, in terms of a Departure, Initiation, and Return? If not, do you think that applying a mythological three-act structure to your story will strengthen your plot?
2. Even the most classical of heroes typically do not go through every stage of Campbell's model. Nevertheless, construct an outline of your script in which your hero goes through *every* stage. Even though this will probably not be a usable outline, the exercise itself may help you realize the strongest and weakest points in your hero's story, or at least give you some ideas for new directions or character developments in your script.
3. If you are writing a script with a female hero, try applying an outline based on Campbell's model to your story, then compare it to an outline based on Murdock's model described in the next chapter. Which outline best represents the heroine you'd like to portray?

### STAGES OF THE HERO'S JOURNEY AT A GLANCE

| STAGES | EXAMPLES FROM FILMS |
| --- | --- |
| The Call to Adventure | Emperor Marcus asking Maximus to democratize Rome |
| Refusal of the Call | Maximus refusing the emperor's charge |
| Supernatural Aid | Wallace's handkerchief / Maximus' figurines |
| Crossing First Threshold | Wallace's first battle |
| The Belly of the Whale | The coliseum for Maximus / The battlefield for Wallace |
| The Road of Trials | Maximus' career as Gladiator / Wallace's career as Warrior |
| Meeting with the Goddess | Maximus & Wallace encountering their deceased wives |
| Woman as the Temptress | Lucilla in *Gladiator* / Princess Isabelle in *Braveheart* |
| Atonement with the Father | Wallace becoming a rebel leader |
| Apotheosis | Wallace being betrayed and wounded at the Battle of Falkirk |
| The Ultimate Boon | Maximus & Wallace realizing their roles as liberator heroes |
| Refusal of the Return | Wallace refusing to rejoin with the nobles |
| The Magic Flight | Wallace agreeing to help the nobles |
| Rescue from Without | Wallace being captured and taken to London |
| Crossing Return Threshold | Maximus & Wallace martyring themselves willingly |
| Master of the Two Worlds | Wallace becoming an inspiring mentor to Robert the Bruce |
| Freedom to Live | Maximus & Wallace liberating their peoples |

*Chapter Eleven*

# THE HEROINE'S JOURNEY

Though the hero has had a thousand faces, his sex invariably has been the same... a male. But modern mythology reflects modern people. Film — as the modern showcase and generator of mythology — has provided many myths of the female hero. But in large part, the movie heroine typically has been just a female inserted into the traditionally male role of hero. The inversion of sex in the hero formula does not necessarily change the structure. When modern filmmakers attempt to cast female characters as heroes, they typically give them the traditional male heroic qualities. "Girl-power Movies" such as *Charlie's Angels* (2000), *Lara Croft: Tomb Raider* (2001), and *Kill Bill* (2003) embody the notion that simply casting a sexy girl in the hero's role fulfills the function of the female hero. However, female strengths and male strengths are inherently different. Furthermore, the needs and desires of women are inherently different than the needs and desires of men.

In her book, *The Heroine's Journey* (1990), Maureen Murdock reconfigures Joseph Campbell's traditionally "androcentric" structure of the male hero's myth, creating a mythic structure for heroines that addresses the particular needs, struggles, and desires of modern women in a modern age. The tremendously popular film *Erin Brockovich* (2000), will be used as a running example of the heroine's journey. Just like the hero in Campbell's paradigm, Erin (Julia Roberts) encounters and integrates different archetypes at each stage of her journey.

### STAGE ONE: SEPARATION FROM THE FEMININE

The modern heroine's journey begins with a **rejection of traditional feminine values**. The feminine stereotypes of weakness, dependence, sensitivity, and emotionality are perceived as being retrograde and demeaning. Erin's struggle to find a job in the beginning of the film represents her need to leave behind her old life of being a housewife and stay-at-home mother. Rather than remaining dependent on her ex-husbands to support herself and her children, Erin decides to become self-supportive by achieving independence in the traditionally male realm of work in the outside world. Her need is increased when her caring and nurturing neighbor moves, leaving Erin without a babysitter. The babysitter's departure represents Erin's separation from the feminine. The babysitter is a traditional stay-at-home mother and housewife with no personal ambitions other than the raising and nurturing of children. Though Erin loves her kids, she also wants more out of life than playing out the traditional feminine roles that have been laid out for her. The first stage for Erin is a separation from the traditional archetype of **Mother Goddess**, exemplified physically by her maternal babysitter.

### STAGE TWO: IDENTIFICATION WITH THE MASCULINE

After separating from the feminine archetype, the heroine must find a new mentor to guide her in the male dominated realm of work in the outside world. The new mentor must be a male, a function played by the traditional **Wise Old Man** archetype. The wise old man in *Erin Brockovich* is Ed (Albert Finney), the crusty old lawyer who gives Erin a job and initiates her into the realm of male competition... the field of legal combat.

### STAGE THREE: THE ROAD OF TRIALS

Once initiated into the world of adventure, the heroine embarks on a road of trials much like the male hero's. At this stage, Erin must encounter and integrate her **Animus** – the archetypal masculine strengths of determination, rational intellect, courage, and fortitude. By internalizing these strengths into her character, the heroine overcomes the consummate female weaknesses. Murdock delineated these female weaknesses as the following "false myths" historically applied to women: **The Myth of Dependency**, **The Myth of Female Inferiority**, and **The Myth of Romantic Love**. The tasks of debunking these myths are illustrated as the heroic acts of slaying different monster archetypes.

### SLAYING THE TWO-HEADED DRAGON

Erin debunks the Myth of Dependency by proving that she can succeed and achieve her goals in the traditionally male realm of legal combat. The Two-Headed Dragon is the conflicting needs of her job and her children. Work and family both demand her time and attention. The heroine must juggle both tasks at once, just as the hero fighting the two-headed dragon must battle both heads at once. By finding a balance between work and family, the heroine slays the Two-Headed Dragon.

## SLAYING THE OGRE TYRANT

Erin debunks the Myth of Female Inferiority by not only succeeding in her own goals, but by triumphing over P. G. & E. — the huge, heartless, multi-billion-dollar utility corporation, which is the epitome of male despotic power. While P. G. & E. is the external representation of the "Ogre Tyrant," the real male monster archetype is inside of the heroine. Erin must slay her inner tyrant by controlling her own need to succeed at all costs. She needs to restrain her obsession with work, which is progressively destroying her relationships with her children and her boyfriend, George (Aaron Eckhart).

## SLAYING THE KNIGHT IN SHINING ARMOR

The Myth of Romantic Love is the one told in fairy tales and princess stories. The myth tells impressionable young girls that one day, a handsome prince charming will come and awaken you with a kiss. He'll lift you onto his noble white steed and carry you off — solving all of your problems and taking care of your every need forever and ever. The Knight in Shining Armor is not a monster, he is an illusion. For the heroine, the illusion of a man who will solve all of her problems is more dangerous than the most vicious monster. By giving into this illusion, the heroine regresses all the way back to the beginning of her journey. She ceases to be a modern heroine, and becomes the traditional **maiden in distress**, who waits passively on a bed of roses for the brave hero to rescue her.

When Erin's struggle with P. G. & E. dominates all of her time, George gives her an ultimatum... *"you gotta' either find a new job or a new man."* Erin debunks the Myth of Romantic Love by refusing to give in to George's ultimatum. She tells George that she doesn't need him to take care of her. Though she loves him, she refuses to let a man confine her identity and run her life. She confirms her status as a strong, vital, and independent woman.

## STAGE FOUR: THE ILLUSORY BOON OF SUCCESS

At the highpoint of her journey, the heroine may feel that she has achieved dominance over her struggles. However, the heroine at this point is suffering a delusion, a lack of insight that Murdock calls the "**superwoman mystique**." The heroine harbors "false notions of the heroic," believing that she can be both a champion of the masculine world and queen of the feminine world simultaneously. The superwoman mystique is the false belief that one person can excel in two things at once. The superwoman can be a super-worker at her job, while also being a super-mom at home. But the mystique is a delusion, an illusion of balance, a denial of the fact that the heroine is human, not a superhuman being. Eventually, she must realize that something has to give. Erin's realization of her illusory boon of success comes when George tells her over the telephone that her baby spoke her first words while Erin was busy at work.

### Stage Five: Strong Women Can Say No

When the heroine realizes that she is suffering from the delusion of the superwoman mystique, she must restrict her own ambitions by saying "no" to some of the demands on her time and attention. The archetype that the heroine encounters at this stage is the "**King**" – the representations of male demandingness that are tearing her in two. The heroine must stand up to her boss, husband, boyfriend, etc., and say "No." Erin displays her strength by saying no to George when he gives her his ultimatum, and she also says no to Ed when he tries to take her off the P. G. & E. case. But while the King archetype is the external representation of male demandingness, the real King that the heroine must face are the demands of her own "inner male." The heroine must "**silence the inner tyrant**," by saying "no" to her own unrealistic demands on herself.

While the external symbols of the King are represented well in *Erin Brockovich*, the internal King is never really dealt with. In the traditional male hero style, Erin merely pushes herself harder and harder throughout the film, never really giving in or admitting weakness. The "silencing of the inner tyrant" theme is represented more directly in *Baby Boom* (1987), in which the heroine, J. C. (Diane Keaton), realizes that she cannot be a super mother and a super business woman at the same time. J. C. says "no" to her CEO by refusing a big corporate career. She also says "no" to herself, realizing that her new baby is more important to her than a high-powered position.

## STAGE SIX: THE INITIATION AND DESCENT TO THE GODDESS

At one point in her journey, the heroine re-encounters a version of the **Goddess** archetype that she disconnected herself from in the first stage. The goddess that Erin encounters is Donna (Marg Helgenberger), an ailing mother who is suffering from toxin poisoning as a result of P. G. & E.'s negligence. Erin's sympathy for the ailing mother sets her on an external journey to battle P. G. & E. in order to gain a settlement that will heal the ailing mother. The external legal battle is symbolic of Erin's inner journey to heal the ailing mother within herself. She desperately wants to be a good mother to her children. Her inner mother, however, feels neglected and malnourished, because Erin is focusing all of her energy and attention on her career.

## STAGE SEVEN: URGENT YEARNING TO RECONNECT WITH THE FEMININE

The encounter with the goddess awakens a realization in the heroine that she has lost a crucial part of her feminine identity in dedicating herself so wholeheartedly to the goal of success in the male realm. The "urgent yearning to reconnect with the feminine" is symbolized by a need to encounter and reintegrate the Anima archetype. **Anima** integration in the heroine means reconnecting with the feminine body, feminine feeling, feminine passion, and emotion. For many heroines, it is the reawakening of love, sex, and passion in her character. J. C.'s anima is awakened in *Baby Boom* when she falls in love with a new man. Erin's anima is awakened when she falls in love with George.

## THE WILD WOMAN ARCHETYPE

In her enormously popular bestseller, *Women Who Run With the Wolves: Myths and Stories of the Wild Woman Archetype* (1992), Clarissa Pinkola Estés speaks of the "wild woman archetype" – the passionate, emotional, impulsive side of the female Self that represents the "instinctual nature of women." To an extent, Erin is in touch with her "wild woman" from the beginning. She is impulsive, strong, passionate, and comfortable with her feminine sexuality. She uses her seductive persona to con the weak men she encounters to help her on her journey, and she uses her passion to plow through the barriers put in front of her. Erin's inner "wild woman" is seen in full force during her love scene with George, in which she wears a tiara that she won as a teenager in a beauty contest. But Erin's yearning to reconnect with the feminine is most deeply connected with her realization that she is neglecting her children and missing their childhood. She yearns to reconnect with the traditional feminine archetype – the nurturing, caring, loving mother who is devoted to her children rather than outside goals.

## STAGE EIGHT: HEALING THE MOTHER/DAUGHTER SPLIT

In Murdock's model, the heroine's final reconnection with the Mother Goddess is facilitated by a mediating figure – the symbolic representation of ancestral feminine wisdom and healing embodied in the "**Grandmother Spider**" archetype. The Grandmother is a benign figure, a woman who understands the needs of both mother and daughter, and therefore the most expedient healer of the mother/daughter split. Erin does not encounter an external Grandmother figure, but she symbolically heals her own mother/daughter split by healing Donna, the ailing mother, with a big settlement check from P. G. & E. While the money is a great boon, it is clear in the final scene between Erin and Donna that the real healing for both characters is not accomplished through money, but through the caring relationship established between the two women.

## STAGE NINE: FINDING THE INNER MAN WITH HEART

The function of the heroine's love interest typically parallels the anima's function in the male hero's journey. In *Erin Brockovich*, George displays the traditionally feminine qualities usually associated with the anima. He is sensitive, supportive, loving, empathic, nurturing, and mothering to both Erin and her children. George also delivers the typical anima message of emotional wisdom to Erin – that her obsession with work is disintegrating her relationships with her family and loved ones. Though his male sex places him in the role of the animus, his function as the hero's love interest is more closely in tune with the function of the anima, which inspires the hero to reintegrate the feminine forces of intimacy, sensitivity, and love in her Self.

## STAGE TEN: BEYOND DUALITY

As in the hero's journey, the integration of the opposite sex archetype is tantamount to a "hieros gamos" or **sacred marriage** – resulting in "the **birth of the divine child**." As the embodiment of both feminine and masculine character traits, the fully developed heroine is the "**Master of Two Worlds**." She has found success in the business world, and fulfillment in her personal world. According to Jung, the mythological archetype that represents psychological androgyny is the **Hermaphrodite** — a common figure in myth and dreams. The hermaphrodite archetype represents a sense of personal completeness that goes "beyond duality," because he/she is one figure, not a duality but a *singularity*. For Murdock, the principal symbol at the final stage is the circle. As a "perspective for life," the circle is all-inclusive. It represents the eternal cycle of life, the concentric sphere of human relationships, and rebirth within the circular enclosure of the womb.

Murdock's and Campbell's models are both very similar and very different, yet oddly complementary. While Campbell's mythological male hero integrates his archetypes in order to achieve legendary status in death, Murdock's contemporary female heroine integrates her archetypes in order to achieve psychological balance in life.

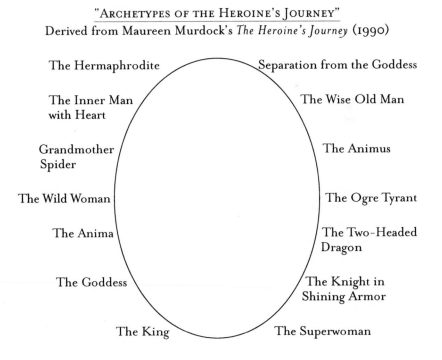

"ARCHETYPES OF THE HEROINE'S JOURNEY"
Derived from Maureen Murdock's *The Heroine's Journey* (1990)

The Hermaphrodite     Separation from the Goddess

The Inner Man with Heart     The Wise Old Man

Grandmother Spider     The Animus

The Wild Woman     The Ogre Tyrant

The Anima     The Two-Headed Dragon

The Goddess     The Knight in Shining Armor

The King     The Superwoman

## CHAPTER ELEVEN SUMMARY POINTS

+~+

- The heroine's journey is Maureen Murdock's reconfiguration of Campbell's hero's journey model. Murdock's model is especially relevant to the challenges of modern "liberated" women in contemporary society.
- Murdock's heroine integrates her archetypes in order to achieve a sense of *psychological balance* between the contrasting goals of success in the world of personal competition – (the masculine realm) – and contentment as a traditional mother, wife, and caregiver – (the feminine realm).
- Stage one, *separation from the feminine*, is a rejection of traditional feminine values. This stage is typically accomplished by a separation from a traditional mother, housewife, or caregiver – represented by the *Goddess* archetype.
- Stage two, *identification with the masculine*, is a meeting with a male mentor who fulfills the role of the father figure or wise old man archetype.
- In Stage three, *the road of trials*, the heroine must debunk the three false myths of femininity.
- The *myth of dependency* is debunked when the heroine slays the *two-headed dragon*. She demonstrates that she can master both her personal life and professional life without having to rely on a man.
- The *myth of female inferiority* is debunked when the heroine slays the *ogre tyrant*, demonstrating that she can be just as powerful as a man in the realm of competition.
- The *myth of romantic love* is debunked when the heroine slays the *knight in shining armor*. She demonstrates that she is not an old-fashioned "maiden in distress" and that she does not need a handsome prince charming to rescue her. She can rescue herself.
- In Stage four, *the illusory boon of success*, the heroine confronts her own "false notions of the heroic." She sees that she is trying to live up to the *"superwoman mystique,"* the false belief that she can be a champion of both the male and female realms simultaneously.
- In Stage five, *strong women can say "no,"* the heroine debunks her own false myth by saying "no" to some of the unrealistic demands that she has put on herself. The heroine encounters and renounces the king archetype, either by saying "no" to a demanding male figure in her external life or by *"silencing the inner tyrant"* within herself.

- In Stage six, *the initiation and descent to the goddess*, the heroine re-encounters a version of the goddess archetype that she separated herself from in the first stage. She begins to identify with some of the traditional feminine roles that she rejected earlier.
- In Stage seven, *urgent yearning to reconnect with the feminine*, the heroine encounters the *anima* archetype – the representation of feminine beauty, emotion, sensitivity, and passion that she needs to reintegrate into her Self.
- In Stage eight, *healing the mother/daughter split*, the rift between traditional and contemporary versions of the feminine is healed, and the heroine becomes "whole." This stage of healing is often facilitated by a compassionate mediator... the *Grandmother Spider* archetype.
- In Stage nine, *finding the inner man with heart*, the heroine encounters and integrates her *animus* archetype, typically represented by a sensitive male love interest
- In the final stage, *beyond duality*, the heroine has integrated all of her archetypes. She has found psychological balance and a sense of "wholeness." The fully developed heroine represents the "androgynous" balance of both feminine and masculine personality traits.

## CHAPTER ELEVEN EXERCISES
✦

1. Identify five movie heroines and analyze their journeys in reference to Murdock's model.
2. Identify the stage of "separation from the feminine" in *Gorillas in the Mist*.
3. Identify the stage of "identification with the masculine" in *G. I. Jane*.
4. Identify the stage of "the road of trials" in *The Wizard of Oz*.
5. Identify the stage of "the illusory boon of success" in *Working Girl*.
6. Identify the stage of "strong women can say no" in *There's Something About Mary*.
7. Identify the stage of "initiation and descent to the goddess" in *White Oleander*.
8. Identify the stage of "urgent yearning to reconnect" with the feminine in *How to Make an American Quilt*.
9. Identify the stage of "healing the mother/daughter split" in *Girl, Interrupted*.

10. Identify the stage of "finding the inner man with heart" in *Alice Doesn't Live Here Anymore*.

11. Identify the stage of "beyond duality" in *Gone With the Wind*.

## ADDRESSING THE HEROINE'S JOURNEY IN YOUR SCRIPT

1. In *Erin Brockovich*, the first stage of Separation from the Feminine is not seen explicitly, though it could be inferred.  How do you address this stage in your heroine's story?  Would the heroine's story be strengthened by a more explicit separation from a real feminine figure?

2. The masculine archetype in *Erin Brockovich* is represented by a traditional father figure − a surly, but good-hearted, older man.  Consider the masculine archetype in your heroine's story.  Would you be better off with a more traditional father figure or a less traditional one?  Should he be completely positive or should he offer negative values as well?

3. While Erin faces a few rivals, there is no real villain in her story − as is typical of heroines' journeys according to Murdock's model.  If P. G. & E. were represented by a physical character, would Erin's story be stronger, or was it better to leave the huge utility corporation as a faceless, menacing specter?

### STAGES OF THE HEROINE'S JOURNEY AT A GLANCE

| STAGES | EXAMPLES/ARCHETYPES FROM *ERIN BROCKOVICH* |
| --- | --- |
| Separation from the Feminine | Erin loses her babysitter and searches for a job |
| Identification with the Masculine | Erin's new boss, Ed |
| The Road of Trials | Erin works on the P.G. & E. case |
| The Illusory Boon of Success | Erin "balances" success at work with family life |
| Strong Women Can Say No | Erin stands up to George and Ed |
| Initiation & Descent to the Goddess | Erin identifies with Donna |
| Yearning to Reconnect with Feminine | Erin falls in love with George |
| Healing the Mother/Daughter Split | Erin "heals" Donna with the P. G. & E. settlement |
| Finding the Inner Man with Heart | George displays archetypal qualities of the anima |
| Beyond Duality | Success in business world & fulfillment at home |

# PART FIVE

*Alfred Adler*

*Chapter Twelve*

# THE INFERIORITY COMPLEX

Alfred Adler was a colleague of Freud's who, like Jung, was also banished from Freud's inner circle of psychoanalysts when his theories began to diverge from the original interpretations of the "Master's." Specifically, Adler proposed two concepts that were considered subversions of orthodox theory. First, Adler believed that deep-seated feelings of inferiority and a need to compensate for these feelings were the primary root of neurotic conflict, rather than the basic drives. Second, Adler believed that the rivalry between siblings for the love and attention of parental figures is often a greater unconscious motivational force than the Oedipal rivalry between father and son. By supplanting the Oedipal complex with the inferiority complex, and by placing Sibling Rivalry over Oedipal rivalry as the primary neurotic conflict, Adler earned the status of persona non grata in Sigmund Freud's address book. Nevertheless, Adler went on to become an extremely influential and significant theorist in the field of analysis, and his theories of the Inferiority Complex and Sibling Rivalry became as popular as any theory originally composed by "the Master."

## THE INFERIORITY COMPLEX

According to Adler, *"we all experience feelings of inferiority, since we all find ourselves in situations we wish we could improve."* We deal with our feelings of inferiority through **compensation**, the natural inclination to succeed in other areas in order to cover our lacking in the areas in which we feel inferior. Just as a blind man will compensate for his lack of sight by developing a superior sense of hearing, the individual compensates for his inferiority complex by developing in the areas of life in which he can feel superior. Consequently, the instinctive reaction to an inferiority complex "will always be a compensatory movement toward a feeling of superiority."

## HAMARTIA

A common element of the hero's character in mythic structure is the "hamartia," the tragic flaw that the hero must overcome. The term

"Achilles' Heel" refers to Achilles' hamartia, the only part of his body that was vulnerable, because his heel was covered when he was dipped in the mystical river Styx. The most common hamartia among the classical heroes was **hubris**, the arrogance and conceit that would naturally afflict heroes with great powers and demi-god status.

Hamartia is the root of the inferiority complex, the basic weakness, flaw, or foible that the hero must overcome. In films, the inferiority complex is often depicted as a character overcoming great personal adversity to achieve superiority in a particular field. In *Shine* (1996), a man (Geoffrey Rush) goes on to become a great pianist despite a serious psychiatric illness. In a similar story — *A Beautiful Mind* (2001) — a man (Russell Crowe) overcomes a serious psychiatric illness to become a Nobel Prize winning mathematician. And in *My Left Foot* (1989), a man (Daniel Day-Lewis) overcomes severe cerebral palsy to become a great writer. In all of these stories, the heroes compensate for their disabilities by focusing with great initiative and determination on a field in which they can succeed. In addition, these characters are driven by a need to feel superior in the fields that they have chosen.

## THE SUPERIORITY COMPLEX

Naturally, extreme feelings of inferiority will produce extreme reactions toward superiority. These extreme reactions are called "**overcompensa-tion.**" While compensation is a normative way of dealing with the neurosis of inferiority, overcompensatory behaviors are pathological and maladaptive. Perpetual or generalized overcompensation can even lead to a "**superiority complex**," a personality disorder in which the individual expresses a pathological need to dominate and humiliate others around him. Certainly, Adolf Hitler's need to feel racially and genetically superior to others, and his pathological desire to dominate, humiliate, and exterminate those whom he considered his inferiors, could be considered a worst case scenario of a superiority complex gone wild. His madness inspired and possessed an entire generation.

In an Adlerian analysis, Hitler's overcompensatory behaviors were an extreme reaction to a severe *inferiority* complex. Just a brief glance at Hitler's personal biography, along with some historical background relating to the extreme poverty, depression, unemployment, chaos, and widespread humiliation of post-WWI Germany, would seem to support an Adlerian interpretation of the Nazi movement as an extreme reaction to both a personal and collective inferiority complex. Much depth can be added to the character of someone with a superiority complex (typically the villain), by **revealing the inferiority complex** behind his overcompensatory behavior. When this is achieved, the villain ceases to function as a one-dimensional character. The audience understands why the villain is evil, and feels pity, as well as hatred, for his character.

In *One Hour Photo* (2002), Sy (Robin Williams) is an atypical villain – an insecure misfit whose dangerous obsession with a family becomes twisted and violent. But when the root of his behaviors is revealed, we realize that the torture he inflicts on the father of the family he is obsessed with is actually overcompensated revenge against his own father, who abused and tortured him. By revealing this layer of inferiority within the villain, depth is added to his character, and the level of conflict is raised within the mind of the viewer. Feelings of disgust and contempt are now mingled with pity and empathy... the villain becomes a tortured soul, as well as a torturing sadist.

## SUPERVILLAINS

The "supervillains" in superhero movies are often deformed, mutated characters who are tortured by their own disabilities and driven by a need to dominate others. The Joker (Jack Nicholson) in *Batman*, The Green Goblin (Willem Dafoe) in *Spider-man*, and Big Boy Caprice (Al Pacino) in *Dick Tracy* (1990) are all "freaks." Their physical deformities represent their raging inferiority complexes. Their subsequent superiority complexes are driven by overcompensation. By dominating, controlling, and destroying others, the supervillain quells his feelings of shame, anger, and disgust with himself. While the supervillain is an extreme example of overcompensation and the superiority complex, these drives and conflicts are common motivations in *all* characters. They can be just as effective means of character motivation in heroes (especially tragic heroes), rivals, supporting characters, or even mentors. For example, the coach who drives his team with a psychotic need for victory in order to compensate for his own failed career as a player is an archetypal example of the superiority complex in the mentor character.

## CHILDHOOD FANTASIES

According to Adler, all children experience a sense of inferiority in one way or another. The universality of the inferiority complex in children is a natural result of the child's small size, weakness, lack of experience, powerlessness, and complete dependence on adults. Children have a heightened desire to see stories about heroes that they can relate to, that is, heroes overcoming inferiority. The child hero formula in film is especially adept at piquing the child's imagination. Disney's "Princess Series" is directly marketed toward little girls, who naturally resonate toward the Princess Hero formula. Movies marketed toward little boys tend to have heroes who recall the classical male heroes of the Greek and Medieval tradition, such as the heroes in *Hercules* (1997) and *The Sword in the Stone* (1963). The princess fantasy in girls and superhero fantasy in boys relate to an innate **"goal of superiority"** that exists in all people, but is particularly acute in the minds of children — because of their natural state of physical, intellectual, and social inferiority.

## THE DISNEY MYSTIQUE

By capturing a child's imagination, you capture a child's heart. The Disney Corporation has built an empire by appreciating and exploiting the fact that children feel especially powerless and demoralized in a world controlled by adults. By supplying a hero formula that is carefully designed to symbolize the psychological trials and tribulations of childhood, Disney acquires loyal customers at their most suggestible age. The attachment and special intimacy felt by Disney fans for all Disney products is created in childhood, and so the Disney brand itself becomes a treasured childhood memory, as well as an integral part of the individual's identity. The purity of the individual's association between the Disney logo and that idealistic state of mind remembered as "childhood" results in lifelong customers who'll pay through the nose to recapture the feelings of innocence and youth that they felt as children. And, since parents re-experience cherished childhood memories through their own children, parents will line-up by the thousands to instill the same associations from their childhoods into their own children.

## THE CHILD HERO'S CONFLICT

The greatest and most ubiquitous conflict in childhood is **powerlessness**. Children are small and weak. Adults control every aspect of their existence. Children are not allowed to control where they live, what they do, who they see, and how they spend their time. Every action a child takes is supervised and controlled by a dominating adult. *"Brush your teeth!"* *"Eat your greens!"* *"Go to bed!"* *"Wear a sweater!"* *"Do your homework!"* *"Make your bed!"* *"Go to school!"* *"Turn off the TV!"* These are the externally enforced imperatives that fill a child's life, leaving little room for independence or individuality – much less adventure, danger, or excitement. Hence, children can relate to the conflict of little Simba in *The Lion King* (1994), when Simba is exiled from his pride of lions by his evil uncle, and must overcome his own powerlessness in order to overthrow his uncle.

While powerlessness is the essence of the child hero's conflict, many adult heroes face moments of powerlessness at crucial points in their stories, as well. In *Raiders of the Lost Ark* (1981), Indiana Jones (Harrison Ford) is tied to a post during the dramatic sequence when the holy ark is uncovered. In *The Empire Strikes Back*, Luke is shackled and powerless when his closest ally, Han Solo, is frozen into a carbon block. By making the hero (typically the most proactive member of the cast), powerless at a critical moment, a great deal of tension is added to the plot.

## ORPHAN HEROES

The child hero formula begins with a child who is suddenly freed of the domineering presence of parents or other adult authority figures. The formula begins with a basic **wish fulfillment** – the child hero is free – and independence is sweet. *Pinocchio* (1940) runs off to the stage to become an actor. *Dumbo* (1941) gets to enjoy life on his own in the topsy-turvy world of the circus. Mowgli in *The Jungle Book* (1967) never knows his parents at all; like a jungle animal, he is born free. Simba in *The Lion King* goes off into the exciting forest to experience life away from the watchful eye of Mother and Father. Arthur in *The Sword in the Stone*, Moses in *The Prince of Egypt* (1998), Dorothy in *The Wizard of Oz*, Harry Potter, Cinderella, and Snow White are all orphan heroes.

The childhood fantasy of becoming an orphan expresses various wishes. For some children, it is an unconscious wish to punish their parents for their cruelty. For others, it expresses a wish for freedom from possessive and dominating parents. And for others, the dream of being an orphan represents a desire to form an independent identity completely separate from the identity of their parents. Often times, child heroes in these fantasies grow up with surrogate parents. Princess heroes such as Cinderella and Snow White grow up with evil stepmothers, while Sleeping Beauty grows up with her fairy godmothers. Other heroes – Luke in *Star Wars*, Arthur, Jesus,

Moses, Cyrus, Perseus, Hercules, etc. – grow up with surrogate parents because their real parents are royal or even divine figures. The childhood fantasy expressed in the stories of these child heroes is the desire for a grand, illustrious sense of identity beyond the boring and mundane world of the child's real parents.

After becoming freed from their parents, the child heroes learn their most important lesson first: they love their parents and miss their homes. The first stage of development is the realization that **home** is where the heart is, and that Mommy and Daddy's tyrannical domination is really just their way of expressing love and care. The goal at this point becomes clear... the heroes must find and fight their way back home. But getting back home is just half the battle. Though the child hero's wish for freedom and independence is fulfilled and the desire resolved, the child's desire for a sense of **power** and **self-determination** still needs to be addressed.

ROLE REVERSAL

In the child's real life, Mom and Dad are the champions. They are the ones who go out and battle the dragons of the world in order to save house and home. The adults are the defenders and the children are the defenseless victims. But in the child's fantasy life, children are the characters imbued with power and strength. In their world, the children must slay the dragon, defeat the witch, conquer the black knight, or destroy the villain. In their world, it is the parent who is powerless, helpless, and completely vulnerable. Only the child hero can save the powerless parents from certain death and destruction. The theme of the child hero saving his parent (and/or the world), is ubiquitous in Disney films. Pinocchio's journey was fulfilled when he saved Gepetto. Simba saved his pride of lions and the entire jungle kingdom from the tyranny of his evil uncle. And in the *Spy Kids* series (2001, 2002, 2003), the child heroes save their parents and/or world in every film.

MARRIAGE SAVING

A child's world is rather small in perspective. The parental marriage and child-parent relationships – the cement of the **family unit** – can seem like the entire universe to a child. In films like *The Parent Trap* (1961 & 1998), the child's world is saved when the family unit is reconnected. Instead of saving the world or their parents' lives, the child heroes save their parents' marriage, which in the children's perspective is tantamount to saving the entire world.

## ANIMAL HEROES

Children are very adept at **imaginary animation** – projecting human qualities onto animals, or even inanimate figures. Hence, movies and stories for children are often animated cartoons featuring animal heroes such as the characters in *Bambi* (1942), *Dumbo*, *Jungle Book*, *Lady and the Tramp* (1955), *101 Dalmatians* (1961 & 1996), *The Lion King*, and countless others. Children also love to project themselves into the roles of fantasy figures such as the monsters in *Monsters, Inc.* (2001). They can even identify with inanimate objects, such as the toys in *Toy Story* (1995) or the household appliances and furnishings in *Beauty and the Beast* (1999), and *The Brave Little Toaster* (1987). In a child's imagination, the extra **suspension of disbelief** required to identify with a character that couldn't even exist in the real world is just that much more fun and fantastic. Absolutely anything could happen! When animals, objects, or monsters symbolizing children save the human adult world, the victory is psychologically rewarding on a variety of levels.

## PINOCCHIO

Disney's rendition of the classic Pinocchio story has become an eternal fixture in the American psyche. The film is a very successful portrayal of the child hero formula because the hero has a quest that all children can identify with. All children have the sense that they are not completely "real," since the adults in their world constantly limit their freedom because they are "just children." The children's fantasy of someday developing into "grown ups" and having all of the freedom they desire is symbolized in Pinocchio's quest of becoming a "real boy." Pinocchio's story begins when he is separated from his "father," Gepetto, (the artisan who created his body). His immediate goal is to reunite and integrate with his father. But to achieve his ultimate goal of becoming a real boy, he must reconnect with his spiritual mother – the Blue Fairy, (the Goddess who gave him life).

Pinocchio's mentor is a talking animal – Jiminy Cricket. In many Disney movies, the hero's **animal mentor** must also overcome an inferiority complex. The Seven Dwarves must overcome their small size and fear of the Evil Queen in order to defend Snow White. The talking mice must overcome their small size and fear of the evil cat in order to defend Cinderella. The Candlestick and other household objects must overcome their small size to battle the invading mob and defend the castle in *Beauty and The Beast*. And Mushu, the miniature talking dragon, must overcome his smallness in order to help Mulan rescue the Emperor. In *Pinocchio*, Jiminy overcomes his self-doubt and smallness by aiding his hero and joining him in battle against the giant whale, Monstro.

Just as the hero in Campbell's model completes his journey by returning home, child heroes typically complete their journeys by reuniting with their parents and returning home. In the end, Pinocchio and Jiminy save Gepetto. Pinocchio is rewarded for his bravery and constancy when he is resurrected by the Blue Fairy and triumphantly transformed into a real boy. However, we get the sense that whether real or wooden, Pinocchio's true triumph came when he was reunited with his loving and devoted father.

# CHAPTER TWELVE SUMMARY POINTS

+~+

- All heroes must overcome something either in themselves or in their environment. In this sense, the *hamartia*, or *inferiority complex*, is a basic part of every hero's character, and *compensation* is a basic element of the hero's motivation.
- Extreme feelings of inferiority may lead to *overcompensation* – maladaptive ways of expressing the need to feel superior that are indicative of the *superiority complex*.
- *Supervillains*, who have an abnormal need to dominate others and the world around them, are extremely potent examples of the superiority complex.
- You can add a lot of depth to a villain character by *revealing the feelings of inferiority* that lie at the root of his superiority complex.
- Movies for children, especially Disney movies, tend to address *childhood fantasies* and psychological needs particular to childhood.
- The superhero fantasy in children relates to their *goal of superiority*, the way children deal with natural feelings of inferiority that arise from being small people in a world run by big people.
- *Powerlessness* is the central conflict in the child-hero formula.
- When adult heroes are rendered powerless at crucial times in their stories, a critical element of tension is added to the plot.
- Child heroes are often cast as *orphans*. This ubiquitous plot device provides an element of *wish fulfillment*, giving the child complete freedom and independence. It also offers a clear goal – to reconnect with the parental archetypes.
- *Role reversals*, in which child heroes must save their parents, are popular with kids because the children get to play the role of powerful defenders while the parents must play the role of defenseless victims.
- *Animal heroes* are extremely common in movies for children, because kids are particularly adept at identifying with animated and animal characters, and readily project themselves into those roles.
- The ultimate goal in most children's films is to *reunite with beloved parental figures*.

## CHAPTER TWELVE EXERCISES

1. Identify five superheroes from movies and analyze their inferiority complexes.
2. How do all of these superheroes compensate for their feelings of inferiority?
3. Identify five supervillains from movies and reveal the feelings of inferiority behind their superiority complexes.
4. How do all of these supervillains overcompensate for their feelings of inferiority?
5. Identify the hamartia – the weakness or critical flaw – in your five superheroes.
6. Identify five child heroes and analyze their primary goals and motivations.  Can all of these themes be related in one way or another to the issue of powerlessness?
7. List all of the great heroes from myth, legend, and film that you can think of.  How many of these heroes are either orphaned or separated from their birth parents in infancy or childhood?
8. Identify 10 films that were marketed toward children that involve a role reversal plot.
9. Identify 10 films that were marketed toward children that have animal heroes or animal characters in principal roles.
10. Analyze the following films and relate the plots to the child-hero formula described in this chapter: *The Lion King, Cinderella, The Prince of Egypt, Snow White, Mulan, Hercules, Toy Story, Dumbo, The Sword in the Stone,* and *The Brave Little Toaster.*

## ADDRESSING THE INFERIORITY COMPLEX IN YOUR SCRIPT

1. What is your hero's hamartia, or inferiority complex? What must your hero compensate for?
2. Is there a character in your script with a superiority complex? If so, how could you add depth to this character by revealing the inferiority complex behind his or her overcompensatory behavior?
3. Could including a scene in which your hero must deal with power-lessness add a level of tension to your plot?

| THE CHILD-HERO FORMULA AT A GLANCE | | |
|---|---|---|
| ELEMENTS | FUNCTION | EXAMPLES |
| Powerlessness | Establishing the need for change, and the need for independence and power | Dorothy's conflict in the 1st Act of *The Wizard of Oz* |
| Wish Fulfillment | Experiencing an exciting adventure Being free of parental control | Pinocchio joining the circus Pinocchio in "Pleasure Island" |
| Orphan Heroes | Freedom from parents A need to reconnect with parents | Pinocchio, Harry Potter, Dorothy, Arthur, Cinderella |
| Role Reversal | Becoming powerful and strong | Spy Kids |
| Marriage / Parent Saving | Resurrecting or preserving the nuclear family unit | *The Parent Trap* *Spy Kids* |
| Animal Heroes | Characters whom children love to imagine and identify with | *Dumbo*, The supporting characters in *Jungle Book* |
| Animal Mentors | Non-threatening, non-dominating, understanding & wise mentor figures | Jiminy in *Pinocchio* Mushu in *Mulan* |
| Reuniting with Parents | Returning to the 1st stage of the journey as a fully developed hero | The final sequences in *Pinocchio* & *The Wizard of Oz* |

*Chapter Thirteen*

# SIBLING RIVALRY

Freud focused on Oedipal rivalry as the primary motivation related to the need for love and approval from the parents. Adler, on the other hand, focused on the rivalry between siblings. Sibling rivalry in myth and legend is an archetypal theme and the mythological progenitor of the ubiquitous rivalry conflict in dramatic structure. Rivalry is also a common theme in hero plots. Great heroes tend to have great rivals or "**nemeses.**" Superman has Lex Luthor, Batman has The Joker, Spider-man has Green Goblin, Sherlock Holmes has Professor Moriarty... and even God himself has Satan — the greatest and most powerful of the angels. Though the elements of the rivalry plot in this chapter will be delineated in relation to the archetypal sibling rivalry theme, the same elements can be generalized to *any* rivalry plot, whether the rivals are siblings, or not.

*Sibling Rivalry: Aron (Richard Davalos) and Cal (James Dean) in* East of Eden *(1955).*

### EAST OF EDEN

The archetypal theme of sibling rivalry in Western mythology is epitomized in the biblical story of Adam's first two sons, Cain and Abel. The
Bible (Genesis 4:16), tells the story of how Cain killed his brother Abel
and was consequently banished by God: Cain "*went out from the lord's presence and lived in the land of Nod, east of Eden.*" The rivalry between Cain
and Abel is not over the love of Adam or Eve, it is over the love of God —
the archetypal father.   Hence, Cain and Abel are best read not as real
brothers, but as archetypal brothers, who are perpetually pitted against
each other in competition for the love of the parental figure.   John
Steinbeck recast the Cain and Abel myth in his novel, *East of Eden*, which
was made into a feature film by Elia Kazan.   In the movie, Cal (James
Dean) and Aron (Richard Davalos) are brothers in rivalry for the love of
their father, Adam (Raymond Massey).

### THE GOOD CHILD/BAD CHILD DUALITY

Cal is the "bad" son and Aron is the "good" son, just as Cain was bad and
Abel was good.  The clear-cut duality between the good child and bad child
is symbolic of the persona/shadow duality within the self.  In a broader
sense, it is symbolic of the conflict between good and bad in everyone, in
the world and in nature itself.  In film, the good child/bad child duality is
often recapitulated in the hero/villain dichotomy.  The hero is supremely
good, while his nemesis, the villain, is unconditionally bad.

In *East of Eden*, badness is related to both sexuality and knowledge of the
inherent selfishness and egoism in people.  Goodness is related to innocence and a naïve idealism in the inherent goodness of others.  In this
sense, Cal and his mother are "bad," while Aron and his father are "good."
When Cal encounters his mother and learns that she left his father in
order to live on her own terms, his newfound knowledge of her validates
his knowledge of himself and makes him stronger.  But when Aron is
forced by Cal to encounter his mother, the knowledge of her existence
destroys him.  He cannot comprehend the notion of having a mother who
abandons her family to run a brothel.  In the end, it is Aron, the good son,
who is banished from Eden, because Aron's view of the world is based on
the bible and not on reality.

## PARENTAL FAVORITISM

The root of the conflict between the rivals is the love of the parent. One child sees himself as good and the other as bad because the parent favors one child and disfavors the other. The child thinks, "*If Father loves me, I must be good;*" or alternatively, "*Father does not love me, so I must be bad.*" The children then cast themselves in the roles of good child and bad child and play out those roles, ostensibly for the rest of their lives. They rival each other over many things, but the root of the conflict remains their jealousy for the love of the parent.

Often times, the conflict over favoritism is complicated when Mother favors one child and Father favors the other. In this case, the parental conflict between Mother and Father is extended into their children, who play out this conflict within a sibling rivalry. In *East of Eden*, Cal, disliked by his father, has always bristled under the role of the bad son. After discovering his mother, the notion of being the bad son doesn't bother him as much, because he sees that he is more like his mother, and therefore favored by her. This knowledge of his mother helps Cal accept himself for who he is, and it motivates him to "atone" with his father – his central quest in the film.

## THE RIVAL/MENTOR SWITCH

While the parent is the primary mentor figure, there is an inextricable link between parents and siblings, which creates a link between the archetypal rival and mentor figures. Consequently, we often see the theme of a former rival becoming an ally and/or mentor. This theme recapitulates the common occurrence in real life of an older brother or sister replacing the parent as a mentor figure when the parent dies, leaves, or becomes otherwise negative or absent. This theme is represented quite comprehensively in the five *Rocky* films.

A. In *Rocky* (1976), Rocky (Sylvester Stallone) is inspired by his mentor (trainer), Mickey (Burgess Meredith), to face his rival, Apollo (Carl Weathers).
B. In Rocky II (1979), Rocky defeats his rival.
C. In *Rocky III* (1982), the death of Rocky's mentor predicates the emergence of a new rival – Clubber Lang (Mr. T) – the man who killed Mickey. Apollo, Rocky's former rival, now becomes Rocky's new mentor.

D. In *Rocky IV* (1985), Rocky becomes Apollo's mentor in Apollo's return-from-retirement bout. (By this point, the former rivals have both become mentors to each other.) Apollo's death now predicates the emergence of a new rival – Ivan Drago (Dolph Lundgren) – the man who killed Apollo. And Apollo's former mentor, Buck (Tony Burton), becomes Rocky's new mentor

E. In *Rocky V* (1990), Rocky becomes a mentor to a young fighter, Tommy, who promptly leaves Rocky for a new mentor – Duke – who was a former mentor to both Rocky and Apollo. Rocky finds himself in a mentorship rivalry with Duke, and a fighting rivalry with Tommy.

The role transformations in the *Rocky* movies represent the fluidity in which the rival and mentor archetypes can change hands. The linking element between the mentor and rival roles is that they both serve essentially the same function – they inspire the hero to compete and succeed.

## ROMANTIC RIVALRY

Another typical element of the sibling rivalry in film is a romantic rivalry over a mutual love interest. In *East of Eden*, both Cal and Aron compete for the love of Abra (Julie Harris). The romantic rivalry is the central conflict for the female love interest, because – while she loves the gentle and kind good son – she is simultaneously attracted and drawn to the sexy and shady bad boy.

## THE NEED FOR APPROVAL

The driving force between the sibling rivalry is the competing need for the parent's love, attention, and approval. In film, the different levels of psychological conflict between siblings are typically played out through a rivalry to attain an **external goal**. This visible goal is the external representation of the rivalry, while the driving unconscious force of the conflict is the internal rivalry for parental approval. A common element within the external goal plot is a **moral conflict** in which the good child/bad child theme is played out.

In *East of Eden*, Cal wants to make money to help his father recover from a failed business venture. He thinks that by doing this, he can win his father's approval and consequently become the favored son. Cal contrives a plan to make quick money through war profiteering. Meanwhile, Aron is openly expressive of his belief that war is immoral, as is anyone who would make a profit from war. The external goal for money becomes tinged by a moral conflict between the siblings over the ethics of war.

In a key scene, Cal surprises his father with the money he earned. The father rejects Cal's gift, just as God rejected Cain's sacrifice. In the same scene, the father is overjoyed with Aron's gift — the news that he and Abra are going to be married. Just as God's rejection of Cain's sacrifice and acceptance of Abel's sacrifice lead Cain to murder Abel in a fit of jealous rage, the father's rejection of Cal's gift and his acceptance of Aron's gift leads Cal to destroy Aron. Both of these plots revolve around the child's desperate need for love and parental approval.

### DUEL IN THE SUN
In King Vidor's epic Western, *Duel in the Sun*, the sibling rivalry is between Jesse (Joseph Cotten) and Lewt (Gregory Peck). The rivalry between brothers exists on all six of the levels listed above.

1. Jesse is the good son — kind, gentle, civilized, and moral. Lewt is the bad son — cruel, violent, savage, and immoral.
2. Jesse is Mother's (Lillian Gish) favorite. Lewt is Father's (Lionel Barrymore) favorite.
3. There is a romantic rivalry over Pearl (Jennifer Jones), the beautiful half-caste whom both Jesse and Lewt desire.
4. There is a psychodynamic rivalry over the love of their father, whose respect and approval they both crave.
5. The rivalry over an external goal is a political conflict over the building of a railroad in their family's territory.
6. The moral conflict involves both the railroad and the brothers' treatment of Pearl. Jesse is for the railroad — a good commodity that will help all of Texas. Lewt is against the railroad, because it conflicts with his father's imperialistic desire to control vast tracts of land. Also, Jesse treats Pearl with honor, kindness, and respect. Lewt brutalizes Pearl. He uses her for sex but refuses to offer her anything more than a physical relationship, because she is a half-caste.

## CHAPTER THIRTEEN SUMMARY POINTS

- The classical theme of sibling rivalry, as epitomized in the biblical story of Cain and Abel and analyzed in the theories of Alfred Adler, provides the template for the ubiquitous rivalry plot in movies.
- The *good child/bad child* duality is the most basic part of the rivalry formula. One child or character is the good guy and the other is the bad guy. This dichotomy is similar to the hero/nemesis duality, in which every great hero has an equally great villain.
- In the classic sibling rivalry theme, one child is typically favored by a parent over the other child. The favoritism element can build some extremely sophisticated levels of conflict, when Mother favors one child and Father favors the other.
- The rival figure is similar in nature to the mentor figure – as both characters provide the hero with motivation to succeed. Often times, a rival can develop into a mentor and vice-versa, as the functions of these two figures are so closely related.
- Another staple of the rivalry formula is a romantic rivalry over a mutual love interest.
- Finally, most rivalries also focus on an external goal... i.e., winning the big game, winning the election, winning the big race.
- Often times, there is a moral element involved in the competition to achieve the external goal, in which the good child/bad child duality is played out. For example, the good child wants to win the election to save the town, while the bad child wants to win the election so he can sell out to the evil oil conglomerate.

## CHAPTER THIRTEEN EXERCISES

1. Identity three films in which there is a classical sibling rivalry theme — brothers and/or sisters conflicting with each other.
2. Do the rivalries in these films contain the plot elements delineated in this chapter?
3. Identity three films in which the sibling rivalry theme is represented less directly — the rivals are not siblings, the rivals are not competing for parental or romantic love, the rivals are not either good or bad, etc.
4. Do the rivalries in these films still contain some or most of the plot elements delineated in this chapter?
5. Analyze the rivalries in the following films: *Whatever Happened to Baby Jane? Crimes and Misdemeanors*, and *The Royal Tennenbaums*.
6. Do you have siblings? Analyze your relationships with your own siblings, and see if you can detect any elements of rivalry. Think about how any of these rivalry issues may have affected your goals and motivations in your own life story.

## ADDRESSING SIBLING RIVALRY IN YOUR SCRIPT

1. Most heroes experience rivalry at some level, whether or not the rival is a sibling or even a main character in the film. In *Shane*, the hero faces a rival early on — a tough cowboy in the saloon. The fight with the minor rival foreshadows the big shootout in the end with Wilson — the primary rival. The rivalry is a showcase for the hero... a chance for him to prove his strength, intellect, skill, or courage. Do you have at least one scene in your script in which your hero is confronted with a rivalry?
2. Rivalry for the love interest is a ubiquitous plot line, even in movies that are not overtly romantic. The romantic rivalry adds tension and conflict to the love interest theme. Does your hero face a rival for the heart of his love interest?
3. There is typically a moral element to the conflict between rivals. In *Shane*, the hero is fighting for the good homesteaders, while his rival — Wilson — is fighting for the evil cattle baron. What is the moral conflict between your hero and his rival?

| SIBLING RIVALRY AT A GLANCE | | |
|---|---|---|
| **ELEMENTS** | **DESCRIPTION** | **EXAMPLES FROM** *EAST OF EDEN* |
| Good Child / Bad Child Duality | One sibling is cast as the good child, the other is cast as the bad child | Aron is the good child Cal is the bad child |
| Parental Favoritism | A parent favors one child over the other. Or, one child is Mother's favorite, the other is Father's favorite | Aron is Father's favorite Cal sees himself as "taking after" his mother |
| Romantic Rivalry | Romantic rivalry between the siblings over a mutual love interest | Cal and Aron rival each other for Abra's love |
| Need for Approval | Underlying rivalry arising from the need for approval from one or more of the parents | Cal's need for Father's approval results in jealousy and rage directed at Aron |
| External Goal | There is a rivalry over achieving some external goal | Cal's need to help his father recover from a failed business venture |
| Moral Conflict | A moral conflict in which the "good child/bad child" theme is played out | Cal's war profiteering & Aron's moral denouncement of war |

*Chapter Fourteen*

# LIFE STYLES

Adler's theory of the superiority drive owes much to **Friedrich Nietzsche** (1844-1900), the philosopher whose incredibly original and provocative ideas inspired and influenced an entire generation of European intellectuals, including Freud, Jung, Erikson, and most of the other great psychoanalytic theorists. Adler used Nietzsche's concept of the "**Will to Power**" to describe the primary drive of superiority as a universal goal in human nature. Like Nietzsche, Adler saw the superiority drive as an innate urge toward perfection, which has as its endpoint a hypothetical ideal, rather than an actual attainable goal. *"The beautiful thing about man,"* Nietzsche wrote, *"is that he is a bridge... a bridge to the Ubermensch!"* From an evolutionary standpoint, individual people cannot attain true perfection. However, evolution provides each individual human being with the drive toward perfection, the goal of superiority that inspires humankind toward greater heights, and makes each living person a "bridge" to the next evolutionary stage of human development.

## UBERMENSCH & UNDERDOG

While the Ancient Greeks preferred classical heroes of royal or divine birth – men who were born with great powers and predestined glory – the **Judeo-Christian** tradition championed the true underdog. As Nietzsche pointed out, the Greeks and Romans were the first and second "Reichs" – their mythologies were being composed as their cultures were becoming powerful empires. The Greco-Romans valued nobility, power, and the belief in divine destiny that could drive one culture to conquer and dominate others. The Judeo-Christian tradition was born out of slave societies that valued humility, service to God, and the belief in a reward after death in return for a life of poverty and subjugation. Nietzsche believed that it was natural for a "**master race**" of conquerors to have a mythology based on the "**master morality**" – in which the strong and powerful deserve to be victorious. Inversely, it was also natural for a "**slave race**" to have a mythology based on the "**slave morality**" – in which the meek shall inherit the earth. Hence, the Greco-Roman hero is an "ubermensch," a superman, while the Judeo-Christian hero could be called an "untermensch"... an underdog.

The battle between ubermensch and underdog is symbolic not only of the individual triumph over personal inferiority, but of the historical triumph of the Judeo-Christian ethic over the Master-Race ethic of the ancient Greeks and Romans, as well as the more recent triumph over the Nazi "uber alles." Films such as *Rocky* address the mythical conflict between ubermensch and underdog in clearly delineated battle scenes. In *Rocky*, the quintessential Judeo-Christian underdog must face a technically superior champion who is appropriately named after a Greek god – "Apollo." WWII films address the ubermensch-underdog conflict by pitting the Judeo-Christian Allies against the Aryan Nazis. The Roman and biblical epics pit the ancient Judaeans and Christians against their imperialist masters – the ancient Egyptians, Romans, and Greeks. In other films, the ubermensch-underdog conflict is an internal struggle experienced by one hero.

## SUPERHEROES

The superhero character in films represents an odd combination of classical and Judeo/Christian character traits. Superheroes typically display features of both superiority and inferiority complexes. They are the Ubermensch and underdog combined into one hero. The superhero's personality split, however, is conveniently distributed into his two identities. In his mortal existence, Clark Kent is "mild-mannered," meek, shy, clumsy, insecure, and ineffectual; but in times of trouble, he transforms into Superman, the "man of steel," who is superior to every other man on Earth. Similarly, Peter Parker is a small, weak, insignificant young man; but when he turns into Spider-man, he is superior to everyone. Viewers, especially children, easily identify with modern superheroes because they represent the same opposing duality that they feel inside themselves. While we struggle with feelings of inferiority and inadequacy (our inner Clark Kent), our dreams of superiority (our inner Supermen), motivate us to do great things.

## THE LIFE STYLES

A central theme in Adler's later theories was his model for the different "life styles" that people use in their struggles to attain superiority. Inspired by Nietzsche's theory of the "will to power," Adler's theory of conflicting life styles provides a model for both intrapersonal neurotic conflict within film characters (internal conflict), and interpersonal conflict between characters (external conflict). Adler distinguished between four fundamental life styles — all but one of them being "mistaken."

1. The "**ruling type**" — the individual drives toward superiority and domination over others.
2. The "**getting type**" — the individual takes from and depends on others rather than providing for others and oneself.
3. The "**avoiding type**" — the individual escapes and avoids challenges, responsibilities, and duties.
4. The "**socially useful type**" — the individual engages in socially constructive activities.

The "socially useful type" is the only type that is not "mistaken," because the superiority drive is directed toward the improvement of oneself and society, rather than selfish pursuits. Notwithstanding the existence of these types, Adler's theories are not pessimistic or deterministic like Freud's. Adler was a humanist. His theories espoused the notion of a "creative self," in which the individual can change and construct his own personality by modifying, or even altering, his life style through the force of his own "will." Film heroes are also "creative selves." Through the course of a film, their characters always develop in some way. Often times, characters display personal growth by developing from one of the mistaken types into the socially useful type.

### A Model for both Intrapersonal and Interpersonal Conflict

Many films depict these life-style types as *interpersonal conflict*. In a movie with a classical hero, the hero usually starts out as a fully developed moral individual. In these stories, the hero is the socially useful type, the allies that he recruits are initially the avoiding types before they join the hero and become socially useful, the villain is the ruling type, and the villain's cronies are the getting type. This formula is standard template for "band of heroes" movies such as Kurosawa's *Seven Samurai*, in which a ronin samurai (socially useful type), pulls together a ragtag band of warriors(avoiding type), in order to defeat the greedy bandits (getting type), and their evil master (ruling type).

Other films depict the life styles as *intrapersonal conflict*. The antihero figure in movies usually starts out as the getting type — an outlaw or gunslinger out for himself. He then epitomizes the avoiding type when a call
to adventure is made for him to save the town, and he refuses the call. But
he eventually becomes the socially useful type by accepting the call and
destroying the evil villain — who is typically the embodiment of the ruling
type. The hero in Kurosawa's *Yojimbo* is a ronin samurai looking to make
a few bucks as a hired sword, (the getting type). At first he avoids helping
the poor townspeople (the avoiding type), but eventually he dedicates himself to the cause of saving the town (the socially useful type), which he does
by killing the evil mob bosses who are ruling the village, (the ruling types).

### SPARTACUS

Crassus (Lawrence Olivier), the ruthless patrician in *Spartacus*, is the
embodiment of the ruling type. He treats the slaves and subordinates
around him like toys in his own personal game of pleasure. Slaves are not
human to Crassus, they are objects whose only purpose is to satisfy his perverse
and sadistic appetites for sexual and psychological domination. Batiatus
(Peter Ustinov), the avaricious master of the gladiator academy, epitomizes
the getting type. He would sell his own mother for a few pieces of gold.
When buying and appraising his slaves, Batiatus affects the posture of a
patrician. He is head-and-shoulders in class above his slaves and servants,
but his position is that of a bourgeois shop owner, who buys valuable stock
at wholesale and sells them to the ruling class at resale. Batiatus's grasping
and selfish nature is evident in the scene in which he encounters Crassus
and his patrician pals. He immediately disaffects all of his pride and pre-
tense to bow to Crassus and serve his every whim. Batiatus even sells his
most precious possession to Crassus, the exquisite Varinia (Jean
Simmons), catering to the senator's sexual desire. Moreover, Batiatus,
despite his better judgment, yields to Crassus' order for a gladiator fight to
the death within the academy itself. He cannot refuse Crassus, because his
type can always be bought for a pot of gold. Making the gladiators-in-
training fight to the death in their own home is the straw that breaks the
back of the downtrodden slaves. The fight leads to a mutiny and
full-scale slave rebellion, all because of Crassus' lust for power and
Batiatus' lust for gold.

In the 1st act, while still a slave in the gladiator academy, Spartacus plays the
role of the avoiding type. He knows, all too well, his place in the world,

and has even tasted the bitter pill of punishment. In the opening
sequence, Spartacus is tethered to a rock to die of sun exposure as penalty
for attacking a guard in defense of a fellow slave. He barely escapes this fate
when he is bought at discount by Batiatus, who is out on a shopping spree.
Spartacus is not about to stick his neck out again for anyone. But
Spartacus overcomes his avoiding ways when he is inspired by the courage
and martyrdom of a fellow slave, and when he is enraged by the sight of his
beloved Varinia being taken away from him by his heartless masters. By
inciting and leading the greatest slave rebellion in recorded history,
Spartacus depicts the leadership and social interest indicative of the socially
useful type. Even in death, Spartacus continues his social usefulness, his
legend standing as a beacon and inspiration for slaves everywhere.

## THE ROBE

The biblical epic *The Robe* (1953) depicts a character who progresses
through all four of Adler's life styles. Tribune Marcellus Gallio (Richard
Burton) is a Roman patrician, a member of the elite ruling class that owns
slaves and dominates other nations as the self-proclaimed "Masters of the
World." Gallio starts out as a prototype for the classical Greco-Roman
hero, but in this extremely religious film, Gallio must overcome his superiority complex in order to become a Judeo-Christian hero. In the first
act, Gallio is the epitome of the ruling type. His own superiority complex
leads him into a bidding contest over a slave in which he butts heads with
Caligula, the heir apparent to the throne of the Roman empire. As punishment, Gallio is given an officer's commission in the Roman army and sent off
to an obscure post in the uncivilized realm of Judea.

Gallio's journey of personal transformation begins after he crucifies Jesus.
Gallio's guilt at having destroyed such a pure and divine being is physically
retained in Jesus' robe. The guilt is initially a curse that drives Gallio mad.
He tries to evade the curse by leaving Judea and returning to Rome.
Gallio's evasiveness at this stage of his journey embodies the life style of the
avoiding type. Gallio's madness, however, follows him to Rome. The
imperial soothsayer diagnoses Gallio with a curse bewitched upon him by
Jesus, the "sorcerer" whom he executed. Emperor Tiberius gives Gallio an
imperial commission to return to Judea in order to find and destroy Jesus'
robe. While doing so, Gallio must also uncover the leaders of the new
seditious Christian movement, so that they may all be executed. The
imperial commission transforms Gallio once again into the getting type.

Rather than ruling others or avoiding responsibility, Gallio's life style is now completely focused on getting something in order to satisfy a personal need at the expense of others. While he is now just a servant of the ruling class, a messenger boy carrying out the emperor's orders, Gallio is out for himself. His only purpose in life is to get.

Gallio returns to Judea and finds the robe, but the holy cloth and the guilt it embodies transforms Gallio once again, turning him into a socially useful type. The symbolic relationship between guilt and the robe signifies the essential difference between the Roman and Christian moralities. The Roman ethic is based on pride and the idealization of dominance, nobility, and strength. The Judeo-Christian ethic is based on guilt and the consequent idealization of social responsibility and humility, especially in relation to the lowest rung of society... the poor, the crippled, the enslaved, and the oppressed. In Nietzschean terms, pride is the psychological force behind the "master morality," and guilt is the psychological force behind the "slave morality." After converting to Christianity, Gallio renounces his old proud ways and embraces the humility of Christian guilt.

In the 3rd act, Gallio displays his newfound social usefulness. He fights against his old Roman allies in order to rescue his former slave (Victor Mature), a fellow Christian. In a final dramatic display of his life-style reversal, Gallio selflessly sacrifices his own life in order to save the slave that he bought in the beginning of the film in an act of pride, hubris, and superiority. Gallio's martyrdom is doubly significant, because he — a Roman patrician — sacrifices his life for the life of a lowly slave. Gallio's self-sacrifice is also a literal emulation of the Christian ideal performed by Jesus himself. By willingly sacrificing himself for the poorest member of society, Gallio displays his complete identification with Jesus as a mentor, and his ultimate devotion to the Christian ideal.

# CHAPTER FOURTEEN SUMMARY POINTS

- Drawn from Nietzschean philosophy, Adler's theory of conflicting *life styles* provides a model for both internal and external conflict. The theory delineates four different personality types based on life style – the way people express their drive toward superiority.
- The *Ruling Type* strives to feel dominant and superior over others.
- The *Getting Type* takes from others or depends on them to satisfy his needs.
- The *Avoiding Type* runs away from his duties and avoids obligations or responsibilities.
- And the *Socially Useful Type* engages in selfless, socially useful activities.
- Some films depict these life style types as *interpersonal conflict*. For example, the hero is the socially useful type, his reluctant sidekick or allies are the avoiding type, the villain is the ruling type, and the villain's cronies are the getting type.
- Other films depict the life styles as *intrapersonal conflict*. For example, the antihero figure usually starts out as the getting type. He epitomizes the avoiding type when a call to adventure is made and he refuses the call. But he eventually becomes the socially useful type by accepting the call and destroying the evil villain – who is typically the embodiment of the ruling type.

## CHAPTER FOURTEEN EXERCISES

1. Using your knowledge of film, identify five movie characters who epitomize the life style of the getting type.
2. Identify five movie characters who epitomize the life style of the avoiding type.
3. Identify five movie characters who epitomize the life style of the ruling type.
4. Identify five movie characters who epitomize the life style of the socially useful type.
5. Find and analyze a film in which there is interpersonal conflict between the four different character types delineated in this chapter.
6. Find and analyze a film in which there is intrapersonal conflict – inner conflict within a character that drives him to develop from one type of life style into another. See if you can find a film in which the protagonist develops through all four of the life style types delineated in this chapter.

## ADDRESSING ADLER'S LIFE STYLES IN YOUR SCRIPT

1. Would you define the hero in your script as a Greco-Roman hero (an Ubermensch) or as a Judeo-Christian hero (an underdog)? Why, or why not?
2. Does your hero develop into someone who is more socially useful? If not, do you think that this sort of character development may add something to your script?
3. Analyze the hero's character development in films such as *Spider-man* (2002), *Mad Max 2: The Road Warrior* (1981), and *The Fisher King* (1991), in terms of Adler's model of life styles.

## ADLER'S LIFE STYLES AT A GLANCE

| Life Styles | Character Traits | Examples |
|---|---|---|
| Ruling Type | Needs to feel dominant or superior over others | Crassus in *Spartacus*<br>Gallio in the 1st act of *The Robe* |
| Getting Type | Takes from or depends on others | Batiatus in *Spartacus* |
| Avoiding Type | Escapes or avoids responsibilities and duties | Spartacus before his rebellion<br>Peter in the 1st act of *Spider-man* |
| Socially Useful Type | Engages in socially useful activities | Spartacus after his rebellion<br>Gallio in the 3rd act of *The Robe* |

# PART SIX

*Rollo May*

*Chapter Fifteen*

# EXISTENTIAL CONFLICT

Rollo May was a psychoanalyst with a strong background in theology and existential philosophy. May saw a link between psychoanalysis and existentialism, realizing that neurotic anxiety is often directly related to what existentialists called "angst," or existential despair. He became the leader of a new movement in existential psychoanalysis by redefining anxiety as an existential malady that transcends the purely personal. Anxiety as an existential conflict refers to the agitating feeling that one is out of place in the world. It is the conflict between the basic belief that there should be some purpose or meaning in the universe, and the realization that one has no sense of purpose or meaning in one's own life.

## THE BALLGAME METAPHOR

The conflict of existential meaning is often analogized to the conflict of the **spectator** versus the conflict of the **player**. In a baseball game, there are moments of great anxiety – such as the 9th inning of a tie game. The player's anxiety is great, but he can do something about it — hit the ball, throw the ball, catch the ball, etc. The spectator's anxiety is great, but he really can't do anything about it except clap or yell, actions that have essentially no impact on the game. Hence, the spectator's anxiety is even greater than the player's anxiety, because the spectator's neurotic energy cannot be channeled into any meaningful action. Rollo May pointed out that existential conflict is similar to the spectator's anxiety. When we feel that life is passing us by, that things are happening around us but we have no control over them, we feel anxious. The problem, according to May, is that we are viewing our own lives as spectators rather than as players. Instead of taking an active stance in our own existence, we stand aside passively as other forces determine our identities, our destinies, and our purposes in life.

Though existential conflict in real life is incredibly sophisticated and complex, existential conflict in film is quite simple. The hero is confused, anxious, depressed, or agitated because he feels that his life is useless, point-less, meaningless, or absurd. But by finding a specific purpose or objective to chase after (an external goal), the hero defines and creates meaning in his own existence. His negative anxiety is turned into positive energy that fuels his journey. The hero starts out as a spectator, but finishes not only as a player, but as the champion in the ballgame of his own life.

## SELF-CONSCIOUSNESS

May's solution for the modern problem of anxiety is self-consciousness, the process of becoming aware of one's own predicament, and taking steps to overcome it. The existential neurotic must change his perspective on life from the spectator role to that of the player role. Once his perspective is changed, his feelings about himself will change, his behaviors will change, and his life will change. He will overcome the absence of meaning in his life by defining meaning in a personally resonant way, and then creating meaningful goals that provide purpose in his formerly purposeless life. For May, this process is achieved primarily though self-analysis, introspection, and insight. In film, self-consciousness is typically depicted as an interacting combination of external forces and internal character development.

## STAGES OF SELF-CONSCIOUSNESS

In his classic book, *Man's Search for Himself* (1953), May delineated four stages of self consciousness:
1. Innocence — "*... before consciousness of self is born.*"
2. Rebellion — "*... trying to become free to establish some inner strength...*"
3. Ordinary Consciousness of Self — "*... a healthy state of personality.*"
4. Creative Consciousness of Self — "*ecstasy...* "*to stand outside one's self*"*...*"

May's last stage is not a state of being, but a transitory moment of transcendence, in which a person goes beyond a purely subjective view of himself, and sees himself from an objective perspective, as an external, omniscient observer looking at his own life and providing new insights and meaning to his own existence.

## STAGES OF SELF-CONSCIOUSNESS IN CHARACTER DEVELOPMENT

Though May proposed his model in relation to the different stages of life, the model also can be related to the stages of character development in film.

1. Innocence – the hero is **uninvolved**, ignorant, or indifferent to any problem within himself or out in the world.
2. Rebellion – A problem from the external world triggers a realization of existential conflict, which leads to introspection and **soul searching**.
3. Ordinary Self-Consciousness – The hero dedicates himself to a meaningful, significant **external goal**, and goes on a journey to accomplish this goal.
4. Creative Self-Consciousness – The hero's journey climaxes with an internal realization – an **"epiphany"** – about himself.

In the film version of the stages, there is a constant interchange of conscious energy from internal conflict to external goals. In the 1st stage, conscious energy is dormant. In the 2nd stage, an external problem initiates an internal conflict. In the 3rd stage, the internal conflict is externalized into a specific goal. In the 4th stage, proximity to, or achievement of, the external goal results in an internal flow of conscious energy, in which the hero realizes the vital essence of his own character. May referred to this climactic transcendent experience with the classical psychological term, "*ecstasy*." For our purposes, the classical dramatic term of "epiphany" is more appropriate. By the final stage of epiphany, the hero has accomplished his external goal – but more importantly – he also has discovered his true identity and special purpose in the universe.

### STAGE ONE: INNOCENCE

In the first stage of the hero's development, he is innocently uninvolved with conflict on either the internal or external level. The hero's lack of involvement, however, does not mean that he is unaware of the existence of conflict. In *Star Wars*, Luke starts out as an innocent boy on a secluded desert planet. Though he is aware of the external conflict in the galaxy between the evil Empire and the rebels, he is not involved in it. And though he is vaguely aware of the deep-seated feelings of restlessness and impatience heating up inside of him, his internal conflict has not yet reached its boiling point. In your script, the first stage of your hero's character is the setup for everything to come. Though your hero is not an adventurer yet, he should be ready for his adventure – whether he knows it or not. At this stage, your protagonist is a hero in waiting – an emergent hero – who only needs an external trigger to set off the heroic nature inside of him.

## STAGE TWO: REBELLION

In the 2nd stage, something arises from the external world to pull the hero out of his state of existential dormancy. The **external goal** is a signal to the hero that he isn't living up to his potential – that he has a purpose in the world, but he isn't achieving it. The hero experiences in full the anxiety of the spectator, who is distressed by the conflict on the field but feels that he cannot do anything about it. The internal conflict for the hero at this stage is to rebel against the forces that are keeping him dormant, and to become actively engaged as a player in the field of external combat.

## DEATH OF THE INNOCENT

Often times, the end of the innocence stage is predicated by the death of an innocent figure in the hero's life. In *Star Wars*, Luke's aunt and uncle are killed by imperial storm troopers. These innocent bystanders become victims in the external conflict between the Empire and the rebellion. Luke has no choice now – he must become an active player in the fight. His aunt and uncle were the last things holding him back. In Luke's story, the death of these two innocents represents the death of his own innocence. The same plot device was used in *Braveheart*, *Gladiator*, and dozens of other films as a means of stirring the hero into action, while also cutting his emotional ties to his initial world of innocence.

## FORCES OF VENGEANCE

The death of the innocent also provides a vital element of character motivation for the hero. As psychological motives go, **revenge** may be the strongest. All a film needs is one scene in the 1st act in which a character suffers a terrible injustice, and the audience will identify and stay with its tortured, vengeance driven hero for the rest of the film. The audience will wait for hours for the final act of vengeance, because revenge is a dish best served cold. For many heroes, such as Wyatt Earp, revenge is a driving force, but not the only motivation. Earp accepts the post as marshal of

Tombstone to avenge the death of his brother. But once he becomes marshal, he starts to care about bringing order to the lawless town. For other heroes, vengeance remains the primary motive. In *Death Wish* (1974), the hero's (Charles Bronson) wife is murdered and his daughter raped by a band of thugs. His psychological need for vengeance is so desperate that it drives him on a rampage of murderous vigilantism that persists not only throughout the 2nd and 3rd act, but through four more sequels, as well.

### THE DAEMONIC

A desire for vengeance gives the hero an initial mission and purpose. Though this purpose is dark and selfish, it is an extremely vital motivation, especially in the early stages of the hero's story. The problem arises when the vengeance motive becomes the hero's singular obsession. May referred to any unhealthy obsession as a **possession by the "daemonic"** – the "daemon" being an inner demon that devours the soul of the one it

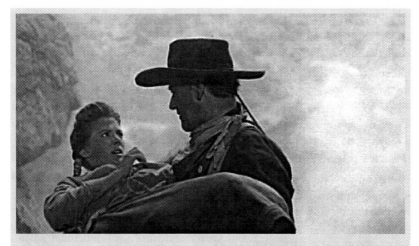

*Daemonic Possession: Ethan (John Wayne) and his niece (Natalie Wood) in* The Searchers *(1956).*

possesses. In *The Searchers* (1956), Ethan (John Wayne) is motivated at first by a desire to rescue his nieces from the wild Commanches who raided his family's house. Gradually, his motivation to rescue his niece is replaced by a daemonic possession – the need to avenge himself against the Commanches and the dark desire to kill his niece, because after years among the Commanche, she has become one of them.

If the hero's rebellion is instigated by a dark motif such as revenge, rage, destruction, or hatred, he must at one point overcome his daemonic possession and become dedicated to a "prosocial" or non-egoistic cause. Though Luke is initially motivated by a desire to avenge the deaths of his aunt and uncle, he soon dedicates himself to the cause of rescuing the maiden in distress (Princess Leia), and eventually allies himself with the broader cause of defeating the Empire. And though Ethan is motivated by a desire to kill his niece (Natalie Wood), he overcomes his dark possession in a moment of epiphany.

### STAGE THREE: ORDINARY SELF-CONSCIOUSNESS

At the third stage of development (usually the 2nd act of the script), the hero, as Joseph Campbell would say, is in "full career of his adventure." He is no longer burdened by reluctance. The hero is fully active in the field of battle and completely dedicated to the task at hand. Existential conflict is no longer an issue for the hero, because he defines the purpose of his existence as the achievement of the goal he is pursuing. This stage of development typically culminates with a **catharsis**, the release of emotional tension and anxiety that occurs when the external goal is achieved.

Catharsis is even more dramatic when it co-occurs with the death of the villain who killed the innocent soul in the 1st act. At the moment of catharsis, the hero earns his vengeance and achieves the goal that he's been chasing throughout his journey. But while the external conflict is resolved, the internal conflict still needs to be dealt with. In a sense, the internal conflict reemerges as a direct result of the catharsis and resolution of the external conflict. Once the hero has achieved his goal, the question becomes: *"What is my purpose in life now?"* How can the hero define meaning in his life, now that the goal which has defined meaning for him up until this point no longer exists?

### STAGE FOUR: CREATIVE SELF-CONSCIOUSNESS

The common theme of identity loss in films, especially in the ubiquitous **amnesia** plot, represents the hero's search for his true identity. The heroes in *The Bourne Identity* (2002), *Spellbound* (1945), *Memento* (2000), and *Angel Heart* (1987) are all searching for their true identities. Their moments of **epiphany** occur when they realize whom they truly are. In essence, all heroes' internal journeys are exactly the same – they are searching for their true identities. Luke's journey begins with the external goals of avenging his aunt and uncle and saving Princess Leia. But after Luke rescues the princess, he experiences a personal epiphany related to his true identity. Luke realizes that he is destined to become a great Jedi knight like his father. Though his initial goals are completed, Luke rededicates himself to the broader goals of the rebellion – engraining his character with significance and meaning that will last the rest of his life.

## CONFLICT RESOLUTION AS DENOUEMENT

Rededication to new goals and the hero's realization of a true sense of identity are crucial factors in the hero's development. These issues must be addressed as part of the film's **denouement** – the "untying" of all the plot lines at the end of the script. If all of the different plot lines in the script are not resolved, then emotional tension will still exist at the end of the film, and the audience will experience an underlying sense of unease or dissatisfaction. The plot lines involving the hero are the most important. Though the story essentially ends with the resolution, the characters presumably live on after the film is over. Therefore, the function of the resolution is to wrap up the story, while the function of the denouement is to wrap up the problem of **character development**. This is achieved by showing the audience how the character has changed and how his life will be different from that point on.

While the resolution of the plot answers the question, "What happened?" – the denouement answers the question, *"What happens next?"* Unless your hero dies in the end (in classic mythological fashion), the denouement in your script should address the hero's new sense of identity and his new commitment or rededication to heroic, meaningful causes.

Often times, the inertia toward resolution is so great by the end of the film that complete denouements can be accomplished in a cursory fashion. The denouement is frequently just a final scene, a character, or voice over that relates information, something to the effect of: *"so the bad guy died, the town was saved, and the hero and maiden lived happily ever after..."* The fact that audiences are willing to accept almost any ending to a film is not an excuse for laziness. As much thought and care should be put into your denouement as was put into your 1st act.

## CHAPTER FIFTEEN SUMMARY POINTS

+∾+

- According to Rollo May, the only cure to *"existential anxiety"* is an awakening to one's own will, desire, and determination… which he called *"self-consciousness."*
- The first stage of self-consciousness is *"Innocence."* In film, this stage is represented by the protagonist who is uninterested or uninvolved in any meaningful cause.
- At this stage, the protagonist is an *"emergent hero."* He is psychologically ready to experience life on a more meaningful level, he just needs a push in the right direction.
- The second stage of self-consciousness is *"Rebellion,"* in which the protagonist realizes his own existential conflict and is motivated to do something about it.
- The stage of rebellion is typically triggered by an *external goal* or problem.
- Often times, the *death of an innocent*, such as a loved one, is the trigger that sets the hero off.
- Heroes are often driven by *vengeance motives*. This destructive motivation is a dark obsession, similar to what May called *"Daemonic possession."* Typically, the hero must exorcise himself of his daemonic possession before resolving his story.
- The third stage of self-consciousness is *"Ordinary Self-Consciousness"* – the hero is dedicated to his cause and actively pursuing it.
- The third stage often will culminate with a *"catharsis,"* an emotional release of anxiety and neurotic energy that occurs when the cause is achieved, the villain is destroyed, or the hero in some way accomplishes his goal.
- The fourth stage of self-consciousness is a moment of clarity, or *"epiphany"* that May called *"Creative Self-Consciousness."* The hero understands himself and his identity, not just in reference to the cause he dedicated himself to, but as a function of some deeper understanding of his own character.
- Ideally, the resolution of the plot leads to a *"denouement,"* in which all of the tension within the story and the hero's character is resolved. While the resolution of the plot answers the question, "What happened?" – the denouement answers the question, "What happens next?"

## CHAPTER FIFTEEN EXERCISES

1. Identify 10 film heroes who are "forces of vengeance" — driven by a daemonic possession to kill or destroy.
2. How do these vengeful heroes exorcise their daemons?
3. Analyze each of your examples and decide whether the moment when the daemon is purged is the same moment as the hero's emotional catharsis.
4. Using the four-stage model of self-consciousness delineated in this chapter, analyze the character development of five of your favorite film heroes.
5. Using the four-stage model of self-consciousness delineated in this chapter, analyze the character development of the heroes in the following films: *Braveheart*, *Mad Max*, *The Matrix*, *Lord of the Rings: The Fellowship of the Ring*, and *Legend*.
6. Identity five film heroes whose primary conflict is the issue of identity loss.
7. How does each of these characters achieve epiphany?
8. Analyze the film *Memento* from an existential point of view. Pay special attention to the intricate interplay between the hero's sense of identity loss, his moments of epiphany, and his daemonic possession.

## ADDRESSING EXISTENTIAL CONFLICT IN YOUR SCRIPT

1. The murder or death of innocent loved ones in the 1st act is an archetypal theme for the hero. It provides the vital motivation of vengeance, and it also cuts the hero's emotional ties with his home. In what way does your hero experience either a literal death of innocence, or a figurative death of innocence in the 1st act of your script?

2. Heroes in the 2nd Act are often "possessed by the daemonic" – driven by dark obsessions of vengeance, hatred, rage, or destruction. As part of the hero's development, he must overcome his own daemonic possession. Does your hero overcome his internal daemons, like Luke in *Return of the Jedi*? Or does he remain daemonically possessed, like Harry Callahan in the *Dirty Harry* movies?

3. A common problem at the end of a film is an abrupt ending lacking complete resolution and denouement. The audience needs to know not only how the story ends, but also what will happen after the movie is over. Now that your hero has completed his journey, how will his life be different? Is he dedicated to a new cause? Does he rededicate himself to the same cause, but at a higher level? In what way is it clear that the hero has changed on his journey, and has become a better person?

### EXISTENTIAL CONFLICT AT A GLANCE

| STAGES | PLOT DEVICES | EXAMPLES FROM *STAR WARS* |
|---|---|---|
| Innocence | The Emergent Hero | Luke's longing to leave his home planet |
| Rebellion | Death of the Innocents | The Murder of Luke's aunt & uncle |
| | Daemonic Possession | Luke's drive toward vengeance |
| Ordinary Self-consciousness | The Selfless External Goal | Rescuing Princess Leia & Defeating Vader |
| | Catharsis | Destroying the Death Star |
| Creative Self-consciousness | Epiphany | Luke's realization of his identity as a Jedi |
| | Denouement | Luke's rededication to the cause of rebellion |

*Chapter Sixteen*

# ARCHETYPES FOR THE AGE OF NARCISSISM

In his later writings, May refined his theories and focused on the problem of **"narcissism"** as the endemic existential illness of modern times. He declared the latter half of the 20th Century the **"Age of Narcissism,"** an age of self-centeredness that stems from the **American myth** of intense individualism, independence, and isolationism. The ideal American hero needs no one, lives in solitude and has no values other than his own. May argues that these narcissistic character traits result in personal separation, distantiation, loneliness, violence, greed, and depression – symptoms of **existential despair** that are typically self-treated through drug use and alcoholism. The archetypes of the age of narcissism are the product of America's idealization of independence and individualism, qualities that are engrained in the American hero depicted in Hollywood films – the primary medium for contemporary American mythology.

## THE AMERICAN HERO

The American archetypal hero is best known within the context of the classical American mythological setting – the Wild West – but he also can be seen in many other settings. In times of war, the American Hero dons an army uniform. When Westerns became less popular, the American Hero traded in his horse for a squad car, and his 10-gallon hat for a policeman's cap. George Lucas even transplanted the traditional American Hero into an outer space setting. But whether he is rustling cattle or blasting through intergalactic wormholes, American heroes all have the same common archetypal traits. They are rugged, stubborn, violent, and single-minded. They don't always follow the rules (in fact, they usually break them), but American heroes have their own **codes of honor** that they hold fast to, no matter the circumstances. And though American heroes may be brash, ignorant, impudent, and reckless – they rarely run from a fight, and can be counted on for bravery, righteous-ness, and determination. In short, the American hero is far from perfect, but he's the kind of guy you'd want in your corner when the going gets rough. Most importantly, he's the kind of character that makes for good movies.

### THE COWBOY HERO

Though John Wayne will forever be the king of the cowboys, the same cowboy hero type was played by almost every actor who worked in film during the Golden Age of Westerns. Henry Fonda, Gregory Peck, Charlton Heston, Tyrone Power, James Stewart, Gary Cooper, Clark Gable, Marlon Brando, Rock Hudson, Alan Ladd, Kirk Douglas, Burt Lancaster, Montgomery Clift, Paul Newman, and William Holden are just some of the stars who frequently mounted horses to play cowboy leads. Cowboy Heroes are usually men who travel alone. They are rugged individualists who need nothing but a horse, a gun, and an open range. Whether they uphold the law as marshals, sheriffs, and rangers, or break the law as outlaws, robbers, and rustlers – they all live independently and proudly, according to their own codes of honor.

### THE LONE CRUSADER

In *High Noon* (1952), Gary Cooper plays a marshal who is about to retire when a violent criminal returns to town. When the chips are down, all the representatives of civilized society prove themselves to be impotent. His friends, the judge, the pastor, his deputy, his wife (Grace Kelly), and even his mentor, the former marshal (Lon Chaney, Jr.), tell Will to get out of town – to run from danger rather than confront it. In the lone crusader's world, only the brave man who holds strong to his code of honor is able to bring justice and order to a world of chaos. The lone crusader hero, epitomized by the Lone Ranger and the cowboy heroes molded after him, appears in urban settings as well....

### THE RENEGADE COP

As the Western genre began to decline in popularity in the 1960s and 70s, the cowboy hero began to appear in the big city. John Wayne hung up his spurs for city cop roles in *Brannigan* (1975) and *Mc.Q.* (1974), and other cowboy heroes followed suit in films such as *Bullitt* (1968) with Steve McQueen and *The Stone Killer* (1973) with Charles Bronson. Clint Eastwood brought his ultra-violent lone drifter persona into the cop genre in the Dirty Harry movies: *Dirty Harry* (1971), *Magnum Force* (1973), *The*

*Enforcer* (1976), *Sudden Impact* (1983), and *The Dead Pool* (1988). He also played the same type of cop hero in movies such as *The Gauntlet* (1977), *Tightrope* (1984), *City Heat* (1984), and *Blood Work* (2002).

While the cop hero is on the side of the law, he is still an outlaw because he invariably breaks all the rules to get his man. The viewer is constantly reminded, typically through the frequent chastisements of his irate police chief, that the hero is a renegade cop who has no respect for proper methods and procedure. The renegade cop archetype was epitomized in the 1980s and 90s by Mel Gibson in the *Lethal Weapon* series, Eddie Murphy in the *Beverly Hills Cop* trilogy and Bruce Willis in the *Die Hard* films. Like the Western hero, the renegade cop is a violent maverick who operates according to his own code of honor. The archetype has even spawned a popular television parody in the ultra-violent character on *The Simpsons*, "McBain." The fact that renegade cop movies are so ripe for parody may signify that this genre has become trite and stale. The current top contenders for lead roles in the renegade cop genre are Vin Diesel and Mark Wahlberg. But unless some new pictures arise that redefine and revitalize the genre in the ways that *Butch Cassidy and the Sundance Kid* (1969), *The Wild Bunch* (1969), and *Unforgiven* revitalized the Western, the renegade cop archetype may simply fade away.

## GANGSTER HEROES

Outlaw heroes can live in the city as well as the Wild West. James Cagney epitomized the gangster hero in Depression Era classics such as *The Doorway to Hell* (1930), *The Public Enemy* (1931), *The Mayor of Hell* (1933), and *Lady Killer* (1933). Though gangster films were made before the 1930s (most notably by Tod Browning), the outlaw became a particularly intriguing figure for Depression Era audiences, who saw no escape from their impoverished situations and dreamed of getting rich quick through larceny. While the Western outlaw typically rides off into sunset at the end of the film, the gangster usually gets his comeuppance. The gangster's fate is a product of his environment — the big city — where a man cannot hide. He is trapped by the city and the people he exploits. This sense of being trapped, surrounded by evil and bound by a dark and foreboding fate is the essence of film noir.

### THE GUMSHOE DETECTIVE

Just as Cagney epitomized the film noir gangster, Humphrey Bogart epitomized the gumshoe detective as Sam Spade in John Huston's *The Maltese Falcon* (1941) and Philip Marlowe in Howard Hawk's *The Big Sleep* (1946). The gumshoe is a poor but respectable detective who fights crime on his own terms. Since he is not a cop, he does not have to conform to police procedures. Like the cowboy, he plays his own game by his own rules. Furthermore, the gumshoe is an outcast among outcasts. Neither a cop nor a criminal, he walks the line between good guy and bad guy, often times getting threatened and beaten by representatives from both sides of the law – all for a few dollars a day plus expenses.

### GOOD COP, BAD COP

Policemen dwell in perilous environments. Surrounded by crime and corruption, they are constantly in danger of becoming infected by the same depravity that they have sworn to fight. In some films, the cop hero's worst enemies are his comrades, or even himself. In *Serpico* (1973) and *Cop Land* (1997), good cops become immersed in a system in which everyone is corrupt. The cop heroes must overcome their temptation to join their colleagues and go "on the take." Their conflict is extremely acute, because in order to honor their duty, they must betray the men who share the same uniform, and break the unwritten "blue code of silence." *Bad Lieutenant* (1992) took this structure one step further. The cop hero starts out completely corrupted. His challenge is to somehow redeem himself and earn forgiveness for all of his bad deeds.

### THE MAD SCIENTIST

A final archetype of the age of narcissism is a product of the 20th Century obsession with scientific discovery. The mad scientist was depicted in *The Cabinet of Dr. Caligari* (1920), *Metropolis* (1927), *The Invisible Man* (1933), and the many versions and remakes of *Dr. Jekyll and Mr. Hyde* and *Frankenstein*. He is an **isolated genius** – so dedicated to his work that he uses people as machines – ignoring their inherent humanity. The mad scientist's narcissistic devotion to his maniacal science projects causes him to isolate himself in his intellectual universe. Often times, the mad scientist is concocting diabolical plots to destroy or conquer the world, symbolizing his need to control everyone and everything. The greatest mistake made by the narcissistic type is that he alienates himself from

*Mad Scientist: John Barrymore in* Dr. Jekyll and Mr. Hyde *(1920).*

others and from his own feelings by focusing so single-mindedly on his egoistic schemes.   His work, in turn, is narcissistic — mega-pompous attempts at creating life in ungodly experiments that are as arrogant as they are sacrilegious.

Mary Wollstonecraft Shelley's full title for her novel, *Frankenstein: The Modern Prometheus*, alludes to the narcissistic quality of her hero's character, as well as his wicked subversion of the natural order through modern science. The mad scientist has a classic superiority complex. He sees himself as superhuman, and others as subhuman. The superiority complex in the mad scientist archetype is elevated to a "god complex." He rationalizes his own superior intelligence as a justification to ignore the customs of society, to use people as objects and to create or manipulate life without taking into account the perilous consequences for himself and others.

### THE ISOLATED GENIUS
Dr. Hartdegen in *The Time Machine* (2002) is a scientist who becomes an isolated genius when his fiancé, Emma (Sienna Guillory), dies.  His mad experiment in time travel is a desperate attempt to get Emma back.  Dr. Hartdegen's quest is symbolic of the quest of every isolated genius.  This archetype's challenge is to become **un-isolated** — to reintegrate love into

his life and reconnect himself with the rest of the world. In *Frankenstein* (1931), Dr. Frankenstein (Colin Clive) only realizes the error of his ways after his monster nearly kills both him and his fiancé. Dr. Jessup (William Hurt) in *Altered States* (1980), is only able to tell his wife that he loves her after his demented experiment nearly alters both of them into evolutionarily regressed primates. And Dr. Nash (Russell Crowe) in *A Beautiful Mind* (2001) is constantly hamstringing his marriage because of his egotistical obsession with his mathematical theories. In all of these films, self-awareness and epiphany only come about when the mad scientist's cold, objective work turns against him, and he must choose between love and science.

### EXISTENTIAL REVERSAL

The mad scientist archetype represents the particularly American proclivity toward "workaholism" and unhealthy obsessions with external goals. He embodies the narcissistic archetype because he is possessed by the daemonic – his own egomaniacal need to play god and prove to the world how brilliant and powerful he is. The moral taught by this type of hero is that an integrated personality requires a balance of love and work ("lieben und arbeiten"). The isolated genius must realize that his work, though important, is not the center of his existence. Character development for the isolated genius is accomplished through an existential reversal. Rather than sacrificing his personal relationships for his work, he must sacrifice his work for the people he loves. Most often, this epiphany and apotheosis come about only after the mad scientist's creation runs amok and comes to the brink of destroying not only himself, but his true love, as well. In the climax of the film, the mad scientist typically must destroy his cherished (albeit demented) creation, in order to save the life of the woman he loves.

### FRANKENSTEIN MONSTERS

The relationship between the mad scientist and his creation is symbolic of the relationship between father and son. Moreover, it is symbolic of the relationship between God, the ultimate creator archetype, and God's creation – the human race. In this sense, the mad scientist movie represents the supreme issue of the Age of Narcissism: Man's negation of the existence of God in favor of science and reason. In the early half of the 20th Century, the mad scientist's creation, **the monster**, represented the ordinary man's basic fear of technology and the unnerving acknowledgement that the modern age is gradually replacing God with science.

Consequently, the mad scientist's creations are sympathetic creatures. They represent the hapless human race adrift in a godless world.

The zombie in *The Cabinet of Dr. Caligari*, the workers in *Metropolis*, Dr. Moreau's mutated creations in *The Island of Lost Souls* (1933), and the monster in *Frankenstein* are **exploited automatons** contrived by irresponsible creators. They embody the anxiety of the exploited masses in the post-Industrial Age, their resentment of the ruling class, their mistrust of science and modern technology, and their repressed rage – which will ultimately rise up in an orgy of violence, destroying both their creators and themselves. The only way in which the mad scientists can avoid this calamitous fate is to realize their narcissistic error, abandon their unholy projects, and devote themselves to human relationships rather than scientific obsessions.

## THE CREATOR ARCHETYPE

Existential questions abound in films – especially in the science-fiction and horror genres – in which humans act like gods by creating Man. In his essay, "Answer to Job," Carl Jung addresses the interrelationship between God and Man, explaining that: *"The encounter with the creature changes the creator."* Whether or not this was true for Job and God, the concept of character change through encounter is an archetypal theme in myth and film, especially in the science-fiction genre. The mad scientist plays God, acts like God, believes himself to be a god, and even becomes a god when he creates a man in his own image. However, the creature that he creates is a projection of the shadow within his Self – a walking testament to his own narcissism and social isolation. When the mad scientist encounters his shadow, when creator encounters creature, epiphany is achieved, and the mad scientist finally sees the error of his own ways. In destroying the creature, the mad scientist purges himself of his own narcissism and hubris, and the isolated genius becomes reintegrated into the whole of society. He becomes human again.

## THE WILLING LAMB

Development for the narcissistic hero must resolve in a reversal of character, in which he sacrifices himself for others. By placing the collective in front of the individual, the hero renounces his individualism and independence and dedicates himself completely to the needs of the whole. So, while Shane rides off as a loner in the end, he demonstrates his dedication to the whole by sacrificing his dreams of a new life to help the homesteaders. Mythological heroes like Wallace in *Braveheart* and Maximus in *Gladiator* are willing lambs in the last stages of their journeys, sacrificing their own lives for the freedom of their people.

The literal sacrifice theme is often played out by the hero's mentor. In *Star Wars*, Obi Won puts down his light saber and dies willingly at the hand of Darth Vader, becoming an even stronger inspiration for Luke. The mentor's ultimate sacrifice inspires the hero to renounce his own needs and dedicate himself completely to others. The hero does not have to die in order to display the ultimate heroic quality of sacrifice – he only has to be inspired by the sacrifice of another – and then put himself in harm's way to defend the holy cause. In this way, every hero's journey is a recasting of the quintessential hero stories, such as the stories of Moses, Jesus, and Arthur... heroes and mentors who sacrificed themselves in order to inspire their people.

## CHAPTER SIXTEEN SUMMARY POINTS

- Rollo May referred to 20th Century America as the "*Age of Narcissism.*" He was referring in large part to the archetype of the narcissistic American hero, who embodies the qualities of fierce independence, rugged individualism, and unabashed isolationism.
- The *American hero* archetype appears most predominantly in the landscape of American mythology – the movie screen – especially in Westerns.
- The *cowboy hero* is a lone crusader who upholds his personal code of honor, typically using extreme violence.
- The *renegade cop* archetype in films represents the traditional American hero, transplanted into an urban setting.
- *Gangster heroes* and *gumshoe detectives* in film noir movies are also traditional American antiheroes in urban settings.
- The *mad scientist* archetype is an *isolated genius* who must reintegrate into society in order to redeem himself.
- The mad scientist is a particularly resonant archetype for the age of narcissism, because he arrogantly *plays God* to further his unholy experiments, he isolates  himself from loved ones in a haze of *self-centered workaholism*, and his *megalomaniacal schemes* endanger himself and the innocent people around him.
- The mad scientist's hapless *creature* is a poignant symbol for modern man. The creature is an exploited automaton manipulated by an irresponsible master.
- The creature's dilemma symbolizes the *alienation* of the exploited masses in a post-Industrial age, and the *disillusionment* of an increasingly faithless society in a modern age of science.
- In the resolution of the mad scientist's story, the *creator encounters and integrates his creature*, symbolically uniting the masses with the master, and the mortals with the immortal.

## CHAPTER SIXTEEN EXERCISES

+ɔ+

1. Using your knowledge of film, identify five movie characters who embody the cowboy hero type.
2. Identify five movie characters who embody the renegade cop type.
3. Identify four movie characters who embody the gangster hero type.
4. Identify three movie characters who embody the gumshoe detective type.
5. Identify five movie characters who embody the mad scientist type.
6. How do the stories of your mad scientist characters' resolve? Do they in some way encounter and integrate their mad creations?

## ADDRESSING MODERN ARCHETYPES IN YOUR SCRIPT

+ɔ+

1. Would you define the hero in your script as an American hero? Why, or why not?
2. Which elements of narcissism does your hero portray? Do these narcissistic character elements represent strengths or weakness in your hero's character? If they are weaknesses, does you hero over-come his narcissism at one point in your script?
3. Rebellion against a narcissistic character is also an archetypal theme in movies. For example, Ethan (John Wayne) in *The Searchers* is an archetypal narcissist – a lone crusader cowboy hero. Martin (Jeffrey Hunter) is his young squire, who is always bristling under Ethan's narcissistic mastery. Is there a character in your script who stands up to a narcissistic hero, villain, mentor, love interest, or supporting character? If not, think of how you can add an element of narcissism into one of the aforementioned characters in your script. Then add an element of rebellion in a contrasting character to create conflict.

| MODERN ARCHETYPES AT A GLANCE | | |
|---|---|---|
| ARCHETYPES | PLOT DEVICES & CHARACTERS | EXAMPLES |
| American Hero | The independent individualist | Scarlet O'Hara in *Gone With the Wind* |
| Cowboy Hero | The wandering knight with a personal code of honor | The title character in *Shane* Ethan in *The Searchers* |
| Lone Crusader | The violent man who stands up alone against evil & corruption | Marshal Kane in *High Noon* Terry Malloy in *On the Waterfront* |
| Renegade Cop | Breaking the police rules in order to be a good policeman | Sgt. Riggs in *Lethal Weapon* Inspector Callahan in *Dirty Harry* |
| Gangster | The big city outlaw anti-hero | Tony in *Scarface* |
| Gumshoe Detective | Two parts renegade cop, one part gangster hero | Humphrey Bogart in *The Maltese Falcon* and *The Big Sleep* |
| Conflicted Cop | The good cop who doesn't go "on the take," and doesn't want to inform on the bad cops | The title character in *Serpico* Sheriff Heflin in *Cop Land* Daniel Ciello in *Prince of the City* |
| Mad Scientist/ Creator | Isolated Genius who plays god and creates an unholy creature | The title character in *Frankenstein* Title character *Dr. Jekyll & Mr. Hyde* |
| Monsters/ Creations | Exploited automatons created by an irresponsible creator | The workers in *Metropolis* The mutants in *Island of Lost Souls* |

# CONCLUSION

*"Whoever speaks in primordial images speaks with a thousand voices;*
*he enthralls and overpowers, while at the same time he lifts the idea*
*he is seeking to express out of the occasional and the transitory*
*into the realm of the ever-enduring...*
*That is the secret of great art and its effect upon us.*
*The creative process... consists in the unconscious activation of an*
*archetypal image,*
*and in elaborating and shaping this image into the finished work.*
*By giving it shape, the artist translates it into the language of the pres-*
*ent,*
*and so makes it possible for us to find our way back to the deepest springs*
*of life."*

— Carl Gustav Jung
"On the Relation of Analytical Psychology to Poetry," (1922)

As with any creative endeavor, screenwriting is a largely unconscious process. Where do our ideas for stories and characters come from? They come from within... from the dark recesses of unconscious memory, emotion, and experience that we may be only partially aware of on a conscious level. Some writers and artists believe that a rational understanding of the unconscious functions behind image making and storytelling could be detrimental to the creative process. This author cannot disagree more strongly!

Personally, I have found that a thorough knowledge and appreciation of the psychological principles behind the creative act have helped me tremendously and offered me guidance, structure, ideas, and support for every sentence I've ever written. The psychological theories explained in this book are invaluable wellsprings for both my work, and my life, and I can only hope that the ideas I've laid out in the preceding chapters can offer the same kind of inspiration to you. Each theory in this book provides a somewhat different approach to creating conflict, plot structure, and character development in your script. This was my intention. The old saying, *"there's more than one way to skin a cat,"* is especially relevant to screenwriting — a field that's plagued with formulaic plots, hackneyed character types, trite dialogue, and tired, overused scenarios. I structured this book to offer many different psychological perspectives on screenwriting, in order to offer you a variety of approaches to your work. The wider your palette as a writer, the more freedom you will have in your creativity.

In a sense, structure and creativity are both complementary and antagonistic elements in the screenwriting process. While you need structure to organize your ideas about character and plot into a cohesive story, too much structure can stifle your creativity, closing the doors to original or unique characters and plots. That's why you, as a writer, should always be on the look out for new ways to approach your art. If you discover and apply a different perspective or structure to your writing, then (in Joseph Campbell's words), *"doors will open where there were no doors before."* This book, I hope, will offer not just one, but many doors of creativity to working screenwriters.

It is important to note that none of the theories in this book is a rigid template for conflict, plot structure, or character development within a screenplay. This is because such a template — a "cookie-cutter" for movie scripts — simply does not exist. Yes, there are formulas for structure, as well as established character types and plot lines, but simply cranking out formulas and types will get you nowhere fast. Screenwriting is a creative process, and in order to be even minimally successful in the field, you must offer producers new, inventive, original, and unique stories and characters. So, while this book provides psychological analyses of most of the basic formulas for structure, plot lines, and character types found in the major movie genres, the analyses are intended to increase your ability to understand these elements as a springboard for creating original and unique stories and characters. If you're not interested in the creative process of screenwriting, a deeper understanding of its psychological elements will not help you.

As a final thought, I'd like to offer an answer to a question that's been asked of me many times: "*Which psychological approach should I take for the specific character and story that I'm writing now?*" As a developmental psychologist, I learned early on in my work that the basic answer to any question about individual psychology or human development is the same basic answer to the question asked above. Unfortunately, it's not a very satisfying answer. The answer is: "*It depends.*" The best approach to writing your character and story depends on the individual character and story that you're writing. Every character is an individual, just as every human being is an individual. And every story is unique, just as every human being's life story is unique. I can't tell you which approach is best, because there are billions and billions of characters and stories, and only you know the true nature of the beast.

To recall an old architectural adage: "*form follows function.*" Your approach to the character and plot that you're writing *depends entirely* on the function they have in your particular story. If you impose a theory or form onto your characters and plot without carefully fitting it to their function in your story, then the script will simply not be as good as it could be. The purpose of this book is to supply you with a variety of psychologically resonant and compelling forms, and the understanding to apply these forms in order to create a story that functions in the way you want it to function. In the end, the story is inside of you. The theories of the master psychologists in this book are merely tools to help you reveal the story that you, yourself, have hidden in your mind.

# ABOUT THE AUTHOR

William Indick earned his bachelors degree in psychology (1993) and masters degree in music therapy (1996) from New York University. After working as a special education teacher and as a creative arts therapist, he earned his Ph.D. in developmental psychology (2001) from Cornell University. Dr. Indick is an active screenwriter, author, screenwriting consultant, and an Assistant Professor of Psychology at Dowling College in Oakdale, New York, where his courses include: "Psychology in Film," "The Western," "Identity Issues in Film," and "Construction of Personal Identity." He is also the author of the upcoming, *Analyzing Film: Revealing the Psychological Symbolism in Movies*. You may contact Dr. Indick through his Web site at: *http://dowling.edu/faculty/Indick/*.

# ILLUSTRATIONS

The author acknowledges the copyright owners of the following motion pictures from which single frames have been used in this book for purposes of commentary, criticism, and scholarship under the Fair Use Doctrine. No endorsement or sponsorship of this book by the copyright owners is claimed or implied.

CHAPTER ONE

*Harold & Maude*, © 1971 Paramount Studios

CHAPTER TWO

*Star Wars*, © 1977 Twentieth Century Fox

CHAPTER THREE

*Citizen Kane*, © 1941 Warner Home Video

*Psycho*, © 1960 Universal Studios

CHAPTER FOUR

*The Searchers*, © 1956 Warner Brothers Studios

CHAPTER SEVEN

*Ikiru*, © 1952 The Criterion Collection

CHAPTER EIGHT

*Blazing Saddles*, © 1974 Warner Brothers Studios

CHAPTER THIRTEEN

*East of Eden*, © 1955 Warner Home Video

CHAPTER FIFTEEN

*The Searchers*, © 1956 Warner Brothers Studios

CHAPTER SIXTEEN

*Dr. Jekyll & Mr. Hyde*, © 1920 Gotham Distribution

# FILMOGRAPHY

**101 Dalmatians** (1961). *Directed by* Clyde Geronimi, Hamilton Luske (as Hamilton S. Luske), Wolfgang Reitherman. *Writing Credits*: Dodie Smith (novel *The One Hundred and One Dalmatians*), Bill Peet (story). *Starring*: Rod Taylor (voice), Betty Lou Gerson (voice), Cate Bauer (voice).

**101 Dalmatians** (1996). *Directed by* Stephen Herek. *Writing Credits*: Dodie Smith (novel), John Hughes (screenplay). *Starring*: Glenn Close, Jeff Daniels, Joely Richardson.

**About Schmidt** (2002). *Directed by* Alexander Payne. *Writing Credits*: Louis Begley (novel), Alexander Payne (screenplay) & Jim Taylor (screenplay). *Starring*: Jack Nicholson, Hope Davis, Dermot Mulroney, Kathy Bates.

**African Queen, The** (1951). Directed by John Huston. *Writing Credits*: C. S. Forester (novel) & James Agee (adaptation). Starring: Humphrey Bogart, Katharine Hepburn, Robert Morley. *Academy Awards*: Humphrey Bogart (Best Actor in a Leading Role).

**Age of Innocence, The** (1993). *Directed by* Martin Scorsese. *Writing Credits*: Edith Wharton (novel), Jay Cocks (screenplay) & Martin Scorsese (screenplay). *Starring*: Daniel Day-Lewis, Michelle Pfeiffer, Winona Ryder, Alexis Smith, Geraldine Chaplin.

**Alice in Wonderland** (1951). *Directed by* Clyde Geronimi & Wilfred Jackson. *Writing Credits*: Lewis Carroll (novels) & Winston Hibler. *Starring*: Kathryn Beaumont (voice), Ed Wynn (voice), Richard Haydn (voice).

**Alice** (1990). *Directed by* Woody Allen. *Writing Credits*: Woody Allen (written by). *Starring*: Joe Mantegna, Mia Farrow, William Hurt.

**All the King's Men** (1949). *Directed by* Robert Rossen. *Writing Credits*: Robert Rossen & Robert Penn Warren (novel). *Starring*: Broderick Crawford, John Ireland, Joanne Dru, John Derek. *Academy Awards*: Broderick Crawford (Best Actor in a Leading Role), Mercedes McCambridge (Best Actress in a Supporting Role).

**Altered States** (1980). *Directed by* Ken Russell. *Writing Credits*: Paddy Chayefsky (novel) & Paddy Chayefsky. *Starring*: William Hurt, Blair Brown, Bob Balaban.

**American Beauty** (1999). *Directed by* Sam Mendes. *Writing Credits*: Alan Ball (written by). *Starring*: Kevin Spacey, Annette Bening, Thora Birch, Wes Bentley, Mena Suvari, Peter Gallagher, Allison Janney, Chris Cooper, Scott Bakula. *Academy Awards*: Kevin Spacey (Best Actor in a Leading Role), Conrad L. Hall (Best Cinematography), Sam Mendes (Best Director), Bruce Cohen & Dan Jinks (Best Picture), Alan Ball (Best Writing, Screenplay Written Directly for the Screen)

**American Pie** (1999). *Directed by* Paul Weitz & Chris Weitz. *Writing Credits:* Adam Herz (written by). *Starring*: Jason Biggs & Chris Klein.

**Angel Heart** (1987). *Directed by* Alan Parker. *Writing Credits*: William Hjortsberg (novel) & Alan Parker. *Starring*: Mickey Rourke, Robert De Niro, Lisa Bonet, Charlotte Rampling.

**Animal House** (1978). *Directed by* John Landis. *Writing Credits*: Harold Ramis (written by), Douglas Kenney (written by) & Chris Miller (written by). *Starring*: John Belushi, Tim Matheson, Tom Hulce, Stephen Furst, Mark Metcalf.

**Annie Hall** (1977). *Directed by* Woody Allen. *Writing Credits*: Woody Allen and Marshall Brickman. *Starring*: Woody Allen, Diane Keaton, Tony Roberts, Carol Kane, Paul Simon, Shelley Duvall. *Academy Awards*: Diane Keaton (Best Actress in a Leading Role), Woody Allen (Best Director), Charles H. Joffe (Best Picture), Woody Allen & Marshall Brickman (Best Writing, Screenplay Written Directly for the Screen).

**Babe** (1995). *Directed by* Chris Noonan. *Writing Credits*: Dick King–Smith (novel), George Miller (screenplay) & Chris Noonan (screenplay). *Starring*: Christine Cavanaugh (voice), James Cromwell & Miriam Margolyes (voice). **Baby Boom** (1987). *Directed by* Charles Shyer. *Writing Credits*: Nancy Meyers (written by) & Charles Shyer (written by). *Starring*: Diane Keaton, Sam Shepard, Harold Ramis.

**Back to the Future** (1985). *Directed by* Robert Zemeckis. *Writing Credits*: Robert Zemeckis (written by) & Bob Gale (written by). *Starring*: Michael J. Fox, Christopher Lloyd, Lea Thompson, Crispin Glover, Thomas F. Wilson, Claudia Wells, Marc McClure.

**Bad and the Beautiful, The** (1952). *Directed by* Vincente Minnelli. *Writing Credits*: George Bradshaw (story) & Charles Schnee. *Starring*: Lana Turner, Kirk Douglas, Walter Pidgeon, Dick Powell. *Academy Awards*: Gloria Grahame (Best Actress in a Supporting Role). Charles Schnee (Best Writing, Screenplay).

**Bad Lieutenant** (1992). *Directed by* Abel Ferrara. *Writing Credits*: Abel Ferrara & Zoë Lund. *Starring*: Harvey Keitel, Brian McElroy, Frankie Acciarito.

**Bad News Bears, The** (1979). *Directed by* Norman Abbott, William Asher, Bruce Bilson, Jeffrey Ganz, Lowell Ganz, Jeffrey Hayden, Alan Myerson, Gene Nelson. *Writing Credits*: Bill Lancaster (characters). *Starring*: Jack Warden, Catherine Hicks, Phillip R. Allen.

**Bambi** (1942). *Directed by* David Hand. *Writing Credits*: Felix Salten (novel), Larry Morey (story adaptation), Perce Pearce (story direction). *Starring*: Hardie Albright (voice), Stan Alexander (voice).

**Basic Instinct** (1992). *Directed by* Paul Verhoeven. *Writing Credits*: Joe Eszterhas. *Starring*: Michael Douglas & Sharon Stone.

**Beautiful Mind, A** (2001). *Directed by* Ron Howard. *Writing credits*: Sylvia Nasar (book) & Akiva Goldsman (written by). *Starring*: Russell Crowe, Ed Harris, Jennifer Connelly, Christopher Plummer. *Academy Awards*: Jennifer Connelly (Best Actress in a Supporting Role), Ron Howard (Best Director), Brian Grazer & Ron Howard (Best Picture), Akiva Goldsman (Best Writing, Screenplay Based on Material Previously Produced or Published).

**Beauty and the Beast** (1991). *Directed by* Gary Trousdale & Kirk Wise. *Writing Credits*: Roger Allers (story) & Kelly Asbury (story). *Starring*: Paige O'Hara (voice), Robby Benson (voice), Richard White (voice).

**Big** (1988). *Directed by* Penny Marshall. *Writing Credits*: Gary Ross (written by) & Anne Spielberg (written by). *Starring*: Tom Hanks, Elizabeth Perkins, Robert Loggia.

**Big Chill, The** (1983). *Directed by* Lawrence Kasdan. *Writing Credits*: Barbara Benedek & Lawrence Kasdan. *Starring*: Tom Berenger, Glenn Close, Jeff Goldblum, William Hurt, Kevin Kline, Mary Kay Place, Meg Tilly.

**Big Lebowski, The** (1998). *Directed by* Joel Coen. *Writing Credits*: Ethan Coen (written by) & Joel Coen (written by). *Starring*: Jeff Bridges, John Goodman, Julianne Moore, Steve Buscemi.

**Big Sleep, The** (1946). *Directed by* Howard Hawks. *Writing Credits*: Raymond Chandler (novel), William Faulkner (screenplay), Leigh Brackett (screenplay) & Jules Furthman (screenplay). *Starring*: Humphrey Bogart, Lauren Bacall, John Ridgely.

**Blame it on Rio** (1984). *Directed by* Stanley Donen. *Writing Credits*: Charlie Peters and Larry Gelbart. *Starring*: Michael Caine, Joseph Bologna, Valerie Harper, Michelle Johnson, Demi Moore, José Lewgoy.

**Blazing Saddles** (1974). *Directed by* Mel Brooks. *Writing Credits*: Andrew Bergman (also story), Mel Brooks, Richard Pryor, Norman Steinberg, Alan Uger. *Starring*: Cleavon Little, Gene Wilder, Slim Pickens.

**Blob, The** (1958). *Directed by* Irvin S. Yeaworth Jr. *Writing Credits*: Kay Linaker (as Kate Phillips), Irving H. Millgate (story), Theodore Simonson. *Starring*: Steve McQueen, Aneta Corsaut, Earl Rowe.

**Blood Work** (2002). *Directed by* Clint Eastwood. *Writing Credits*: Michael Connelly (novel) & Brian Helgeland (screenplay). *Starring*: Clint Eastwood, Jeff Daniels, Anjelica Huston.

**Blue Velvet** (1986). *Directed by* David Lynch. *Writing Credits*: David Lynch. *Starring*: Isabella Rossellini, Kyle MacLachlan, Dennis Hopper, Laura Dern.

**Boogie Nights** (1997). *Directed by* Paul Thomas Anderson. *Writing Credits*: Paul Thomas Anderson (written by). *Starring*: Luis Guzmán, Burt Reynolds, Julianne Moore, Rico Bueno, John C. Reilly, Nicole Ari Parker, Don Cheadle, Heather Graham, Mark Wahlberg, William H. Macy.

**Bourne Identity, The** (2002). *Directed by* Doug Liman. *Writing Credits*: Robert Ludlum (novel), Tony Gilroy (screenplay) and W. Blake Herron (screenplay) (as William Blake Herron). *Starring*: Matt Damon, Franka Potente, Chris Cooper, Clive Owen, Brian Cox, Adewale Akinnuoye-Agbaje, Gabriel Mann.

**Brannigan** (1975). *Directed by* Douglas Hickox. *Writing Credits*: Michael Butler, William P. McGivern, William W. Norton, Christopher Trumbo. *Starring*: John Wayne, Richard Attenborough, Judy Geeson.

**Brave Little Toaster, The** (1987). Directed by Jerry Rees. *Writing Credits*: Thomas M. Disch (book) & Thomas M. Disch (story). *Starring*: Jon Lovitz (voice), Timothy Stack (voice), Timothy E. Day (voice).

**Braveheart** (1995). *Directed by* Mel Gibson, *Writing Credits*: Randall Wallace (written by). *Starring*: Mel Gibson, James Robinson, Sean Lawlor. *Academy Awards*: Mel Gibson (Best Director).

**Breakfast Club, The** (1985). *Directed by* John Hughes. *Writing Credits*: John Hughes. *Starring*: Emilio Estevez, Paul Gleason, Anthony Michael Hall, John Kapelos, Judd Nelson, Molly Ringwald, Ally Sheedy.

**Brewster's Millions** (1985). *Directed by* Walter Hill. *Writing Credits:* George Barr McCutcheon (novel), Herschel Weingrod & Timothy Harris. *Starring:* Richard Pryor, John Candy, Lonette McKee, Stephen Collins.

**Buffy the Vampire Slayer** (1992). *Directed by* Fran Rubel Kuzui. *Writing Credits:* Joss Whedon (written by). *Starring:* Kristy Swanson, Donald Sutherland, Paul Reubens.

**Bullitt** (1968). *Directed by* Peter Yates. *Writing Credits:* Robert L. Pike (novel Mute Witness), Alan Trustman (screenplay) (as Alan R. Trustman) and Harry Kleiner (screenplay). *Starring:* Steve McQueen, Robert Vaughn, Jacqueline Bisset, Don Gordon, Robert Duvall. *Academy Awards:* Frank P. Keller (Best Film Editing).

**Butch Cassidy and the Sundance Kid** (1969). Directed by George Roy Hill. *Writing Credits:* William Goldman (written by). *Starring:* Paul Newman, Robert Redford, Katharine Ross. *Academy Awards:* William Goldman (Best Writing, Story and Screenplay Based on Material Not Previously Published or Produced).

**Cabinet of Dr. Caligari, The** (1920). *Directed by* Robert Wiene. *Writing Credits:* Hans Janowitz, Carl Mayer. *Starring:* Werner Krauss, Conrad Veidt, Friedrich Feher.

**Cape Fear** (1962). *Directed by* J. Lee Thompson. *Writing Credits:* John D. MacDonald (novel) & James R. Webb. *Starring:* Gregory Peck, Robert Mitchum, Polly Bergen.

**Cape Fear** (1991). *Directed by* Martin Scorsese. *Writing Credits:* John D. MacDonald (novel *The Executioners*), James R. Webb (earlier screenplay), Wesley Strick (screenplay). *Starring:* Robert De Niro, Nick Nolte, Jessica Lange, Juliette Lewis, Joe Don Baker, Robert Mitchum, Gregory Peck.

**Captain Kidd** (1945). *Directed by* Rowland V. Lee. *Writing Credits:* Robert N. Lee (story) & Norman Reilly Raine. *Starring:* Charles Laughton, Randolph Scott, Barbara Britton.

**Casablanca** (1942). *Directed by* Michael Curtiz. *Writing Credits*: Murray Burnett (play) and Joan Alison (play), Julius J. Epstein, Philip G. Epstein, Howard Koch. *Starring*: Humphrey Bogart, Ingrid Bergman, Paul Henreid, Claude Rains. *Academy Awards*: Michael Curtiz (Best Director), Hal B. Wallis (Best Picture), Julius J. Epstein, Philip G. Epstein & Howard Koch (Best Writing, Screenplay).

**Changing Lanes** (2002). *Directed by* Roger Michell, *Writing Credits*: Chap Taylor (story), Chap Taylor (screenplay) and Michael Tolkin (screenplay). *Starring*: Ben Affleck, Samuel L. Jackson, Kim Staunton, Toni Collette, Sydney Pollack.

**Charlie's Angels** (2000). *Directed by* McG. *Writing Credits*: Ivan Goff (TV series) and Ben Roberts (TV series), Ryan Rowe (written by), Ed Solomon (written by) and John August (written by). *Starring*: Cameron Diaz, Drew Barrymore, Lucy Liu, Bill Murray, Sam Rockwell, Kelly Lynch, Tim Curry, Crispin Glover, Luke Wilson, John Forsythe, Matt LeBlanc, Tom Green, L L Cool J, Sean Whalen.

**Chinatown** (1974). *Directed by* Roman Polanski. *Writing Credits*: Robert Towne. *Starring*: Jack Nicholson, Faye Dunaway, John Huston. *Academy Awards*: Best Writing, original Screenplay Robert Towne.

**Christmas Carol, A** (1938). *Directed by* Edwin L. Marin. *Writing Credits*: Charles Dickens (short story) & Hugo Butler (screenplay). *Starring*: Reginald Owen, Gene Lockhart, Kathleen Lockhart.

**Cinderella** (1950). *Directed by* Clyde Geronimi, Wilfred Jackson, Hamilton Luske. *Writing Credits*: Ken Anderson & Homer Brightman. *Starring*: Ilene Woods, Eleanor Audley, Verna Felton.

**Citizen Kane** (1941). *Directed by* Orson Welles. *Writing Credits*: Herman J. Mankiewicz and Orson Welles. *Starring*: Orson Welles, Joseph Cotten, Dorothy Comingore, Agnes Moorehead. *Academy Awards*: Herman J. Mankiewicz & Orson Welles (Best Writing, original Screenplay).

**City Heat** (1984). *Directed by* Richard Benjamin. *Writing Credits*: Blake Edwards (story) (as Sam O. Brown), Blake Edwards (as Sam O. Brown) and Joseph Stinson (as Joseph C. Stinson). *Starring*: Clint Eastwood, Burt Reynolds, Jane Alexander.

**Cocoon** (1985). *Directed by* Ron Howard. *Writing Credits*: Tom Benedek & David Saperstein (novel). Don Ameche, Wilford Brimley, Hume Cronyn, Brian Dennehy. *Academy Awards*: Don Ameche (Best Actor in a Supporting Role).

**Cop Land** (1997). *Directed by* James Mangold. *Writing Credits*: James Mangold (written by). *Starring*: Sylvester Stallone, Harvey Keitel, Ray Liotta, Robert De Niro, Peter Berg, Janeane Garofalo, Robert Patrick, Michael Rapaport, Annabella Sciorra.

**Crimes and Misdemeanors** (1989). *Directed by* Woody Allen. *Writing Credits*: Woody Allen (written by). *Starring*: Bill Bernstein, Martin Landau, Claire Bloom.

**Crush, The** (1993). *Directed by* Alan Shapiro. Writing Credits: Alan Shapiro. *Starring*: Alicia Silverstone, Cary Elwes.

**Dave** (1993). *Directed by* Ivan Reitman. *Writing Credits*: Gary Ross (written by). *Starring*: Kevin Kline, Sigourney Weaver, Frank Langella.

**Dead Poets Society** (1989). *Directed by* Peter Weir. *Writing Credits*: Tom Schulman (written by). *Starring*: Robin Williams, Robert Sean Leonard, Ethan Hawke, Josh Charles. *Academy Awards*: Tom Schulman (Best Writing, Screenplay Written Directly for the Screen).

**Dead Pool, The** (1988). *Directed by* Buddy Van Horn. *Writing Credits*: Harry Julian Fink (characters), Rita M. Fink (characters) (as R.M. Fink), Steve Sharon (story), Durk Pearson (story), Sandy Shakiocus (story) (as Sandy Shaw), Steve Sharon (screenplay). *Starring*: Clint Eastwood, Patricia Clarkson, Liam Neeson.

**Death Wish** (1974). *Directed by* Michael Winner. *Writing Credits*: Brian Garfield (novel) & Wendell Mayes. *Starring*: Charles Bronson, Hope Lange, Vincent Gardenia.

**Devil's Brigade, The** (1968). *Directed by* Andrew V. McLaglen. *Writing Credits*: Robert H. Adleman (novel), William Roberts, George Walton (novel). *Starring*: William Holden, Cliff Robertson, Vince Edwards.

**Dick Tracy** (1990). *Directed by* Warren Beatty. *Writing Credits*: Chester Gould (characters in Dick Tracy comic strip), Jim Cash (written by) & Jack Epps Jr. (written by). *Starring*: Warren Beatty, Charlie Korsmo, Michael Donovan O'Donnell.

**Die Hard** (1988). *Directed by* John McTiernan. *Writing Credits*: Roderick Thorp (novel *Nothing Lasts Forever*), Jeb Stuart (screenplay) and Steven E. de Souza (screenplay). *Starring*: Bruce Willis, Alan Rickman, Bonnie Bedelia. *Academy Awards*: Frank J. Urioste & John F. Link (Best Film Editing).

**Dirty Dozen, The** (1967). *Directed by* Robert Aldrich. *Writing Credits*: E. M. Nathanson (novel), Nunnally Johnson, Lukas Heller. *Starring*: Lee Marvin, Ernest Borgnine, Charles Bronson, Jim Brown.

**Dirty Harry** (1971). *Directed by* Don Siegel. *Writing Credits*: Harry Julian Fink (story) & Rita M. Fink (story). *Starring*: Clint Eastwood, Harry Guardino, Reni Santoni.

**Doorway to Hell, The** (1930). *Directed by* Archie Mayo. *Writing Credits*: Rowland Brown (story) & George Rosener. *Starring*: Lew Ayres, Charles Judels, Dorothy Mathews.

**Dr. Strangelove** (1964). *Directed by* Stanley Kubrick. *Writing Credits*: Peter George (novel) & Stanley Kubrick (screenplay). *Starring*: Peter Sellers, George C. Scott, Sterling Hayden.

**Dracula** (1931). *Directed by* Tod Browning. *Writing Credits*: John L. Balderston (story), Hamilton Deane (story), Bram Stoker (novel). *Starring*: Bela Lugosi, Helen Chandler.

**Drugstore Cowboy** (1989). *Directed by* Gus Van Sant. *Writing Credits*: James Fogle (novel), Gus Van Sant (screenplay) (as Gus Van Sant Jr.) and Daniel Yost (screenplay). *Starring*: Matt Dillon, Kelly Lynch, James LeGros, Heather Graham.

**Duel in the Sun** (1946). *Directed by* King Vidor & Otto Brower. *Writing Credits*: Niven Busch (novel), Oliver H. P. Garrett (adaptation). *Starring*: Jennifer Jones, Joseph Cotten, Gregory Peck, Lionel Barrymore.

**Dumbo** (1941). *Directed by* Ben Sharpsteen. *Writing Credits*: Helen Aberson (book) Otto Englander (story). *Starring*: Herman Bing (voice), Billy Bletcher (voice).

**East of Eden** (1955). *Directed by* Elia Kazan. *Writing Credits*: Paul Osborn. *Starring*: Julie Harris, James Dean, Raymond Massey, Burl Ives, Richard Davalos, Jo Van Fleet. *Academy Awards*: Jo Van Fleet (Best Actress in a Supporting Role).

**El Dorado** (1966). *Directed by* Howard Hawks. *Writing Credits*: Harry Brown (novel) & Leigh Brackett (screenplay). *Starring*: John Wayne, Robert Mitchum, James Caan.

**Elephant Man, The** (1980). *Directed by* David Lynch. *Writing Credits*: Sir Frederick Treves (book *The Elephant Man and Other Reminiscences*), Ashley Montagu (book), Christopher De Vore (screenplay) & Eric Bergren (screenplay). *Starring*: Anthony Hopkins, John Hurt, Anne Bancroft, John Gielgud.

**Enforcer, The** (1976), *Directed by* James Fargo. *Writing Credits*: Harry Julian Fink (characters), Rita M. Fink (characters) (as R. M. Fink), Gail Morgan Hickman (story), S. W. Schurr (story), Stirling Silliphant (screenplay), Dean Riesner (screenplay). *Starring*: Clint Eastwood, Tyne Daly, Harry Guardino.

**Erin Brockovich** (2000). *Directed by* Steven Soderbergh. *Writing Credits*: Susannah Grant (written by). *Starring*: Julia Roberts, David Brisbin, Albert Finney. *Academy Awards*: Julia Roberts (Best Actress in a Leading Role).

**Escape From Alcatraz** (1979). *Directed by* Don Siegel. *Writing Credits*: J. Campbell Bruce (novel), Richard Tuggle. *Starring*: Clint Eastwood, Patrick McGoohan.

**Excalibur** (1981). *Directed by* John Boorman. *Writing Credits*: Thomas Malory (book *Le Morte d'Arthur*), Rospo Pallenberg (adaptation), Rospo Pallenberg (screenplay) and John Boorman (screenplay). *Starring*: Nigel Terry, Helen Mirren, Nicholas Clay.

**Face in the Crowd, A** (1957). *Directed by* Elia Kazan. *Writing Credits*: Budd Schulberg (also story *The Arkansas Traveler*). *Starring*: Andy Griffith, Patricia Neal, Anthony Franciosa, Walter Matthau.

**Falling Down** (1993). *Directed by* Joel Schumacher. *Writing Credits*: Ebbe Roe Smith (written by). *Starring*: Michael Douglas, Robert Duvall, Barbara Hershey.

**Fatal Attraction** (1987). *Directed by* Adrian Lyne. *Writing Credits*: James Dearden (also earlier screenplay) & Nicholas Meyer. *Starring*: Michael Douglas, Glenn Close, Anne Archer.

**Fiddler on the Roof** (1971). *Directed by* Norman Jewison. *Writing Credits*: Sholom Aleichem (book *Tevye's Daughters* and play Tevye der Milkhiker as Sholem Aleichem), Joseph Stein (libretto and screenplay). *Starring*: Topol, Norma Crane, Leonard Frey.

**Finding Forrester** (2000). *Directed by* Gus Van Sant. *Writing Credits*: Mike Rich (written by). *Starring*: Sean Connery, Rob Brown, F. Murray Abraham, Anna Paquin, Busta Rhymes.

**Flowers in the Attic** (1987). *Directed by* Jeffrey Bloom. *Writing Credits*: Virginia C. Andrews (novel) & Jeffrey Bloom. *Starring*: Louise Fletcher, Victoria Tennant, Kristy Swanson.

**Frankenstein** (1931). *Directed by* James Whale. *Writing Credits*: Mary Shelley (novel), Peggy Webling (play). *Starring*: Colin Clive, Mae Clarke, John Boles.

**Freaky Friday** (1976). *Directed by* Gary Nelson. *Writing Credits*: Mary Rodgers (also novel). *Starring*: Barbara Harris, Jodie Foster, John Astin, Patsy Kelly, Dick Van Patten.

**Freaky Friday** (2003). *Directed by* Mark S. Waters. *Writing Credits*: Mary Rodgers (novel), Heather Hach (screenplay) and Leslie Dixon (screenplay). *Starring*: Jamie Lee Curtis, Lindsay Lohan, Mark Harmon, Harold Gould, Chad Michael Murray, Stephen Tobolowsky, Christina Vidal.

**French Connection, The** (1971). *Directed by* William Friedkin. *Writing Credits*: Robin Moore (novel) & Ernest Tidyman (screenplay). *Starring*: Gene Hackman, Fernando Rey, Roy Scheider. *Academy Awards*: Gene Hackman (Best Actor in a Leading Role), William Friedkin (Best Director), Ernest Tidyman (Best Writing, Screenplay Based on Material from Another Medium).

**Friday the 13th** (1980). *Directed by* Sean S. Cunningham. *Writing credits*: Victor Miller. *Starring*: Betsy Palmer & Adrienne King.

**From Here to Eternity** (1953). *Directed by* Fred Zinnemann. *Writing Credits*: James Jones (novel) & Daniel Taradash. *Starring*: Burt Lancaster, Montgomery Clift, Deborah Kerr, Donna Reed, Frank Sinatra. *Academy Awards*: Frank Sinatra (Best Actor in a Supporting Role), Donna Reed (Best Actress in a Supporting Role), Fred Zinnemann (Best Director), William A. Lyon (Best Film Editing), Daniel Taradash (Best Writing, Screenplay).

**G. I. Jane** (1997). *Directed by* Ridley Scott. *Writing Credits*: Danielle Alexandra (story), David Twohy (screenplay) and Danielle Alexandra (screenplay). *Starring*: Demi Moore, Viggo Mortensen, Anne Bancroft.

**Gaslight** (1940). *Directed by* Thorold Dickinson. *Writing Credits*: Patrick Hamilton (play *Angel Street*), A. R. Rawlinson & Bridget Boland. *Starring*: Anton Walbrook, Diana Wynyard, Frank Pettingell.

**Gauntlet, The** (1977). *Directed by* Clint Eastwood. *Writing Credits*: Michael Butler and Dennis Shryack. *Starring*: Clint Eastwood, Sondra Locke, Pat Hingle.

**Gigli** (2003). *Directed by* Martin Brest. *Writing Credits*: Martin Brest (written by). *Starring*: Ben Affleck, Terry Camilleri, David Backus.

**Gladiator** (2000). *Directed by* Ridley Scott. *Writing Credits*: David Franzoni (story), David Franzoni (screenplay), John Logan (screenplay) and William Nicholson (screenplay). *Starring*: Russell Crowe, Joaquin Phoenix & Richard Harris. *Academy Awards*: Best Actor in a Leading Role (Russell Crowe), Best Picture (Douglas Wick, David Franzoni & Branko Lustig).

**Godfather, The** (1972). *Directed by* Francis Ford Coppola. *Writing Credits*: Francis Ford Coppola & Mario Puzo (also novel). *Starring*: Marlon Brando, Al Pacino, James Caan, Richard S. Castellano & Robert Duvall. *Academy Awards*: Marlon Brando (Best Actor in a Leading Role), Albert S. Ruddy (Best Picture), Mario Puzo & Francis Ford Coppola (Best Writing, Screenplay Based on Material from Another Medium).

**Gone with the Wind** (1939). *Directed by* Victor Fleming. *Writing Credits*: Margaret Mitchell (novel) & Sidney Howard. *Starring*: Thomas Mitchell, Barbara O'Neil, Vivien Leigh. *Academy Awards*: Vivien Leigh (Best Actress in a Leading Role), Hattie McDaniel (Best Actress in a Supporting Role), Victor Fleming (Best Director), Hal C. Kern, James E. Newcom (Best Film Editing), Sidney Howard (Best Writing, Screenplay).

**Goodbye, Mr. Chips** (1969). *Directed by* Herbert Ross. *Writing Credits*: James Hilton (novel) & Terence Rattigan (screenplay). *Starring*: George Baker, Peter O'Toole, Petula Clark.

**Goodfellas** (1990). *Directed by* Martin Scorsese. *Writing Credits*: Nicholas Pileggi (book *Wise Guy*), Nicholas Pileggi (screenplay) & Martin Scorsese (screenplay). *Starring*: Robert De Niro, Ray Liotta, Joe Pesci, Lorraine Bracco, Paul Sorvino. *Academy Awards*: Joe Pesci (Best Actor in a Supporting Role).

**Gosford Park** (2001). *Directed by* Robert Altman. *Writing Credits*: Robert Altman (idea), Bob Balaban (idea), Julian Fellowes (written by). *Starring*: Maggie Smith, Michael Gambon, Kristin Scott Thomas, Camilla Rutherford, Charles Dance. *Academy Awards*: Julian Fellowes (Best Writing, Screenplay Written Directly for the Screen).

**Graduate, The** (1967). *Directed by* Mike Nichols. *Writing Credits*: Charles Webb (novel), Calder Willingham (screenplay), Buck Henry (screenplay). *Starring*: Anne Bancroft, Dustin Hoffman, Katharine Ross. *Academy Awards*: Best Director Mike Nichols.

**Great Escape, The** (1963). *Directed by* John Sturges. *Writing Credits*: Paul Brickhill (book), James Clavell (screenplay). *Starring*: Steve McQueen, James Garner, Richard Attenborough, Charles Bronson, Donald Pleasence, James Coburn.

**Greatest Story Ever Told, The** (1965). *Directed by* George Stevens & David Lean. *Writing Credits:* James Lee Barrett & Henry Denker (source writings). *Starring:* Max von Sydow, Michael Anderson Jr., Carroll Baker.

**Gypsy** (1962). *Directed by* Mervyn LeRoy. *Writing Credits:* Arthur Laurents, Gypsy Rose Lee (book *Gypsy, A Memoir*), Leonard Spigelgass. *Starring:* Rosalind Russell, Natalie Wood, Karl Malden.

**Halloween** (1978). *Directed by* John Carpenter. *Writing Credits:* John Carpenter & Debra Hill. *Starring:* Donald Pleasence & Jamie Lee Curtis.

**Hannibal** (2001). *Directed by* Ridley Scott. *Writing Credits:* Thomas Harris (novel *Hannibal*), David Mamet screenplay) and Steven Zaillian (screenplay). *Starring:* Anthony Hopkins, Julianne Moore, Giancarlo Giannini, Gary Oldman, Ray Liotta, Frankie Faison, Francesca Neri.

**Harold & Maude** (1971). *Directed by* Hal Ashby. *Writing Credits:* Colin Higgins. *Starring:* Ruth Gordon, Bud Cort.

**Heist, The** (2001). *Directed by* David Mamet. *Writing Credits:* David Mamet (written by). *Starring:* Gene Hackman, Alan Bilzerian, Richard L. Freidman, Danny DeVito.

**Hercules** (1997). *Directed by* Ron Clements & John Musker. *Writing Credits:* Ron Clements & Barry Johnson (story). *Starring:* Tate Donovan (voice), Joshua Keaton (voice), Roger Bart (voice).

**High Noon** (1952). *Directed by* Fred Zinnemann. *Writing Credits:* John W. Cunningham (story), Carl Foreman (screenplay). *Starring:* Gary Cooper, Thomas Mitchell, Lloyd Bridges, Katy Jurado, Grace Kelly. *Academy Awards:* Gary Cooper (Best Actor in a Leading Role), Elmo Williams, Harry W. Gerstad (Best Film Editing).

**Home Alone** (1990). *Directed by* Chris Columbus. *Writing Credits:* John Hughes (written by). *Starring:* Macaulay Culkin, Joe Pesci, Daniel Stern.

**Hoosiers** (1986). *Directed by* David Anspaugh. *Writing Credits:* Angelo Pizzo (written by). *Starring:* Gene Hackman, Barbara Hershey, Dennis Hopper.

**How Stella Got Her Groove Back** (1998). *Directed by* Kevin Rodney Sullivan. *Writing Credits*: Terry McMillan (novel), Terry McMillan (screenplay) & Ronald Bass (screenplay) (as Ron Bass). *Starring*: Angela Bassett, Taye Diggs, Whoopi Goldberg, Regina King.

**Husbands and Wives** (1992). *Directed by* Woody Allen. *Writing Credits*: Woody Allen (written by). *Starring*: Nick Metropolis, Woody Allen, Mia Farrow, Sydney Pollack, Judy Davis.

**Ikiru** (1952). *Directed by* Akira Kurosawa. *Writing Credits*: Shinobu Hashimoto, Akira Kurosawa, Hideo Oguni. *Starring*: Takashi Shimura, Shinichi Himori, Haruo Tanaka.

**In Dreams** (1999). *Directed by* Neil Jordan. *Writing Credits*: Bari Wood (novel) & Bruce Robinson (screenplay). *Starring*: Annette Bening, Katie Sagona, Aidan Quinn & Robert Downey Jr.

**Invasion of the Body Snatchers** (1956). *Directed by* Don Siegel. *Writing Credits*: Jack Finney (novel) & Daniel Mainwaring. *Starring*: Kevin McCarthy, Dana Wynter, Larry Gates, King Donovan, Carolyn Jones.

**Invisible Man, The** (1933). *Directed by* James Whale. *Writing Credits*: R. C. Sherriff & H. G. Wells (novel). *Starring*: Claude Rains, Gloria Stuart, William Harrigan.

**Island of Lost Souls, The** (1933). *Directed by* Erle C. Kenton. *Writing Credits*: H. G. Wells (novel *The Island of Dr. Moreau*), Waldemar Young & Philip Wylie. *Starring*: Charles Laughton, Richard Arlen, Leila Hyams.

**It Could Happen to You** (1994). *Directed by* Andrew Bergman. *Writing Credits*: Jane Anderson (written by). *Starring*: Nicolas Cage, Bridget Fonda, Rosie Perez, Wendell Pierce, Isaac Hayes.

**It Happened One Night** (1934). *Directed by* Frank Capra. *Writing Credits*: Samuel Hopkins Adams (story) & Robert Riskin. *Starring*: Clark Gable, Claudette Colbert, Walter Connolly. *Academy Awards*: Clark Gable (Best Actor in a Leading Role), Claudette Colbert (Best Actress in a Leading Role), Frank Capra (Best Director), Robert Riskin (Best Writing, Adaptation).

**It's a Wonderful Life** (1946). *Directed by* Frank Capra. *Writing Credits:* Philip Van Doren Stern (story *The Greatest Gift*), Frances Goodrich, Albert Hackett & Frank Capra. *Starring:* James Stewart, Donna Reed, Lionel Barrymore.

**Jaws** (1975). *Directed by* Steven Spielberg. *Writing Credits:* Peter Benchley (also novel) & Carl Gottlieb. *Starring:* Roy Scheider, Robert Shaw, Richard Dreyfuss, Lorraine Gary, Murray Hamilton.

**Jerry Maguire** (1996). *Directed by* Cameron Crowe. *Writing Credits:* Cameron Crowe (written by). *Starring:* Tom Cruise, Cuba Gooding Jr., Renée Zellweger. *Academy Awards:* Cuba Gooding Jr. (Best Actor in a Supporting Role).

**Jesse James** (1939). *Directed by* Henry King & Irving Cummings. *Writing Credits:* Nunnally Johnson (screenplay). *Starring:* Tyrone Power, Henry Fonda, Nancy Kelly, Randolph Scott.

**Jungle Book, The** (1967). *Directed by* Wolfgang Reitherman. *Writing Credits:* Rudyard Kipling (novel) & Larry Clemmons. *Starring:* Phil Harris, Sebastian Cabot, Louis Prima.

**Jurassic Park** (1993). *Directed by* Steven Spielberg. *Writing Credits:* Michael Crichton (novel), Michael Crichton (screenplay) and David Koepp (screenplay). *Starring:* Sam Neill, Laura Dern, Jeff Goldblum, Richard Attenborough.

**Karate Kid, The** (1984). *Directed by* John G. Avildsen. *Writing Credits:* Robert Mark Kamen. *Starring:* Ralph Macchio, Pat Morita, Elisabeth Shue.

**Kill Bill** (2003). *Directed by* Quentin Tarantino. *Writing Credits:* Quentin Tarantino (character The Bride) (as Q), Uma Thurman (character The Bride) (as U), Quentin Tarantino (written by). *Starring:* Uma Thurman, David Carradine, Lucy Liu, Daryl Hannah, Vivica A. Fox, Michael Madsen.

**King of Comedy, The** (1983). *Directed by* Martin Scorsese. *Writing Credits:* Paul D. Zimmerman. *Starring:* Robert De Niro, Jerry Lewis, Diahnne Abbott, Sandra Bernhard.

**Lady and the Tramp** (1955). *Directed by* Clyde Geronimi & Wilfred Jackson. *Writing Credits*: Ward Greene (story) & Erdman Penner. *Starring*: Peggy Lee, Barbara Luddy, Larry Roberts.

**Lady from Shanghai, The** (1947). *Directed by* Orson Welles. *Writing Credits*: Sherwood King (novel) & Orson Welles. *Starring*: Rita Hayworth & Orson Welles, Everett Sloane.

**Lady Killer** (1933). *Directed by* Roy Del Ruth. *Writing Credits*: Lillie Hayward & Ben Markson. *Starring*: James Cagney, Mae Clarke, Margaret Lindsay.

**Lara Croft: Tomb Raider** (2001). *Directed* by Simon West. *Writing Credits*: Sara B. Cooper (story), Mike Werb (story), Michael Colleary (story), Simon West (adaptation), Patrick Massett (screenplay) & John Zinman (screenplay). *Starring*: Angelina Jolie, Jon Voight, Iain Glen, Noah Taylor, Daniel Craig.

**Lethal Weapon** (1987). *Directed by* Richard Donner. *Writing Credits*: Shane Black. *Starring*: Mel Gibson, Danny Glover, Gary Busey.

**Like Father, Like Son** (1987). *Directed by* Rod Daniel. *Writing Credits*: Lorne Cameron & David Hoselton. *Starring*: Dudley Moore, Kirk Cameron, Margaret Colin.

**Like Water for Chocolate** (1992). *Directed by* Alfonso Arau. *Writing Credits*: Laura Esquivel (also novel). *Starring*: Marco Leonardi, Lumi Cavazos, Regina Torné.

**Lion King, The** (1994). *Directed by* Roger Allers & Rob Minkoff. *Writing Credits*: Irene Mecchi (written by) and Jonathan Roberts (written by). *Starring*: Matthew Broderick (voice), Joseph Williams (voice), Jonathan Taylor Thomas (voice).

**Little Princess, The** (1939). *Directed by* Walter Lang & William A. Seiter. *Writing Credits*: Frances Hodgson Burnett (novel), Ethel Hill, Walter Ferris. Starring: Shirley Temple, Richard Greene, Anita Louise.

**Lolita** (1962). *Directed by* Stanley Kubrick. *Writing Credits*: Vladimir Nabokov (novel) & Vladimir Nabokov. *Starring*: James Mason, Shelley Winters, Sue Lyon.

**Lord of the Rings: The Fellowship of the Ring, The** (2001). *Directed by* Peter Jackson. *Writing Credits*: J. R. R. Tolkien (novel *The Fellowship of the Ring*), Frances Walsh (screenplay) (as Fran Walsh), Philippa Boyens (screenplay) & Peter Jackson (screenplay). *Starring*: Elijah Wood, Ian McKellen, Viggo Mortensen, Liv Tyler, Sean Astin, Cate Blanchett, John Rhys-Davies, Billy Boyd, Dominic Monaghan, Orlando Bloom, Christopher Lee, Hugo Weaving, Sean Bean.

**Lost Weekend, The** (1945). *Directed by* Billy Wilder. *Writing Credits*: Charles R. Jackson (novel), Charles Brackett (screenplay) & Billy Wilder (screenplay). *Starring*: Ray Milland, Jane Wyman, Phillip Terry, Howard Da Silva. *Academy Awards*: Ray Milland (Best Actor in a Leading Role), Billy Wilder (Best Director), Charles Brackett & Billy Wilder (Best Writing, Screenplay).

**Love and Death** (1975). **Directed by** Woody Allen. *Writing Credits*: Woody Allen. *Starring*: Woody Allen, Diane Keaton, Georges Adet.

**Magnificent Seven, The** (1960). *Directed by* John Sturges. *Writing Credits*: William Roberts (additions) and Walter Newman. *Starring*: Yul Brynner, Eli Wallach, Steve McQueen.

**Magnum Force** (1973). *Directed by* Ted Post. *Writing Credits*: Harry Julian Fink (characters), Rita M. Fink (characters) (as R. M. Fink), John Milius (story), John Milius (screenplay) and Michael Cimino (screenplay). *Starring*: Clint Eastwood, Hal Holbrook, Mitch Ryan, David Soul, Tim Matheson.

**Malcolm X** (1992). *Directed by* Spike Lee. *Writing Credits*: Alex Haley & Malcolm X (book: *The Autobiography of Malcom X*), Arnold Perl (screenplay) and Spike Lee (screenplay). *Starring*: Denzel Washington, Angela Bassett, Albert Hall, Al Freeman Jr., Delroy Lindo, Spike Lee, Theresa Randle.

**Maltese Falcon, The** (1941). *Directed by* John Huston. *Writing Credits*: Dashiell Hammett (novel) & John Huston (screenplay). *Starring*: Humphrey Bogart, Mary Astor, Gladys George, Peter Lorre.

**Manhattan** (1979). *Directed by* Woody Allen. *Writing Credits*: Woody Allen and Marshall Brickman. *Starring*: Woody Allen, Diane Keaton, Michael Murphy, Mariel Hemingway, Meryl Streep, Anne Byrne Hoffman, Karen Ludwig

**Mayor of Hell, The** (1933). *Directed by* Archie Mayo & Michael Curtiz. *Writing Credits*: Islin Auster (story) & Edward Chodorov (screenplay). *Starring*: James Cagney, Madge Evans, Arthur Byron.

**McQ** (1974). *Directed by* John Sturges. *Writing Credits*: Lawrence Roman. *Starring*: John Wayne, Eddie Albert, Diana Muldaur.

**Memento** (2000). *Directed by* Christopher Nolan. *Writing Credits*: Christopher Nolan & Jonathan Nolan (story). *Starring*: Guy Pearce, Carrie-Anne Moss, Joe Pantoliano, Mark Boone Junior, Russ Fega, Jorja Fox, Stephen Tobolowsky.

**Metropolis** (1927). *Directed by* Fritz Lang. *Writing Credits*: Fritz Lang & Thea von Harbou (also novel). *Starring*: Alfred Abel, Gustav Fröhlich, Brigitte Helm.

**Mexican, The** (2001). *Directed by* Gore Verbinski. *Writing Credits*: J. H. Wyman (written by). *Starring*: Brad Pitt, Julia Roberts, James Gandolfini, J. K. Simmons.

**Mighty Ducks, The** (1992). *Directed by* Stephen Herek. *Writing Credits*: Steven Brill (written by). *Starring*: Emilio Estevez, Joss Ackland, Lane Smith.

**Mildred Pierce** (1945). *Directed by* Michael Curtiz. *Writing Credits*: James M. Cain (novel) & Ranald MacDougall. *Starring*: Joan Crawford, Jack Carson, Zachary Scott. *Academy Awards*: Joan Crawford (Best Actress in a Leading Role).

**Misery** (1990). *Directed by* Rob Reiner. *Writing Credits*: Stephen King (novel) & William Goldman (screenplay). *Starring*: James Caan, Kathy Bates, Richard Farnsworth. *Academy Awards*: Kathy Bates (Best Actress in a Leading Role).

**Mommie Dearest** (1981). *Directed by* Frank Perry. *Writing Credits*: Christina Crawford (book) & Robert Getchell. *Starring*: Faye Dunaway, Diana Scarwid, Steve Forrest.

**Monsters, Inc.** (2001). *Directed by* Peter Docter & David Silverman. *Writing Credits*: Robert L. Baird (additional screenplay material) & Jill Culton (story). *Starring*: John Goodman (voice), Billy Crystal (voice), Mary Gibbs (voice), Steve Buscemi (voice), James Coburn (voice), Jennifer Tilly (voice).

**Mothman Prophecies, The** (2002). *Directed by* Mark Pellington. *Writing Credits*: John A. Keel (novel) & Richard Hatem (screenplay). *Starring*: Richard Gere, David Eigenberg, Bob Tracey, Ron Emanuel, Debra Messing.

**Mr. Deeds Goes to Town** (1936). *Directed by* Frank Capra. *Writing Credits*: Clarence Budington Kelland (story) & Robert Riskin. *Starring*: Gary Cooper, Jean Arthur, George Bancroft. *Academy Awards*: Frank Capra (Best Director).

**Mr. Smith Goes to Washington** (1939). *Directed by* Frank Capra. *Writing Credits*: Lewis R. Foster (story) & Sidney Buchman (screenplay). *Starring*: Jean Arthur, James Stewart, Claude Rains. *Academy Awards*: Lewis R. Foster (Best Writing, original Story).

**Mummy, The** (1932). *Directed by* Karl Freund. *Writing Credits*: Nina Wilcox Putnam (story), Richard Schayer (story) & John L. Balderston. *Starring*: Boris Karloff, Zita Johann, David Manners.

**Mutiny on the Bounty** (1935). *Directed by* Frank Lloyd. *Writing Credits*: Charles Nordhoff (novel), James Norman Hall (novel), Talbot Jennings, Jules Furthman, Carey Wilson. *Starring*: Charles Laughton, Clark Gable, Franchot Tone.

**My Darling Clementine** (1946). *Directed by* John Ford. *Writing Credits*: Samuel G. Engel, Sam Hellman (story), Stuart N. Lake (book *Wyatt Earp, Frontier Marshal*), Winston Miller. *Starring*: Henry Fonda, Linda Darnell, Victor Mature, Cathy Downs, Walter Brennan.

**My Left Foot** (1989). *Directed by* Jim Sheridan. *Writing Credits*: Christy Brown (book), Shane Connaughton & Jim Sheridan. *Starring*: Daniel Day-Lewis, Brenda Fricker, Alison Whelan. *Academy Awards*: Daniel Day-Lewis (Best Actor in a Leading Role), Brenda Fricker (Best Actress in a Supporting Role).

**My Life** (1993). *Directed by* Bruce Joel Rubin. *Writing Credits*: Bruce Joel Rubin (written by). *Starring*: Michael Keaton, Nicole Kidman, Bradley Whitford, Queen Latifah, Michael Constantine.

**Natural, The** (1984). *Directed by* Barry Levinson. *Writing Credits*: Bernard Malamud (novel), Roger Towne, Phil Dusenberry. *Starring*: Robert Redford, Robert Duvall, Glenn Close, Kim Basinger, Wilford Brimley, Barbara Hershey, Robert Prosky, Richard Farnsworth.

**Night of the Hunter, The** (1955). *Directed by* Charles Laughton. *Writing Credits*: James Agee & Davis Grubb (novel). *Starring*: Robert Mitchum, Shelley Winters, Lillian Gish.

**Nightmare On Elm Street, A** (1984). *Directed by* Wes Craven. *Writing Credits*: Wes Craven (written by). *Starring*: John Saxon, Ronee Blakley, Heather Langenkamp.

**North by Northwest** (1959). *Directed by* Alfred Hitchcock. *Writing Credits*: Ernest Lehman. *Starring*: Cary Grant, Eva Marie Saint, James Mason.

**Ocean's Eleven** (2001). *Directed by* Steven Soderbergh. *Writing Credits*: George Clayton Johnson (1960 story), Jack Golden Russell (1960 story), Harry Brown (1960 screenplay), Charles Lederer (1960 screenplay), Ted Griffin (screenplay). *Starring*: George Clooney, Cecelia Ann Birt, Paul L. Nolan.

**Odd Couple, The** (1968). *Directed by* Gene Saks. *Writing Credits*: Neil Simon (also play). *Starring*: Jack Lemmon, Walter Matthau, John Fiedler.

**Of Human Hearts** (1938). *Directed by* Clarence Brown. *Writing Credits*: Honore Morrow (story), Bradbury Foote (screenplay). *Starring*: Walter Huston, James Stewart.

**Officer and a Gentleman, An** (1982). *Directed by* Taylor Hackford. *Writing Credits*: Douglas Day Stewart. *Starring*: Richard Gere, Debra Winger, David Keith, Robert Loggia, Lisa Blount, Lisa Eilbacher, Louis Gossett Jr. *Academy Awards*: Louis Gossett Jr. (Best Actor in a Supporting Role).

**One Hour Photo** (2002). *Directed by* Mark Romanek. *Writing Credits*: Mark Romanek (written by). *Starring*: Robin Williams, Connie Nielsen, Michael Vartan, Dylan Smith, Erin Daniels.

**Ordinary People** (1980). *Directed by* Robert Redford. *Writing Credits*: Judith Guest (novel), Alvin Sargent. *Starring*: Donald Sutherland, Judd Hirsch, Timothy Hutton, M. Emmet Walsh, Elizabeth McGovern. *Academy Awards*: Timothy Hutton (Best Actor in a Supporting Role), Robert Redford (Best Director), Ronald L. Schwary (Best Picture), Alvin Sargent (Best Writing, Screenplay Based on Material from Another Medium).

**Papillon** (1973). *Directed by* Franklin J. Schaffner. *Writing Credits*: Henri Charrière (novel), Dalton Trumbo and Lorenzo Semple Jr. *Starring*: Steve McQueen and Dustin Hoffman.

**Parent Trap, The** (1961). *Directed by* David Swift. *Writing Credits*: Erich Kästner (book) & David Swift. *Starring*: Hayley Mills, Maureen O'Hara, Brian Keith.

**Parent Trap, The** (1998). *Directed by* Nancy Meyers. *Writing Credits*: Erich Kästner (book *Das Doppelte Lottchen*), David Swift (screenplay), Nancy Meyers (screenplay) & Charles Shyer (screenplay). *Starring*: Lindsay Lohan, Dennis Quaid, Natasha Richardson.

**Patriot, The** (2000). *Directed by* Roland Emmerich. *Writing Credits*: Robert Rodat (written by). *Starring*: Mel Gibson, Heath Ledger, Joely Richardson, Jason Isaacs, Chris Cooper.

**Pee Wee's Big Adventure** (1985). *Directed by* Tim Burton. *Writing Credits*: Phil Hartman, Paul Reubens, Michael Varhol. *Starring*: Paul Reubens, Elizabeth Daily, Mark Holton.

**Pinocchio** (1940). *Directed by* Hamilton Luske & Ben Sharpsteen. *Writing Credits*: Aurelius Battaglia (story) & Carlo Collodi (novel). *Starring*: Mel Blanc (voice), Don Brodie (voice).

**Planes, Trains & Automobiles** (1987). *Directed by* John Hughes. *Writing Credits*: John Hughes. *Starring*: Steve Martin, John Candy, Laila Robins, Michael McKean, Kevin Bacon, Dylan Baker.

**Poison Ivy** (1992). *Directed by* Katt Shea. *Writing Credits*: Melissa Goddard (story), Andy Ruben (screenplay) & Katt Shea (screenplay) (as Katt Shea Ruben). *Starring*: Sara Gilbert, Drew Barrymore, Tom Skerritt, Cheryl Ladd.

**Poltergeist** (1982). *Directed by* Tobe Hooper & Steven Spielberg. *Writing Credits*: Steven Spielberg (story), Steven Spielberg (screenplay), Michael Grais (screenplay) & Mark Victor (screenplay). *Starring*: JoBeth Williams, Craig T. Nelson, Beatrice Straight.

**Porky's** (1982). *Directed by* Bob Clark. *Writing Credits*: Bob Clark. *Starring*: Dan Monahan & Mark Herrier.

**Prince of Egypt, The** (1998). *Directed by* Brenda Chapman & Steve Hickner. *Writing Credits*: Ken Harsha (story) & Carole Holliday (additional story). *Starring*: Val Kilmer (voice), Ralph Fiennes (voice), Michelle Pfeiffer (voice), Sandra Bullock (voice), Jeff Goldblum (voice), Danny Glover (voice), Patrick Stewart (voice), Helen Mirren (voice), Steve Martin (voice), Martin Short (voice).

**Psycho** (1960). *Directed by* Alfred Hitchcock. *Writing Credits*: Robert Bloch (novel), Joseph Stefano (screenplay). *Starring*: Anthony Perkins, Vera Miles, John Gavin, Martin Balsam.

**Public Enemy, The** (1931). *Directed by* William A. Wellman. *Writing Credits*: Kubec Glasmon (story *Beer and Blood*), John Bright (story *Beer and Blood*), Harvey F. Thew (adaptation) (as Harvey Thew). *Starring*: James Cagney, Edward Woods, Jean Harlow.

**Quiet Man, The** (1952). *Directed by* John Ford. *Writing Credits*: Frank S. Nugent & Maurice Walsh (story). *Starring*: John Wayne, Maureen O'Hara, Barry Fitzgerald, Ward Bond, Victor McLaglen. *Academy Awards*: John Ford (Best Director).

**Raging Bull** (1980). *Directed by* Martin Scorsese. *Writing Credits*: Jake LaMotta (book) and Joseph Carter (book). *Starring*: Robert De Niro, Cathy Moriarty, Joe Pesci. *Academy Awards*: Robert De Niro (Best Actor in a Leading Role).

**Raiders of the Lost Ark** (1981). *Directed by* Steven Spielberg. *Writing Credits*: George Lucas (story), Philip Kaufman (story) & Lawrence Kasdan. *Starring*: Harrison Ford, Karen Allen, Paul Freeman, Ronald Lacey, John Rhys-Davies, Denholm Elliott, Alfred Molina, Wolf Kahler.

**Rebel Without a Cause** (1955). *Directed by* Nicholas Ray. *Writing Credits*: Nicholas Ray (story), Irving Shulman (adaptation) & Stewart Stern (screenplay). *Starring*: James Dean, Natalie Wood & Sal Mineo.

**Red River** (1948). *Directed by* Howard Hawks & Arthur Rosson. *Writing Credits*: Borden Chase (screenplay), Borden Chase (story *The Chisholm Trail*), Charles Schnee (screenplay). *Starring*: John Wayne, Montgomery Clift, Joanne Dru, Walter Brennan.

**Remains of the Day, The** (1993). *Directed by* James Ivory. *Writing Credits*: Kazuo Ishiguro (novel) & Ruth Prawer Jhabvala (screenplay). *Starring*: Anthony Hopkins, Emma Thompson, James Fox, Christopher Reeve, Peter Vaughan, Hugh Grant.

**Rio Bravo** (1959). *Directed by* Howard Hawks. *Writing Credits*: Leigh Brackett, Jules Furthman, B. H. McCampbell (story). *Starring*: John Wayne, Dean Martin, Ricky Nelson, Angie Dickinson, Walter Brennan.

**Robe, The** (1953). *Directed by* Henry Koster. *Writing Credits*: Lloyd C. Douglas (novel), Gina Kaus (adaptation), Albert Maltz (screenplay) & Philip Dunne (screenplay). *Starring*: Richard Burton, Jean Simmons & Victor Mature.

**Rocky** (1976). *Directed by* John G. Avildsen. *Writing Credits:* Sylvester Stallone. *Starring:* Sylvester Stallone, Talia Shire, Burt Young, Carl Weathers. *Academy Awards:* John G. Avildsen (Best Director).

**Rocky II** (1979). *Directed by* Sylvester Stallone. *Writing Credits:* Sylvester Stallone. *Starring:* Sylvester Stallone, Talia Shire, Burt Young, Carl Weathers.

**Rocky III** (1982). *Directed by* Sylvester Stallone. *Writing Credits:* Sylvester Stallone. *Starring:* Sylvester Stallone, Talia Shire, Burt Young, Carl Weathers.

**Rocky IV** (1985). *Directed by* Sylvester Stallone. *Writing Credits:* Sylvester Stallone. *Starring:* Sylvester Stallone, Talia Shire, Burt Young, Brigitte Nielsen, Carl Weathers.

**Rocky V** (1990). *Directed by* John G. Avildsen. *Writing Credits:* Sylvester Stallone. *Starring:* Sylvester Stallone, Talia Shire, Burt Young, Sage Stallone, Burgess Meredith.

**Romancing the Stone** (1984). *Directed by* Robert Zemeckis. *Writing Credits:* Diane Thomas. *Starring:* Michael Douglas, Kathleen Turner, Danny DeVito, Zack Norman, Alfonso Arau.

**Rosemary's Baby** (1968). *Directed by* Roman Polanski. *Writing Credits:* Ira Levin (novel) & Roman Polanski (screenplay). *Starring:* Mia Farrow, John Cassavetes, Ruth Gordon. *Academy Awards:* Ruth Gordon (Best Actress in a Supporting Role).

**Royal Tennenbaums, The** (2001). *Directed by* Wes Anderson. *Writing Credits:* Wes Anderson (written by) & Owen Wilson (written by). *Starring:* Gene Hackman, Anjelica Huston, Gwyneth Paltrow, Ben Stiller, Luke Wilson, Owen Wilson, Danny Glover, Bill Murray, Alec Baldwin, Seymour Cassel.

**Scarface** (1983). *Directed by* Brian De Palma. *Writing Credits:* Oliver Stone. *Starring:* Al Pacino, Steven Bauer, Michelle Pfeiffer, Mary Elizabeth Mastrantonio & Robert Loggia.

**Schindler's List** (1993). *Directed by* Steven Spielberg. *Writing Credits*: Thomas Keneally (book) & Steven Zaillian (screenplay). *Starring*: Liam Neeson, Ben Kingsley, Ralph Fiennes, Caroline Goodall, Jonathan Sagall, Embeth Davidtz. *Academy Awards*: Steven Spielberg (Best Director), Steven Zaillian (Best Writing, Screenplay Based on Material from Another Medium).

**Score, The** (2001). *Directed by* Frank Oz & Robert De Niro. *Writing Credits*: Daniel E. Taylor (story), Kario Salem (story) (screenplay), Lem Dobbs (screenplay) and Scott Marshall Smith. *Starring*: Robert De Niro, Edward Norton, Marlon Brando, Angela Bassett.

**Seabiscuit** (2003). *Directed by* Gary Ross. *Writing Credits*: Laura Hillenbrand (book) & Gary Ross (screenplay). *Starring*: Tobey Maguire, David McCullough, Jeff Bridges, Paul Vincent O'Connor, Chris Cooper.

**Searchers, The** (1956). *Directed by* John Ford. *Writing Credits*: Alan Le May (novel) & Frank S. Nugent (screenplay). *Starring*: John Wayne, Jeffrey Hunter, Vera Miles.

**Sergeant York** (1941). *Directed by* Howard Hawks. *Writing Credits*: Harry Chandlee & Abem Finkel. *Starring*: Gary Cooper, Walter Brennan, Joan Leslie. *Academy Awards*: Gary Cooper (Best Actor in a Leading Role).

**Serpico** (1973). *Directed by* Sidney Lumet. *Writing Credits*: Peter Maas (book), Waldo Salt, Norman Wexler. *Starring*: Al Pacino, John Randolph, Jack Kehoe.

**Seven Samurai** (1954). *Directed by* Akira Kurosawa. *Writing Credits*: Shinobu Hashimoto & Akira Kurosawa. *Starring*: Takashi Shimura.

**Shane** (1953). *Directed by* George Stevens. *Writing Credits*: Jack Schaefer (story) & A. B. Guthrie, Jr. *Starring*: Alan Ladd, Jean Arthur, Van Heflin, Jack Palance, Ben Johnson. *Academy Awards*: Loyal Griggs (Best Cinematography, Color).

**Shine** (1996). *Directed by* Scott Hicks. *Writing Credits*: Scott Hicks (story) & Jan Sardi. *Starring*: Geoffrey Rush, Justin Braine, Sonia Todd. *Academy Awards*: Geoffrey Rush (Best Actor in a Leading Role).

**Shining, The** (1980). *Directed by* Stanley Kubrick. *Writing Credits*: Stephen King (novel), Stanley Kubrick (screenplay), Diane Johnson (screenplay). *Starring*: Jack Nicholson, Shelley Duval.

**Silence of the Lambs, The** (1991). *Directed by* Jonathan Demme. *Writing Credits*: Thomas Harris (novel) & Ted Tally (screenplay). *Starring*: Jodie Foster, Anthony Hopkins, Scott Glenn, Anthony Heald, Ted Levine. *Academy Awards*: Anthony Hopkins (Best Actor in a Leading Role), Jodie Foster (Best Actress in a Leading Role), Jonathan Demme (Best Director).

**Sleeping Beauty** (1959). *Writing Credits*: Charles Perrault, Erdman Penner, Milt Banta, Winston Hibler. *Starring*: Mary Costa (voice), Bill Shirley (voice), Eleanor Audley (voice).

**Snow White and the Seven Dwarfs** (1937). *Writing Credits*: Ted Sears (story) and Richard Creedon (story). *Starring*: Roy Atwell (voice), Stuart Buchanan (voice), Adriana Caselotti (voice). *Academy Awards*: Walt Disney (Honorary Award).

**Spanking The Monkey** (1994). *Directed by* David O. Russell. *Writing Credits*: David O. Russell (written by). *Starring*: Jeremy Davies, Elizabeth Newett, Benjamin Hendrickson, Alberta Watson.

**Spartacus** (1960). *Directed by* Stanley Kubrick. *Writing Credits*: Howard Fast (novel) & Dalton Trumbo. *Starring*: Kirk Douglas, Laurence Olivier, Jean Simmons, Charles Laughton, Peter Ustinov, John Gavin. *Academy Awards*: Peter Ustinov (Best Actor in a Supporting Role).

**Spellbound** (1945). *Directed by* Alfred Hitchcock. *Writing Credits*: Angus MacPhail (adaptation) & Ben Hecht (screenplay). *Starring*: Ingrid Bergman, Gregory Peck, Michael Chekhov. *Academy Awards*: Miklós Rózsa (Best Music, Scoring of a Dramatic or Comedy Picture).

**Spider-Man** (2002). *Directed by* Sam Raimi. *Writing Credits*: Stan Lee (comic book), Steve Ditko (comic book), David Koepp (screenplay). *Starring*: Tobey Maguire, Willem Dafoe, Kirsten Dunst, James Franco, Cliff Robertson, Rosemary Harris.

**Spy Kids** (2001). *Directed by* Robert Rodriguez. *Writing Credits*: Robert Rodriguez (written by). *Starring*: Antonio Banderas, Carla Gugino, Alexa Vega, Daryl Sabara, Alan Cumming, Tony Shalhoub, Teri Hatcher, Cheech Marin, Robert Patrick, Danny Trejo.

**Spy Kids 2: Island of Lost Dreams** (2002). *Directed by* Robert Rodriguez. *Writing Credits*: Robert Rodriguez. *Starring*: Antonio Banderas, Carla Gugino, Alexa Vega, Daryl Sabara, Alan Cumming, Tony Shalhoub, Cheech Marin, Danny Trejo, Steve Buscemi.

**Spy Kids 3-D: Game Over** (2003). *Directed by* Robert Rodriguez. *Writing Credits*: Robert Rodriguez. *Starring*: Antonio Banderas, Carla Gugino, Alexa Vega, Daryl Sabara, Ricardo Montalban, Holland Taylor, Sylvester Stallone.

**Star Wars** (1977). *Directed by* George Lucas. *Writing Credits*: George Lucas. *Starring*: Mark Hamill, Harrison Ford, Carrie Fisher, Peter Cushing, Alec Guinness.

**Star Wars: Episode I – The Phantom Menace** (1999). *Directed by* George Lucas. *Writing Credits*: George Lucas. *Starring*: Liam Neeson, Ewan McGregor, Natalie Portman, Jake Lloyd.

**Star Wars: Episode II – Attack of the Clones** (2002). *Directed by* George Lucas. *Writing Credits*: George Lucas (story) (Screenplay). *Starring*: Ewan McGregor, Natalie Portman, Hayden Christensen, Christopher Lee, Samuel L. Jackson.

**Star Wars: Episode V – The Empire Strikes Back** (1980). *Directed by* Irvin Kershner. *Writing Credits*: George Lucas (story), Leigh Brackett, Lawrence Kasdan. *Starring*: Mark Hamill, Harrison Ford, Carrie Fisher, Billy Dee Williams.

**Star Wars: Episode VI – Return of the Jedi** (1983). *Directed by* Richard Marquand. *Writing Credits*: George Lucas (story) & Lawrence Kasdan. *Starring*: Mark Hamill, Harrison Ford, Carrie Fisher, Billy Dee Williams.

**Stone Killer, The** (1973). *Directed by* Michael Winner. *Writing Credits*: John Gardner (book) & Gerald Wilson. *Starring*: Charles Bronson, Martin Balsam, Jack Colvin.

**Stranger on the Third Floor** (1940). *Directed by* Boris Ingster. *Writing Credits*: Frank Partos. *Starring*: Peter Lorre, John McGuire, Margaret Tallichet.

**Straw Dogs** (1971). *Directed by* Sam Peckinpah. *Writing Credits*: Gordon Williams (novel *The Siege of Trencher's Farm*) (as Gordon M. Williams), David Zelag Goodman & Sam Peckinpah. *Starring*: Dustin Hoffman, Susan George, Peter Vaughan.

**Sudden Impact** (1983). *Directed by* Clint Eastwood. *Writing Credits*: Harry Julian Fink (characters), Rita M. Fink (characters) (as R.M. Fink), Charles B. Pierce (story), Earl E. Smith (story), Joseph Stinson. *Starring*: Clint Eastwood, Sondra Locke, Pat Hingle.

**Superman** (1978). *Directed by* Richard Donner. *Writing Credits*: Jerry Siegel (comic) & Joe Shuster (comic). *Starring*: Marlon Brando, Gene Hackman, Christopher Reeve, Glenn Ford. *Academy Awards*: Stuart Baird (Best Film Editing).

**Superman II** (1980). *Directed by* Richard Lester, Richard Donner. *Writing Credits*: Jerry Siegel (characters) & Joe Shuster (characters). *Starring*: Gene Hackman, Christopher Reeve.

**Suspicion** (1941). *Directed by* Alfred Hitchcock. *Writing Credits*: Anthony Berkeley (novel *Before the Fact*) (as Francis Iles), Samson Raphaelson, Joan Harrison, Alma Reville. *Starring*: Cary Grant, Joan Fontaine, Cedric Hardwicke. *Academy Awards*: Joan Fontaine (Best Actress in a Leading Role).

**Swimming Pool** (2003). *Directed by* François Ozon. *Writing Credits*: François Ozon (screenplay) & Emmanuèle Bernheim. *Starring*: Charlotte Rampling, Ludivine Sagnier, Charles Dance.

**Sword in the Stone, The** (1963). *Directed by* Wolfgang Reitherman. *Writing Credits:* Bill Peet & T. H. White (book). *Starring:* Karl Swenson (voice), Rickie Sorensen (voice), Sebastian Cabot (voice).

**Tadpole** (2002). *Directed by* Gary Winick. *Writing Credits:* Heather McGowan (story), Niels Mueller (story), Gary Winick (story), Heather McGowan (written by), Niels Mueller (written by). *Starring:* Sigourney Weaver, Kate Mara, John Ritter.

**Terminator 2** (1991). *Directed by* James Cameron. *Writing Credits:* James Cameron (written by) & William Wisher Jr. (written by). *Starring:* Arnold Schwarzenegger, Linda Hamilton, Edward Furlong, Robert Patrick.

**There's Something About Mary** (1998). *Directed by* Bobby Farrelly & Peter Farrelly. *Writing Credits:* Ed Decter (story) (screenplay), John J. Strauss (story) (screenplay), Peter Farrelly (screenplay) & Bobby Farrelly (screenplay). *Starring:* Cameron Diaz, Matt Dillon, Ben Stiller, Lee Evans.

**Tightrope** (1984). *Directed by* Richard Tuggle. *Writing Credits:* Richard Tuggle. *Starring:* Clint Eastwood, Geneviève Bujold, Dan Hedaya, Alison Eastwood.

**Time Machine, The** (2002). *Directed by* Simon Wells. *Writing Credits:* H. G. Wells (novel), David Duncan (earlier screenplay), John Logan (screenplay). *Starring:* Guy Pearce, Mark Addy, Phyllida Law.

**Tin Cup** (1996). *Directed by* Ron Shelton. *Writing Credits:* John Norville & Ron Shelton. *Starring:* Kevin Costner, Rene Russo, Don Johnson & Cheech Marin.

**Titanic** (1997). *Directed by* James Cameron. *Writing Credits:* James Cameron (written by). *Starring:* Leonardo DiCaprio, Kate Winslet, Billy Zane, Kathy Bates, Bill Paxton, Gloria Stuart. *Academy Awards:* James Cameron (Best Director).

**Toy Story** (1995). *Directed by* John Lasseter. *Writing Credits:* John Lassete (story) and Andrew Stanton (story). *Starring:* Tom Hanks (voice), Tim Allen (voice), Don Rickles (voice), Jim Varney (voice).

**Treasure of the Sierra Madre, The** (1948). *Directed by* John Huston. *Writing Credits:* B. Traven (novel) & John Huston. *Starring:* Humphrey Bogart, Walter Huston, Tim Holt, Bruce Bennett. *Academy Awards:* Walter Huston (Best Actor in a Supporting Role), John Huston (Best Director), John Huston (Best Writing, Screenplay).

**Unfaithful** (2002). *Directed by* Adrian Lyne. *Writing Credits:* Claude Chabrol (film *La Femme Infidele*), Alvin Sargent (screenplay) and William Broyles Jr. (screenplay). *Starring:* Diane Lane, Richard Gere, Olivier Martinez.

**Unforgiven** (1992). *Directed by* Clint Eastwood. *Writing Credits:* David Webb Peoples (written by). *Starring:* Clint Eastwood, Gene Hackman, Morgan Freeman, Richard Harris. *Academy Awards:* Gene Hackman (Best Actor in a Supporting Role), Clint Eastwood (Best Director).

**Vertigo** (1958). *Directed by* Alfred Hitchcock. *Writing Credits:* Pierre Boileau (novel) and Thomas Narcejac (novel), Samuel A. Taylor & Alec Coppel. *Starring:* James Stewart & Kim Novak.

**Wall Street** (1987). *Directed by* Oliver Stone. *Writing Credits:* Stanley Weiser & Oliver Stone (written by). *Starring:* Charlie Sheen, Tamara Tunie, Franklin Cover, James Karen, Michael Douglas. *Academy Awards:* Michael Douglas (Best Actor in a Leading Role).

**White Heat** (1949). *Directed by* Raoul Walsh. *Writing Credits:* Virginia Kellogg (story), Ivan Goff & Ben Roberts. *Starring:* James Cagney, Virginia Mayo, Edmond O'Brien.

**Wild Bunch, The** (1969). *Directed by* Sam Peckinpah. *Writing Credits:* Walon Green (story), Roy N. Sickner (story), Walon Green (screenplay) and Sam Peckinpah (screenplay). *Starring:* William Holden, Ernest Borgnine, Robert Ryan, Edmond O'Brien.

**Wild One, The** (1953). *Directed by* László Benedek. *Writing Credits:* John Paxton & Frank Rooney (novel). *Starring:* Marlon Brando, Mary Murphy, Robert Keith, Lee Marvin.

**Wolf Man, The** (1941). *Directed by* George Waggner. *Writing Credits*: Curt Siodmak. *Starring*: Claude Rains, Warren William, Ralph Bellamy.

**Working Girl** (1988). *Directed by* Mike Nichols. *Writing Credits*: Kevin Wade (written by). *Starring*: Harrison Ford, Sigourney Weaver, Melanie Griffith, Alec Baldwin, Joan Cusack.

**Yojimbo** (1961). *Directed by* Akira Kurosawa. *Writing Credits*: Ryuzo Kikushima & Akira Kurosawa. *Starring*: Toshirô Mifune.

**Your Friends & Neighbors** (1998). *Directed by* Neil LaBute. *Writing Credits*: Neil LaBute (written by). *Starring*: Amy Brenneman, Aaron Eckhart, Catherine Keener, Nastassja Kinski, Jason Patric, Ben Stiller.

# Bibliography

Adler, Alfred. (1927). *The Practice and Theory of Individual Psychology.* New York: Harcourt, Brace and World.

Adler, Alfred. (1931). *What Life Could Mean to You.* Boston: Little, Brown.

Adler, Alfred. (1939). *Social Interest.* New York: Putnam.

Adler, Alfred. (1954). *Understanding Human Nature.* New York: Fawcett.

Bettelheim, Bruno. (1982). *Freud and Man's Soul.* New York: Knopf.

Campbell, Joseph. (1988). *The Power of Myth.* New York: Doubleday.

Campbell, Joseph. (1986). *The Inner Reaches of Outer Space: Metaphor as Myth and as Religion.* Toronto: St. James Press.

Campbell, Joseph. (1982). *The Hero's Journey: Joseph Campbell on his Life and Work.* Phil Cousineau, (Ed.). New York: Harper & Row.

Campbell, Joseph. (1974). *The Mythic Image.* Princeton, NJ: Princeton University Press.

Campbell, Joseph. (1949). *The Hero with a Thousand Faces.* NJ: Princeton University Press.

Erikson, Erik. (1963). *Childhood and Society.* New York: Norton.

Erikson, Erik. (1968). *Identity, Youth and Crisis.* New York: Norton.

Erikson, Erik. (1974). *Dimensions of a New Identity.* New York: Norton.

Erikson, Erik. (1982, 1997). *The Life Cycle Completed: A Review.* New York: Norton.

Estes, Clarissa Pinkola. (1992). *Women Who Run With the Wolves: Myths and Stories of the Wild Woman Archetype.* New York: Ballantine Books.

Freud, Anna. (1946). *The Ego and the Mechanisms of Defense.* New York: International Universities Press.

Freud, Anna. (1965). *The Writing of Anna Freud.* New York: International Universities Press.

Freud, Sigmund. (1956). *The Complete Psychological Works: Standard Edition* (24 volumes). J. Strachey, (Ed.). London: Hogarth Press.

Freud, Sigmund. (1900). *The Interpretation of Dreams. (In The Complete Psychological Works: Standard Edition,* Volumes 4 & 5).

Freud, Sigmund. (1901). *The Psychopathology of Everyday Life. (In The Complete Psychological Works: Standard Edition,* Volume 6).

Freud, Sigmund. (1917). *Introductory Lectures on Psychoanalysis. (In The Complete Psychological Works: Standard Edition,* Volumes 15 & 16).

Freud, Sigmund. (1923). *The Ego and the Id. (In The Complete Psychological Works: Standard Edition,* Volume 19).

Freud, Sigmund. (1938). *The Basic Writings of Sigmund Freud.* (A. Brill, Trans. & Ed.). New York: Random House, Inc.

Freud, Sigmund. (1940). *An Outline of Psychoanalysis. (In The Complete Psychological Works: Standard Edition,* Volume 23).

The Internet Movie Database. (2003). *www.IMDB.com.*

Izod, John. (2001). *Myth, Mind and the Screen: Understanding the Heroes of Our Time.* Cambridge: Cambridge University Press.

Jung, Carl G. (1971). *The Portable Jung*. (Joseph Campbell, Ed.). New York: Viking Penguin, Inc.

Jung, Carl G. (1953). *Collected Works*. H. Read, M. Fordham & G. Adler, (Eds.). Princeton: Princeton University Press.

Jung, Carl G. (1936). *Archetypes and the Collective Unconscious*. (In *Collected Works*, Vol. 9).

Jung, Carl G. (1939). *The Integration of the Personality*. (In *Collected Works*, Vol. 11).

Jung, Carl G. (1960). *Psychological Aspects of the Mother Archetype*. (In *Collected Works*, Vol. 9).

Jung, Carl G. (1936). *Synchronicity: An Acausal Connecting Principle*. (In *Collected Works*, Vol. 8).

Jung, Carl G. (1961). *Memories, Dreams and Reflections*. New York: Random House.

Jung, Carl G. (1964). *Man and His Symbols*. New York: Doubleday.

May, Rollo. (1953). *Man's Search for Himself*. New York: Norton.

May, Rollo. (1975). *The Courage to Create*. New York: Norton.

May, Rollo. (1977). *The Meaning of Anxiety*. New York: Norton.

May, Rollo. (1983). *The Discovery of Being*. New York: Norton.

May, Rollo. (1991). *The Cry for Myth*. New York: Norton.

Murdock, Maureen. (1990). *The Heroine's Journey*. Boston: Shambhala Publications.

Rank, Otto. (1914/1959). *The Myth of the Birth of the Hero*. New York: Random House.

Stone, Merlin. (1976). *When God was a Woman*. New York: Dorset Press.

Vogler, Christopher. (1998). *The Writer's Journey*. Los Angeles: Michael Wiese Productions.

# Subject Index

MICHAEL WIESE PRODUCTIONS
*www.mwp.com*

We are delighted that you have found, and are enjoying, our books.

Since 1981, we've been all about providing filmmakers with the very best information on the craft of filmmaking: from screenwriting to funding, from directing to camera, acting, editing, distribution, and new media.

It is our goal to inspire and empower a generation (or two) of filmmakers and videomakers like yourself. But we want to go beyond providing you with just the basics. We want to shake you, inspire you to reach for your dreams, and go beyond what's been done before. Most films that come out each year waste our time and enslave our imaginations. We want to give you the confidence to create from your authentic center, to bring something from your own experience that will truly inspire others and bring humanity to its full potential — avoiding those urges to manufacture derivative work in order to be accepted.

Movies, television, the Internet, and new media all have incredible power to transform. As you prepare your next project, know that it is in your hands to choose to create something magnificent and enduring for generations to come.

This is not an impossible goal, because you've got a little help. Our authors are some of the most creative mentors in the business, willing to share their hard-earned insights with you. Their books will point you in the right direction but, ultimately, it's up to you to seek that authentic something on which to spend your precious time.

We applaud your efforts and are here to support you. Let us hear from you.

Sincerely,

Michael Wiese
Filmmaker, Publisher

Printed in the United States
69530LVS00006B/85-87

9 780941 188876